200 YEARS OF
AMERICAN ILLUSTRATION

200 YEARS OF AMERICAN ILLUSTRATION

Text by Henry C. Pitz
Foreword by Norman Rockwell

Published in Association with the
Society of Illustrators

Random House, Inc.
New York

Copyright © Edward Booth-Clibborn 1977
All rights reserved. No part of this publication may be reproduced,
stored in a retrieval system
or transmitted, in any form or by any means,
electronic, mechanical, photocopying, recording or otherwise,
without the prior permission of the Copyright owners.
Random House, Inc.
201 East 50th Street, New York, N.Y. 10022
Filmset by Filmcomposition
6-10 Valentine Place, London SE1 8QH, England
Photographs by Tom Crozier
Printed in Italy by
Arnoldo Mondadori Editore—Verona

Library of Congress Cataloging in Publication Data

Pitz, Henry Clarence, 1895-1976.
200 years of American illustration.

Bibliography: p.
Includes index.
1. Commercial art—United States. I. Crozier, Bob.
II. Title.
NC998.5.A1P57 1977   741.6'0973   77-5961
ISBN 0-394-41474-8

9   8   7   6   5   4   3   2

First Edition

Contents

Acknowledgements

We wish to thank the following for their financial support in the preparation of this project:
Ralph Hansmann; *Sports Illustrated*; Playboy Enterprises;
Meredith Publishing; Time, Inc.; Boy Scouts of America; *Field and Stream* (CBS);
Rhode Island School of Design; Hallmark Cards;
John Deere & Company; Pioneer-Moss and the Ford Motor Company.
We also wish to thank Exxon Corporation for a generous grant which helped make the exhibition possible.
Warmest appreciation to the dedicated staff members who
have worked with us this past year-and-a-half to help organize the material for this book:
Bob Hansmann, Jennifer Riach, Terry Brown, Jill Bossert and Eve Levy.
Also Chairman Bob Crozier and co Chairman Arthur Weithas. Mary Black has
offered acknowledgment in her Preface to the many institutions that have assisted us by lending works.
We would like to add those private collectors and friends who have offered their generous
advice and assistance in so many welcomed ways:

Howard P. Brokaw	Robert J. Mehlman	Peggy & Howard Samuels
Ellen Cabell	Henry C. Pitz	Murray Tinkelman
Louis Cowan	Walt Reed	Mrs. Jane C. Wilcox
Benjamin Eisenstat	Norman Rockwell	
Mort Künstler	Beverly & Ray Sacks	

With special appreciation to Alvin J. Pimsler, past President of The Society of Illustrators,
who had the enthusiasm and vision to sponsor the motion which authorized the Society to undertake
the exhibition.
To Chuck McVicker, the current President and to the Executive Officers of the Society:

HONORARY PRESIDENT Harold Von Schmidt
EXECUTIVE VICE PRESIDENT Les Thompson
VICE PRESIDENT John Witt
TREASURER Dean Ellis
ASSOCIATE TREASURER Roland Descombes
SECRETARY Warren Rogers
HOUSE CHAIRMAN Gerald McConnell
COUNSELOR Professor M. Carr Ferguson
EXECUTIVE DIRECTOR Arpi Ermoyan

The following friends gave generously of their time to help select the entries and hang the exhibition:

James Alexander	John Crozier	Alvin Grossman	Martin Leifer	Louise Riley
Louann Andersen	R. Ames Crozier	Pomona Hallenbeck	Len Leone	Ted Riley
Roy Andersen	Bernard D'Andrea	Ed Hamilton	Allyson Levy	Diane Rudnick
Jane Bance	Diane Dawson	Ed Hamway	Hal Levy	Richard Sachnis
Bruce Barkley	Harry Diamond	Robert Handville	Anna Marie Magagna	Harold Samuels
Murray Belsky	Diane Dillon	Jack Harring	Jerry McConnell	Peggy Samuels
Harry Bennett	Lee Dillon	Bob Havell	Skip McKinley	Eileen Hedy Schultz
Marshall Berland	Leo Dillon	Mitchell Hooks	Chuck McVicker	Thomas Sgouros
David Bermingham	Naiad Einsel	Evelyn Hungerford	Lucy McVicker	Neil Shakery
John Beveridge	Walter Einsel	Charles Hyman	Bonnie McVicker	Carol Smith
Mary Black	Benjamin Eisenstat	Mr. & Mrs. Bud Johnson	Robert Mehlman	Jim Spanfeller
Edward Booth-Clibborn	Bill Erlacher	Harvey Kahn	Susan Meyer	Walt Spitzmiller
Jill Bossert	Bob Essman	Ken Kansas	John Moodie	D. K. Stone
William Bossert	Bea Feitler	Tanya Kasnar	Don Moss	Ian Summers
Bill Cadge	Charles Ferguson	Robert Kingsley	Howard Munce	Elissia Szymanski
Eugene Calogero	Stanislaw Fernandez	Barbara Kirshon	Fred Otnes	Saul Tepper
Nicholas Canetti	Gordon Fisher	Richard Koke	Arthur Paul	Murray Tinkelman
Robert Clive	William Frazer	Sandy Kossin	Bob Pepper	Jessica Weber
Alan E. Cober	Richard Gangel	Mort Künstler	Alvin Pimsler	Janet Weithas
Ernest Costa	Gerry Gersten	Emma Landau	Norma Pimsler	Ann Wolf
Charles Crozier	Wendy Giuliani	Sal Lazzarotti	Walt Reed	David Yerzy
Ginny Crozier	Meriah Graham	Robert Lee	Mr. & Mrs. W. Richards	

Mary Black

The art of the illustrator, both the work that he does on commission and that created for his own pleasure, is a vital record of the nation's social and cultural life. This giant survey, which covers 200 years of American illustration, most of it designed for use in newspapers, magazines, books, posters, record albums and advertisements, is an overview of its contribution to American art. The greatest number of pieces date from this century, but earlier works by Winslow Homer, John James Audubon, William Guy Wall, Charles B. J. F. de St. Memin, William James Bartlett, Thomas Birch, George Catlin, Thomas Nast, George Harvey, William Rickarby Miller, John William Hill and Frances Flora Palmer are among the precursors that influenced twentieth-century illustration.

Artists, collectors and museums cooperated with the Society of Illustrators to bring this major survey together. Great collections of early illustration—like those of Yale University Art Gallery, the New Britain (Conn.) Museum of American Art, the Museum of the City of New York, the Brooklyn Museum, Amon Carter Museum of Western Art (Fort Worth, Texas), the New York Public Library and the New-York Historical Society—have made important contributions to the historical section of this study. Yet these institutions represent only a small number of the museums who collect the work of the illustrator.

In the late nineteenth century, pictorial advertising changed from genre scenes, representations of products, stores and factories to a conscious art form as illustrators enthusiastically adopted the asymmetrical flowing line and other derivations from the Oriental inspiration of Art Nouveau. In this book, paintings and woodcuts by Edward Penfield, Will Bradley, N. C. Wyeth and Rockwell Kent show this trend.

This change in design style came about at almost the moment that the Society of Illustrators was formed, in 1901, to promote friendship and cooperation among illustrators and for philanthropic purposes. Many of the early officers and members of the Society, among them Charles Dana Gibson, Frederic Remington, Howard Pyle, N. C. Wyeth, W. J. Glackens and Dean Cornwell, are represented in this book. Down to the present day, the work of another member, Howard Pyle, has provided inspiration in the teaching and philosophy of American illustration. Initially, this came through his students, N. C. Wyeth, Thornton Oakley and Frank Schoonover; the influence extended to the production of mid-to-late twentieth century illustrators, Henry Patrick Raleigh, Norman Rockwell, Al Parker and Bernard Fuchs.

Illustration often provided modern artists with a means of livelihood. Despite subject or direction requirements, the examples of painting, print-making and sculpture on view in this book frequently transcend their initial use and are collected as prized works of art. For many artists, the framework of an illustrating commission works as a spur to imagination and yields some of their finest creations.

Almost fifty years ago, in a brief history of the Society of Illustrators, …a permanent exhibition, to be assembled in one of the Public Galleries or Museums of this city' was envisioned. At last this dream of 1928 was achieved. The offerings in this book should bring a new awareness of the cultural insights and aesthetic charm afforded by a very large number of these pieces of art, old and new. Even more than easel paintings, these illustrations offer documentary evidence and an exhilarating vision of 200 years of American life.

Mary Black, Curator
Paintings and Sculpture
The New-York Historical Society

Norman Rockwell

I have always considered myself to be an illustrator. When I was a child at home there were always readings-aloud, often from the works of Charles Dickens. I remember when I was very young sketching Mr. Micawber as I heard him described when my father read aloud.

My hero was Howard Pyle. He seemed to represent to me the world of the true illustrator. His pictures always seemed to me to tell a story. When I looked at one of Pyle's pictures, it was always crammed with detail, each one important to the whole picture and the tale it illustrated.

Much is made today about the difference between the artist and the illustrator. But the distinction has always been clear to me: the illustrator must compress a great deal into his picture. As I began to illustrate stories, I saw that I had to draw and paint pictures that would somehow help the reader to see the characters and events of the story more vividly. And the illustration must convey its own story quickly and without demanding a great deal of scrutiny from the reader. The illustrator has, unlike the painter, a primary interest in telling a story. If he does not do that, he fails. Look at the best work of Howard Pyle or the unique Arthur Rackham: each illustration is complete in itself, a joy to look at, and adds immeasurably to the understanding and enjoyment of the story or book that it illustrates.

There have been disadvantages to being an illustrator. Many who consider themselves serious painters look down their noses at us. We paint for money, against deadlines, our subject matter often prescribed by an editor or an author. I have always felt comfortable working within these confines, however, and I suspect most of the truly great illustrators did, too. The only limit to my work, really, was the limit of my own imagination.

The early work I did for *Boys' Life, St. Nicholas, Young People* and other magazines now looks crude to me. But, as the years went by, I began to see some of the possibilities open to an illustrator. He has to make his viewers see themselves in the situation in the drawing. When I first started painting covers for *The Saturday Evening Post,* they were simple pictures of everyday activities: the boy forced to wheel his baby sister out in a baby carriage when he preferred to play baseball; the boy who cannot believe himself lucky enough to be actually talking with a circus clown. But then, as happens with most illustrators, I found myself drawing and painting a somewhat more complex situation, a story in itself. The old couple sit together and listen to a crystal set: what memories of an era that brings to mind! Or the young clerk at his bookkeeping, his mind far away from his figures, in a different world of ships on far-off seas.

If he is to be successful, the illustrator has to keep up with the world in which he lives. Many people have dismissed my work and that of other illustrators as 'only commercial stuff.' I have no idea what that phrase means, but it certainly sounds as if the artist produced merely a product rather than a painting. I like to think that the best illustrators over the years, even when they did paintings for advertisements, somehow caught the true character of the world in which they lived. And that world has been constantly changing.

All of this may sound very complicated. It really is not. The illustration represents at its best a real-life situation, whether it be based on a story, or whether it tells a story of its own. And as my work developed through the time of the Second World War, I saw further the power that illustration has to change and mold opinion. Because the American public during the heyday of the great illustrated magazines, *The Saturday Evening Post, Look, Life,* was exposed to these publications, many of its ideas were changed (remember this was before television!). When I painted the *Four Freedoms,* for example, I could try to express in my paintings much of what every American felt about his country, but would find it difficult to articulate for himself. That is the final value of the illustration: it enables the viewer to see in concrete terms what he has only vaguely felt or guessed before. Illustration is, simply, the presentation of the familiar face or scene, but with certain added overtones which the artist himself is able to suggest.

What I have said above implies that the illustrator has to work hard at what he does if he is to be a success. Most of those whose work appears in this book fall into that category. They have caught in their painting or drawing something which we can believe. They have been willing to work hard at the innumerable details which make up any successful illustration: background, people, facial expressions, 'props,' lighting and many more. But the total effect of their picture is to make anyone who sees it say, 'Yes, it is true.'

The illustrator has played a very important part in the history of this country, for he has portrayed the life of the people as it was really lived. If, sometimes, he criticizes some phase of it, that only betokens the great love he has for his land and his people. The great band of illustrators—Howard Pyle, Frederic Remington, A. B. Frost, Maxfield Parrish, Edwin Austin Abbey, Charles Dana Gibson and many, many more—have shown us to ourselves.

I am proud and happy to have been one of their company.

Norman Rockwell

Bob Crozier

In 1976, The Society of Illustrators celebrated the seventy-fifth anniversary of its founding. Since that event was concurrent with our nation's bicentennial year, it seemed timely and appropriate that the membership of the Society and the public at large have an opportunity to re-examine both the technical and historical richness and value of American illustration over the past 200 years. A major exhibition was prepared to make this possible.

Illustration has both enjoyed and suffered a reputation in its time. As an art form it has been recognized as both trivial and consequential. Of the untold tens of thousands of original drawings, paintings and engravings created for books, magazines, posters and advertising over the past two centuries, too few have survived and even fewer are available for viewing by the public.

Unlike most art forms, no formal, recognized repository for illustration exists. The Library of Congress began collecting illustration in 1932, and while theirs remains an abundant collection of nineteenth and mid-twentieth century art, this noble effort was terminated nine years later. The bulk of what may remain of the vast reservoir of illustrative works of the past must be searched out by slow, deliberate work, which often ends in antique shops and attics.

Up to this time, no single near-complete reference has been compiled to document the history of the American illustrator and his works. There are numerous museum catalogues, magazine articles and books dealing with individual illustrators from which a large number of works can be identified and located. However, the greatest sources of American illustration art are illustrators themselves and private collectors, whom we have heavily relied upon to help create our exhibit and this book.

In America, illustrative art is more often than not taken for granted. Since the mid-eighteenth century, Americans have been 'rewarded' with illustration as part of their purchase of newspapers, magazines and books. We have come to expect amusing, charming, mystic, clever, romantic, or saucy artwork to accompany much of our reading matter. The casual reader gives little conscious thought to the exploratory research, talent and creative ability that have been commissioned to produce these effects.

The history of illustration closely parallels the history of the country. As the population grew and opened new frontiers, illustrators were there to report their impressions. John James Audubon recorded his brilliant *Birds of America* in the wilderness. Frederic Remington recorded daily life in the West. George Catlin documented the declining civilization of the American Indian. Winslow Homer recorded the more romantic aspects of American life.

This book dates illustration back to the eighteenth-century artists and engravers, Paul Revere and Amos Doolittle. However, illustration as most familiar to us today can be traced to the early part of the nineteenth century. Then, graphic artists were often creating designs for currency and signage as a part-time livelihood while painting, in oil and watercolor, bucolic scenes of the countryside which were later reproduced in hand-colored prints and offered for sale. Some artists did illustration for books, periodicals and newspapers while others created work to be reproduced on stone such as that for Currier & Ives. Unconsciously, each was recording history.

As the population grew from five million in 1800 to twenty-three million in 1850, demand steadily grew for more news, entertainment, products and goods. Growth of the new nation was explosive from the discovery of gold in Colona, California in 1848 to the Philadelphia Centennial Exposition in 1876. There could be little doubt that the enormous natural and human resources of America would have a powerful and lasting influence in a national and international sense. A new responsibility was emerging. All this created new horizons for the illustrator. *Harper's Weekly* published its first issue in 1857, closely following *Frank Leslie's Illustrated News*. Women's magazines flourished. *Godey's* was first published in 1804 and was followed by *Petersen's* in 1842, *McCall's* in 1870, *Ladies' Home Journal* in 1883, *Good Housekeeping* in 1885, *Vogue* in 1892. Book publishers followed Lippincott's early lead of 1792 with Harper's in 1817, Little, Brown in 1837 and Scribner's in 1846. A variety of encyclopedias, bibles and almanacs were published with great frequency. Pictorial books and magazines proliferated in both the city and country. Scribner's carried the first magazine advertising pages in 1887. An art poster craze hit the country in the Nineties, advertising bikes, cameras, typewriters, fountain pens and telephones.

In 1901, the year the Society of Illustrators was founded, Marconi transmitted the first trans-Atlantic signals by wireless from Europe and Teddy Roosevelt was elected the youngest President of the United States. Within the next three years the first automobile would travel coast-to-coast and Orville Wright would make his first successful flight. Forty-five stars flew on our flag. New muscles were being flexed. We were well into the golden years of illustration, which lasted through to the mid-twenties. By this time, illustration had come far from the early and crude newspaper woodcut. Illustrators had become famous—John James Audubon, Winslow Homer, Frederic Remington, Charles Russell, Edwin A. Abbey, Felix Darley, A. B. Frost, Charles Dana Gibson, Howard Pyle and Thomas Nast, who in his twenty-year career created the present day image of Santa Claus and Uncle Sam and became one of the most influential men in America.

Illustration was not confined to men in those early days. Women in print included Dorothy Warren, Ethel Franklin Betts, Anna Whelan and Frances Newton, and their work was especially popular in children's books. 'Fanny' Palmer (Frances Bond Palmer) was a full-time and popular illustrator-in-residence for Currier & Ives.

About the exhibition

When a committee was formed almost two years ago and charged to collect illustration for an exhibition, it was an unprecedented event. No exhibit of such scope had ever been attempted before. While museum exhibitions have been held of the illustrator's work, the majority of those pieces were from the permanent collections of large museums or galleries scattered coast-to-coast.

Our objectives were to unearth the works of popular as well as lesser known, but equally important, illustrators of the past and present. Our search led us to private collectors, galleries, museums and individuals who had a love for illustration. We also had the extensive Society of Illustrators collection to draw upon. The U.S. Army, Navy and Marine Corps have extensive collections of illustration and members of the Society of Illustrators have provided the U.S. Air Force art program with documentary illustrations since 1952. These were made available to us.

What you will see in this book are approximately 850 pieces selected from a total of 9,000 submitted for consideration. Our criterion was to select only one or two pieces from the contemporary illustrator unless that illustrator was considered by our committee to have been an extremely important influence on illustration. In such instances, up to three pieces were accepted. Illustrators of the past, now proven, were allowed even more exposure. Reproductions were photographed only where originals were unobtainable. Winslow Homer drew directly on wood for his illustrations which appeared in *Harper's Magazine*. The originals have long been lost or destroyed. Few of the original drawings or paintings done for Currier & Ives' lithographs exist today, although we show two. We are fortunate indeed to have original drawings and paintings done by John William Hill, William J. Bennett and even John James Audubon since curiously, limited importance was placed on their works during much of their early lifetime. To this day, only one first state proof of Paul Revere's *Boston Massacre* is known to exist. Most were glued, shellacked or nailed to walls or boards and have long since vanished.

When the economics of art are examined, illustrators are often less well paid than the highly publicized painters and printmakers of today. We are all the better for their dedication for we enjoy the full fruits of the illustrator's trade daily. In our homes, we raise our children on magazine and book illustration. We teach them in school with illustrated text books. We have come to accept illustration as part of our lives. An illustrator's concept and interpretation add to our variety of choice. Whether N. C. Wyeth's interpretation of James Fenimore Cooper's *Deerslayer* is better than that of Reginald Marsh is a very personal decision to be made by the reader. One may have been a greater commercial success than the other, but this is hardly a judgment of the quality of illustration.

200 Years of American Illustration cannot be considered a complete collection of American illustration. However, it may be considered the most complete assembly to date. There are hundreds of worthy illustrators whose work is not included in this book: not by choice, but rather because their originals were not readily available to us when our material was gathered. All of us who have worked on this undertaking are painfully aware that there are important omissions that might have been filled had time permitted. We regret this. There are also important sources known to us but neglected: most notably, the Library of Congress, the Smithsonian Institution, the Delaware Art Museum, the Brandywine Museum and many of the large and small museums, universities and publishing houses in the United States which house collections of illustrators' works.

For much of the contemporary work we see in this book, we owe a special debt of gratitude to one giant in the field of illustration, Howard Pyle. His early teaching at Drexel Institute in Philadelphia, Pennsylvania in 1898-1899 and in Chadds Ford, Pennsylvania in 1901 produced a legacy of talents and generous assistance which was passed on to generation after generation of illustrators who followed. Pyle's early students included Frank Schoonover, Violet Oakley, Elizabeth Shippen Green, Jessie Wilcox Smith, Philip R. Goodwin, Thornton Oakley, N. C. Wyeth, Harvey Dunn, George Harding and Harry F. Townsend. Examples of their works are represented in this book.

This collection, spanning 200 years, is additional evidence of the enormous talent, intellect and dedication of the artist, painter, illustrator in his day. Perhaps this book will generate additional interest, support and resources which will further help to preserve what is among our great heritages and treasures—American illustration.

We are honored to have a Preface by Mary Black, Curator of Paintings and Sculpture of the New-York Historical Society where these illustrations were first exhibited from November, 1976 through April, 1977. We are also indebted to Norman Rockwell for his thoughtful Foreword.

I should also like to pay respect to Henry C. Pitz, who passed away the week after the exhibition opened. Henry devoted his life to illustration as a practicing artist and long-time head of the illustration department of the Philadelphia College of Art. He was terribly excited about the concept of the exhibition and book and we deeply regret that he was unable to see the latter completed. I hope this book will serve as a lasting memorial to his considerable talent, dedication and craft.

Bob Crozier

200 YEARS OF
AMERICAN ILLUSTRATION

Chapter 1
The Early Years

Dr. Alexander Anderson (1775–1870). *House of Greenwich, Connecticut. 1795.*
Pen and ink, 4¾″ x 7″. Lent by the New-York Historical Society.

When the former Atlantic provinces began to contend with the consequences of their new achievement as a single, unified country, it was a nation of broad contrasts. It was a long, north to south coastal settlement. This was mostly cultivated country, dotted with flourishing cities and towns, converted from the wilderness in scarcely more than a century. Imbedded in it were cities like Boston, Philadelphia, New York and Charleston—Philadelphia, for instance, was the second largest English-speaking city in the world, at that time.

This was no longer a primitive world. But just over the mountains, the wilderness began. Mile by mile, and year by year, that wilderness would recede. The structures and appurtenances of civilization were springing up overnight. The printing press had arrived with the early shiploads ready to print the word and if possible, the picture.

Those early presses and even later ones like Franklin's, for instance, were little changed from the first one of Gutenberg. The squeeze of the inked type or plate against the paper, page by page, was still done by hand and lever by the printer.

Meanwhile, the print-maker had a choice of possible ways of preparing a printing plate. Earliest and most popular was the woodcut, cut with gouge and chisel in wooden blocks, preferably of soft and even grained wood. This method gave us the first examples of what would be called American illustration, a humble woodcut done of Richard Mather in 1670 and a woodcut map of New England in 1677.

This represented the primitive emergence of the printed image on these shores and little of greater accomplishment can be discovered for a long time. But by the time of our independence, more pictorial competence can be found. The woodcut was still in use, but it was a crude medium and the more sophisticated talents were inclined toward copper engraving. This metal was relatively soft and offered only modest resistance to the engraving tool. The pre-Revolutionary print of Paul Revere's *Boston Massacre* is probably the best known example, although of mediocre artistic attainment.

A copperplate project of far greater scope and accomplishment than any previous one was the colored *Views Of Philadelphia,* issued in 1800 by the English-born father and son William and Thomas Birch. Later, in 1808, they published another excellent series, *The Country Seats of the United States.* Here were pictorial documents of artistic merit and at the same time a social record of importance—a report of the cultivated and even opulent lifestyle of much of the older settled coastal strip.

Year by year, more ambitious illustrative projects were attempted, such as the eighteen volumes of Ree's *Encyclopedia,* with its 543 copperplate engravings. But soon the copperplate had a rival. About 1810 the process of steel engraving was introduced for the printing of bank notes. It was soon adopted for books and other publications for its delicate and clean-cut beauty and because the plates yielded many more impressions than those obtainable from copper. On large runs they were much more economical. This was a period in which much excellent engraving art was produced.

Coincidental with the rise of steel engraving came the work of Alexander Anderson, often called the father of wood engraving in the United States. A former engraver on copper, Anderson was captivated by the 'white line' obtained by engraving on the end grain of a finely grained wood, such as

The BLOODY MASSACRE perpetrated in King—⸻Street BOSTON on March 5th 1770 by a party of the 29th REGT

BUTCHER'S HALL

Engrav'd Printed & Sold by PAUL REVERE BOSTON

Unhappy BOSTON! see thy Sons deplore,
Thy hallow'd Walks besmear'd with guiltless Gore:
While faithless P—n and his savage Bands,
With murd'rous Rancour stretch their bloody Hands;
Like fierce Barbarians grinning o'er their Prey,
Approve the Carnage, and enjoy the Day.

If scalding drops from Rage from Anguish Wrung,
If speechless Sorrows lab'ring for a Tongue,
Or if a weeping World can ought appease
The plaintive Ghosts of Victims such as these;
The Patriot's copious Tears for each are shed,
A glorious Tribute which embalms the Dead.

But know, FATE summons to that awful Goal.
Where JUSTICE strips the Murd'rer of his Soul:
Should venal C—ts the scandal of the Land,
Snatch the relentless Villain from her Hand,
Keen Execrations on this Plate inscrib'd,
Shall reach a JUDGE who never can be brib'd.

The unhappy Sufferers were Messrs. SAML GRAY, SAML MAVERICK, JAMS CALDWELL, CRISPUS ATTUCKS & PATK CARR

Killed. Six wounded; two of them (CHRISTr MONK & JOHN CLARK) Mortally

Paul Revere (1735–1818). *Boston Massacre. 1776.*
Paul Revere's Engravings by Clarence S. Brighton. Hand-tinted copper engraving, 13″ x 9″. Lent by the New-York Historical Society.

Dr. Alexander Anderson (1775–1870). *The Bridewill Prison, City Hall Park. 1800–1810.*
Wash, $3\frac{7}{8}'' \times 6\frac{1}{2}''$. Lent by the New-York Historical Society.

Arthur J. Stansbury (1781–1845). *City Hall Park. 1825.*
Watercolor and pen and ink, $12'' \times 16\frac{1}{2}''$. Lent by the Museum of the City of New York.

boxwood or cherry, as practiced by the English artist Thomas Bewick. The technique was new to this country and speedily became popular. One of Anderson's first major projects was redrawing and engraving 300 of Bewick's own illustrations for the first edition of the *General History of Quadrupeds.* Anderson was by no means the equal of his master, but produced a large body of work during his long and productive life. In the course of a few years a growing company of engravers were incising their white lines and dots on boxwood blocks, and the greater part of America's illustrations were reproduced in this way until the process finally reached its peak in the supreme skills of engravers like Timothy Cole and Henry Wolf in the latter part of the nineteenth century.

The early impulses of the industrial revolution were bringing changes. There was more money in more pockets. All types of education were more widespread. Illiteracy was dwindling rapidly. The appetite for the printed word and picture was growing.

The wherewithal to supply that appetite was assembling. The production of paper was increasing rapidly. The first paper mill was built in 1690 on the banks of the Wissahickon Creek near Philadelphia by William Bradford and Samuel Carpenter, and put in charge of William Rittenhouse, a German paper-maker. From that earliest beginning, paper-making spread rapidly in Pennsylvania until by 1787 the state had forty-eight of the ninety mills then operating in the country. The number of paper mills was increasing rapidly in New England and also in the South.

Printing ink was in plentiful supply, and two German printers had begun the founding of type in Germantown, Pennsylvania in 1775. Propitious social conditions were building up a widespread potential audience for the printed word, but that awaited the advent of the power-press. When it came, it came with a rush early in the nineteenth century, and improvement upon improvement followed rapidly. The first book printed in the United States upon a steam power-press is said to be an *Abridgement of Murry's English Grammar,* in 1823. Seven years later an improved version of this power-driven bed-and-platen press was invented by an American, Isaac Adams; this, it is estimated, handled about ninety per cent of the better type of American book and magazine publishing up to the Civil War. At last the American craving for abundant reading and picture matter was being satisfied.

William James Bennett (1787–1844) and **Nicolino Calyo** (1799–1884). *View of the Ruins after the Great Fire—1836.*
Colored aquatint, 16″ x 23½″. Lent by the Museum of the City of New York.

Jacques Gérard Milbert (1766–1840). *Glens Falls, New York.*
A French Explorer in the Hudson River Valley. 1818. Sepia, 3¾″ x 5¾″.
Lent by the New-York Historical Society.

William James Bennett (1787–1844). *View of New York Harbor from the Battery.*
New York Mirror, February 3, 1844. Watercolor, 11½″ x 17½″.
Lent by the New-York Historical Society.

Currier & Ives. *Life on the Prairie: 'Buffalo Hunt'. Artist—Arthur F. Tait (1819–1905), published 1862.* Lithograph, 20¼″ x 28″. Lent by the Museum of the City of New York.

Amos Doolittle (1754–1832). *Engagement at North Bridge in Concord. 1775.*
Hand-tinted copper engraving, 13″ x 18″.
Lent by the New York Public Library Print Collection.

Amos Doolittle (1754–1832). *View of the South Part of Lexington. 1775.*
Hand-tinted copper engraving, 13″ x 18″.
Lent by the New York Public Library Print Collection.

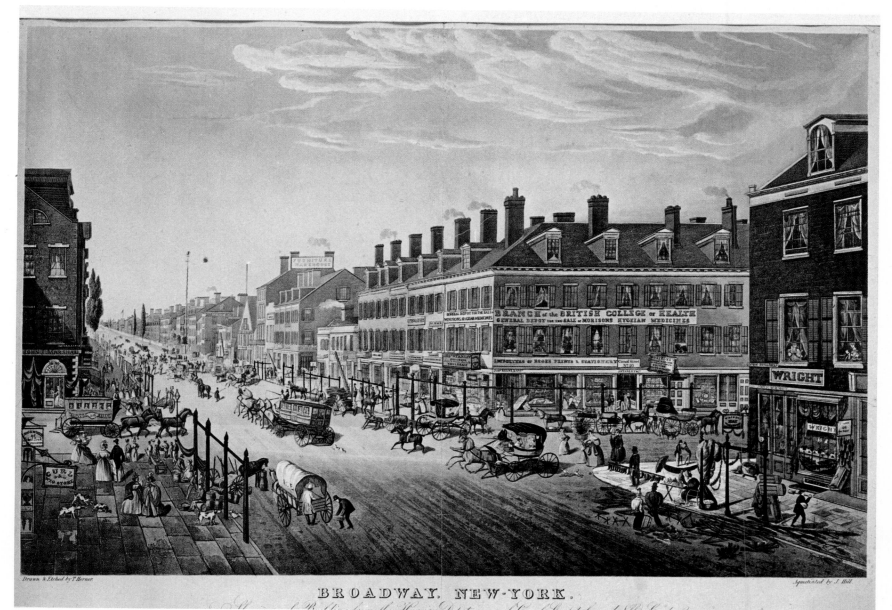

BROADWAY, NEW-YORK.

Thomas Hornor. *Broadway, New-York. Joseph Stanley & Co., 1836.* Print, 17¾" x 27¼". Lent by the New-York Historical Society.

Amos Doolittle (1754–1832). *Battle of Lexington, April 19, 1775.*
Hand-tinted copper engraving, 13" x 18".
Lent by the New York Public Library Print Collection.

Amos Doolittle (1754–1832). *A View of the Town of Concord. 1775.*
Hand-tinted copper engraving, 13" x 18".
Lent by the New York Public Library Print Collection.

21

George Cooke (1793–1849). *West Point from above Washington Valley.*
Published by Lewis P. Clover, 1834. Print, 15⅞" x 22¾". Lent by the New-York Historical Society.

Charles B. J. F. de Saint-Mémin (1770–1852).
View of the City of New York from Mount Pitt. 1794.
Pencil and ink, 16½" x 25⅝". Lent by the New-York Historical Society.

William James Bennett (1787–1844). *View of the High Falls of Trenton, West Canada Creek, New York.*
Published by Lewis P. Clover, 1835. Print, 18″ x 23¼″. Lent by the New-York Historical Society.

William Guy Wall (1792–1864). *View near Sandy Hill.*
The Hudson River Portfolio, 1821–25. Watercolor, 14″ x 21″.
Lent by the New-York Historical Society.

Nicolino Calyo (1799–1884). *The Bakers Cart. 1840–44.*
Watercolor, 9″ x 13″. Lent by the Museum of the City of New York.

Nicolino Calyo (1799–1884). *The Charcoal Cart. 1840–44.*
Watercolor, 9″ x 13″. Lent by the Museum of the City of New York.

Nicolino Calyo (1799–1884). *The Oyster Man. 1840–44.*
Watercolor, 9″ x 13″. Lent by the Museum of the City of New York.

Nicolino Calyo (1799-1884). *The Butcher. 1840–44.*
Watercolor, 12″ x 9½″. Lent by the Museum of the City of New York.

Nicolino Calyo (1799–1884). *Lemon and Orange Stand. 1840–44.*
Watercolor, 9″ x 13″. Lent by the Museum of the City of New York.

John William Hill (1812–1879). *Hudson River Bridge near Waterford, New York. 1832. Watercolor, 9¾" x 13⅞".* Lent by the New-York Historical Society.

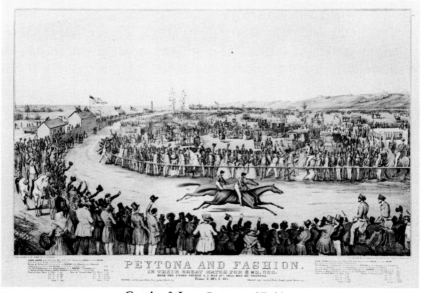

Currier & Ives. *Peytona and Fashion.*
Artist—Charles Severin b. ca. 1808, published 1845. Lithograph, 21" x 30¼".
Lent by the Museum of the City of New York.

Chapter 2

Audubon, Darley and after.

Felix O. C. Darley (1822–1888). *South Street Dock Scene, New York.*
American Bank Note Company, 1878. Pen and ink and wash, 7½" x 9".
Lent by Mrs. Thomas Wilcox.

The second quarter of the nineteenth century was a period of adolescent growth in American illustration. The expanding audience was there, making its wants known; the mechanical means were at hand. The talent was gradually forming. There was promise ahead.

Two strong and diverse talents emerge, high above the general average: John James Audubon and Felix Octavius Carr Darley. They were in striking contrast, both in work and personality. Darley was a self-taught picture-maker of considerable gifts. He was beginning a steady and prolific career that would last over half a century. He would see American illustration develop, grow and compete with the best of Europe.

John James Audubon, too was largely untaught: a brilliant man and a great artist, he won the admiration and applause of not only his own adopted country but of Europe. His fame has been steady, Darley has been well-nigh forgotten.

Audubon's life is a restless chronicle of constant journeying, business ventures and disappointments, plans and frustrations, chronic financial difficulties with intermittent strokes of good fortune and yet, through it all, the unquenchable passion to draw and paint the animals of the New World. Born in Les Cayes, Santo Domingo and living his boyhood years in France, he came to the United States in the summer of 1803. Here, at the age of eighteen, he lived in a pleasant stone farmhouse, Mill Grove, perched on a hill above the waters of the Perkiomen Creek, some twenty miles from Philadelphia.

There was an abundance of birds and other animal life in the area and here began Audubon's passionate dedication to record the wildlife of the New World. From Mill Grove began his restless journeys through the West and the South, piling up his stock of nature drawings and paintings, interrupted at frequent intervals to pick up odd jobs to sustain himself and his wife and then back to his passion again. After years of work he had the paintings assembled for his historic *Birds of America* folio, and he journeyed to England to exhibit them and arranged to have them engraved and published. His dedication to his goal continued up to his last waning years. Other editions of his *Birds* appeared along with the *Ornithological Biography* and the *Viviparous Quadrupeds of North America.* Praise and honor were showered upon him. His fame is secure.

Felix Darley was America's first general illustrator of importance. He was born in Philadelphia in 1822 of English actor parents and he early displayed a natural gift for pictorial dramatization. He never had a formal art lesson and apparently his native gift for free and easy expression of the human figure needed none.

At fourteen he was an apprentice in a counting house, but all his spare time was spent drawing. By the age of twenty he had bulging portfolios of drawings and after taking them on a round of the printing, publishing and engraving houses, his artist's career was launched. Several of these early drawings were reproduced in the *Saturday Museum,* a magazine edited by Edgar Allen Poe. Later Darley made a number of drawings to be reproduced by lithography for a series called *Scenes in Indian Life.* The drawings were in outline and quite a bit below the high level that Darley's work would reach in a few more years, but Poe praised them, saying, 'They abound in spirit and are in all respects meritorious.'

Darley's work improved rapidly, for talent was there in abundance and driven by great adaptability and an enormous capacity for hard work. It was soon apparent that he was the most gifted illustrator in the field, and when Carey and Hart published their *Library of Humorous American Works* in 1846, the series bore the imprint, 'Illustrated by Darley.' This was unusual for its time; scarcely any illustrators were given recognition by name.

Darley was coming into his mature ability at a time when rapid and relatively inexpensive methods of reproduction were on trial. The fine older methods of etching, mezzotint, aquatint and copper engraving were generally too costly and time consuming. The choice seemed to narrow down to wood engraving, steel engraving and the newly discovered technique of lithography. Steel engraving could be beautiful, but expensive. Although many German lithographers were emigrating to America, lithography was less familiar and less trusted by conservative printers than wood engraving. The bulk of the illustration of the time would pass through the hands of the wood engravers.

Darley seemed at home in all three processes—he was a born illustrator. He was showered with work. At this time the young republic was in a mood to celebrate its past in text and picture, and Darley became famous for his American themes. Washington Irving admired his work and became his friend, and was happy to see his *Sketch Book* (containing *Rip Van Winkle* and *The Legend of Sleepy Hollow*) and *The Knickerbocker History of New York* illustrated by Darley. Many of the important authors of the

time—Henry Wadsworth Longfellow, Francis Parkman, Mary Mapes Dodge, James Fenimore Cooper, Harriet Beecher Stowe, N. P. Willis, Donald Grant, Mitchell and George Lippard—had their works illustrated by Darley and became his friend.

Because Darley was our first illustrator of outstanding ability, it is possible that his Americanism has been exaggerated. Certainly a large portion of his themes were American and can be said to have a certain native touch. But it must be remembered that he had no tradition of American illustration behind him. He was himself beginning its creation. In fact he looked largely to the fine British school of illustration of that time for nourishment. And concurrent with his depiction of American themes, were his illustrations for Scott, Dickens, Laurence Sterne and Tennyson.

His diversity was notable. It ranged from designs for bank notes to pictures for a wide variety of the rapidly upspringing new magazines: *Riverside Magazine*, *Every Saturday*, *Harper's Monthly Magazine*, *Harper's Weekly*, *Our Young Folks* and *Health and Home*. He illustrated and wrote a book of his European travels and illustrated books like *Peter Ploddy*, *Picking from the Picayune* and *Yemassee* and *Some Adventures of Captain Simon Suggs Late of the*

Felix O. C. Darley (1822–1888).
Father Entertains His Children by the Fireside. 1889.
Pencil, 9" x 8¼". Lent by Mrs. Thomas Wilcox.

Felix O. C. Darley (1822–1888). *The Fight in the Lake.*
Leather Stocking Tales by James Fenimore Cooper, 1875.
Pencil and charcoal, 7" x 5¼". Lent anonymously.

John James Audubon (1785–1851). *Pileated Woodpecker.*
Birds of America, John J. Audubon, 1827–1838. Watercolor, 38⅛" x 25".
Lent by the New-York Historical Society.

Tallapossa Volunteers, notable for their titles rather than their texts.

Darley's ceaselessly productive life spanned almost a half century. During that period he witnessed great change and growth and was part of it. Shortly after he began his professional career he saw the production of what has been called the first really ambitious illustrated book, Harper's *Illuminated Bible* of 1846, with its 1,600 engravings. Darley's last important work was the steel-engraved illustrations for the Stratford edition of Shakespeare in 1886. He had seen the beginnings of the revolutionary half-tone, the proliferation of the weekly and monthly magazine like *Harper's* and *Leslie's,* and the emergence of a sizable corps of younger illustrators. Time had revealed that he was a prototype of the new breed of illustrator.

The relentless demands of the new publications for almost overnight material was putting a premium on rapid pictorial conception and execution. The quality of standards was also rising. American illustration was moving speedily from the tentative to the plane of great accomplishment.

John James Audubon (1785–1851). *Carolina Paroquet.*
Birds of America, John J. Audubon, 1827–1838. Watercolor, 29½" x 21¼". Lent by the New-York Historical Society.

Chapter 3

The Civil War Years

Allen Carter Redwood (1834–1922). *The Battle of Shiloh.*
The Century Magazine, February 1885. Print, 10½" x 14".
Lent by the American Heritage Publishing Company.

Our Civil War, that great convulsion that shook the country to its roots, was of its nature bound to leave its mark upon every aspect of American life. Looking back upon the accumulation of reproduced art of the great conflict, it is scarcely possible to claim artistic merit for much of that spate of pictures. What was accomplished was a further acceleration in the whole process of pictorial reporting to an anxiously demanding public.

At the beginning of the conflict, the mechanism for quick creation and distribution of the printed picture on a wide scale was rapidly shaping itself toward the giant accomplishments of its future. The half century prior to the outbreak of war had been a time of amazingly rapid development of the whole world of printing—the designing and cutting of type punches, of type casting, the power-press moving from improvement to improvement, better inks and widespread expansion in the production of paper.

As a result of all this, the illustrated weekly and monthly magazines had appeared to satisfy a swelling audience. The daily newspapers were also finding a need for the reproduced picture. The war had aroused the public demand for pictorial reporting to fever pitch. Poised for the first hostile shot were the country's two notable magazine publishers, *Frank Leslie's Illustrated Newspaper* and the *Harper's Weekly* and *Monthly* magazines. Events had organized a great war's opening like a stage setting, the confrontation between the mainland batteries clustered about Charleston's harbor and those of Fort Sumter, out in the bay. Frank Leslie had the English artist William Waud

ready with crayon and paper on the Charleston shore. Several of the Federal officers in the fort had been sending sketches to *Harper's Weekly* and would be called on for more. It is doubtful if the opening of any other war was so readily under the artist's watchful eyes.

That was the beginning of four years of pictorial reporting. Particularly in the early days of the war, the war artists at the front were greatly outnumbered by those safely at work in their cubby-holes in lower Manhattan, but more artists would be dispatched as battleground after battleground opened up across more than half the breadth of the continent. Most would come from the more industrialized North, but the South did what it could. The photographers, of course, were there, chiefly the famous Mathew Brady, and their records are priceless, although because of the limitations of the earlier cameras, their reports were mainly of camp life—such as the before and after of battle.

Usually the word could be transmitted quite rapidly from the front to the publication headquarters by telegraph; not so the picture report. The sketch at the front made under all kinds of trying conditions, usually hasty and incomplete from the average reader's point of view, had to be taken to a railhead, and hopefully transported by train to New York. There, in the publisher's workshop, came its transformation into a printing surface. Almost always it had to be worked over and brought to a state of completion by one of the stay-at-home artists, either before or after being traced onto a block of boxwood for engraving purposes. Many of these artists were skilled, some were not. The retouching artisan, a creature of his time, tended to think of the war through a haze of sentimental ardor and patriotism. So did the publishers who employed him and the public who awaited his efforts. All the influences were in the direction of glorification and theatricality.

The artist at the front was very close to the real thing, but not completely involved. He lived with the soldiers but he was not one of them. He may have depicted a charge but it is scarcely likely he took part in it. He may have stepped over the stricken and disordered heaps after the charge and been heart-broken at what he saw but he would not have made a drawing of it. Or if he had, he would not have sent it to his publisher—neither publisher nor public was ready for that. So there was much sword waving and gallant gesturing in the earlier pictures. The engraver bent over his block of close-grained boxwood, with his triangular pointed engraving tool in his hand, and translated the artist's drawing to a new medium. A pen and ink drawing could hope for nearly literal reproduction, but not a tonal drawing of blacks and greys. Tones had to be translated into dots and hair-lines and in skilled hands the end effect was remarkably close, but never entirely true, to the original. Block engraving, of its nature, could not be a rapid operation. Sometimes it would require a week to engrave a large and intricate drawing. This time-hampering factor could be alleviated somewhat by the careful sawing of such a block into quarters, each of which was given to a different engraver. Each engraver tooled his quarter block except for a thin strip of about one-eighth of an inch in width along the two sides of the block that abutted against its two neighboring blocks. When completed, the quarters were brought together and fastened to a tight fit by light iron rods. The thin, eighth-inch strips of untouched wood were then worked over by a master-engraver who reconciled his cuts to those on either side to conceal the fact of separation. So, in spite of high

Henry A. Ogden (1856–1936). *A Louisiana Private.*
Battles and Leaders of the Civil War, Century Publishing Company, 1888. Reprint, 10½″ x 14″.
Lent by the American Heritage Publishing Company.

skills, ingenuity, and brilliant and continual new inventions, the pictorial report of a battle could only reach its audience many days after the last guns had been fired.

As the war months slowly passed by, something of the fervor and expectation of an early spectacular victory faded, as can be traced in many of the war pictures. There began to be less of wild theater in them and something more of cruel reality.

The reproduced picture was now an American necessity. Even though the numbers seem small by comparison with today's figures, a normal issue of *Harper's Weekly* in the war years had a circulation of about 125,000 copies, which could be run from the press in two days. Special issues might reach 300,000 copies. But copies were usually treasured and handed from person to person in a way now unknown to us.

The most accomplished and celebrated of the Civil War artists was Winslow Homer (1836-1910). At twenty-one he was a freelance illustrator working for the pictorial press, chiefly Ballou's and Harper's. He was sent to Washington to sketch the first Lincoln inauguration and then to Yorktown in 1862 to picture the Peninsula campaign. His time at the front was relatively short but he continued to draw and paint from that experience for some years.

Alfred R. Waud (1828–1891). *Destruction of an Ammunition Train.*
Battles and Leaders of the Civil War, Century Publishing Company, 1888. Reprint, 10½″ x 14″.
Lent by the American Heritage Publishing Company.

Edwin Forbes (1839–1895). *Meeting Jackson's Flank Attack, Chancellorsville.*
The Century Magazine, September 1886. Reprint, 10½″ x 14″. Lent by the American Heritage Publishing Company.

Another famous name linked with the Civil War times is that of Thomas Nast (1840-1902). His parents had brought him to New York at the age of six, and at fifteen he was drawing for *Frank Leslie's Illustrated Newspaper.* At twenty-one he was making drawings of wartime activities in Washington, but he never drew from the armies in the field. His gift was toward the satirical which found its full expression in his later powerful political cartoons.

Neither Homer nor Nast made long and detailed records of the war; that was done by other less famous illustrators who lived and worked with the armies in the field, who followed through fortune and misfortune and who came to know intimately the life of the fighting men. These artists created a considerable body of work, much of it reproduced.

Two such artists were the brothers William and Alfred R. Waud. Except for their English birth, little is known of their early background. William was in Charleston in the early days of suspense, awaiting the first shot of the war. Later he was sketching the war in the Western campaigns and in the South. His brother Alfred seems to have followed the fighting in Virginia from the defense of Washington and the first Bull Run to

the closing days at Appomattox. The brothers made thousands of on-the-spot sketches and fortunately many of them have been preserved.

Another prolific field artist was Edwin Forbes, who not only followed the armies during the war, but devoted the rest of his creative life to preserving his memories in paintings and etchings. There were fewer field artists on the Confederate side. Probably the most important was Conrad Wise Chapman. Trained in Italy, he hastened back to his homeland upon news of impending war and enlisted in a Confederate regiment. Wounded at Shiloh, he began his career as field artist after recovery, piling up hundreds of sketches of army life and military portraits.

The war's field artists were not unsung, at least in the North. Close to the war's end, *Harper's Weekly* paid tribute to the men who had risked their lives, pencil in hand:

(They) have not been less busy and scarcely less imperiled than the soldiers. They have made the weary marches and dangerous voyages. They have shared the soldiers' fare: they have ridden and waded, and climbed and floundered, always trusting in lead-pencils and

Theodore R. Davis (1840–1894). *Federal Lines, Vicksburg.*
Battles and Leaders of the Civil War, Century Publishing Company, 1888. Reprint, 10½″ x 14″. Lent by the American Heritage Publishing Company.

keeping their powder dry. When the battle began, they were there. They drew the enemy's fire as well as our own. The fierce shock, the heaving tumult, the smoky sway of battle from side to side, the line, the assault, the victory—they were a part of all, and their faithful fingers, depicting the scene, have made us a part also.

The greater part of the old drawings are gone. Perhaps only a few thousands are left. Most of those that came north to the publishers, to be traced on to the boxwood blocks, were probably dropped into wastebaskets. Some, drawn upon a poor grade of paper, have disintegrated. But there are some sizable collections around the country.

The Library of Congress has the largest collection of the work of the Waud brothers, Edwin Forbes, and some others. The Cooper Hewitt Museum has a group of Winslow Homer sketches done for *Harper's*. The New York Public Library has a small collection of war drawings made for *Leslie's Weekly*. The only considerable Confederate collection seems to be that in the Valentine Museum in Richmond, Virginia, by the artist Conrad Wise Chapman. Even the *Illustrated London News* sent their artist, Frank Vizetelly, across the sea to the battlefields, and twenty-nine of his drawings are owned by Harvard University.

Of course, pictures of our Civil War did not stop with Lee's surrender. About a generation later *The Century* magazine, anxious to record the reminiscences of some of the many participants still living, began its famous 'War Papers.' Within six months of the printing of the first articles, the circulation of the magazine had increased by 100,000 copies. The series included papers from participants ranging from General Grant to foot soldiers from the ranks. A few years later the material was gathered together in a large, horizontal book of *Battles and Leaders of the Civil War*, more familiarly known as *The Century War Book*. It was filled with pictures, not only those of the original war artists but from a younger generation such as James E. Taylor, E. W. Kemble, Gilbert Gaul, J. O. Davidson and R. F. Zogbaum.

Civil War themes have and will continue to animate the pencils and brushes of American artists. Just as Howard Pyle later painted his large mural of the 'Battle of Nashville' in the Minnesota State Capital and N. C. Wyeth his stirring color paintings for Mary Johnson's two Civil War novels, *The Long Roll* and *Cease Firing,* it remains the role of the illustrator to illuminate the past as well as comment upon his own day.

Chapter 4
The Wild West

George Catlin (1796–1872). *Athapasca Indians.*
Outlines of North American Indians by George Catlin, 1858–1869.
Pen and ink, 18⅜″ x 24⅜″. Lent by the New-York Historical Society.

The West of the frontier is gone, but with the years its power as myth has grown. Our imaginations have played upon it ever since the early days when the West lay just over the hump of the Alleghenies. We are still at work on the myth. Both the written word and the picture have been largely fictional and the motion picture and television have added their great resources of dramatization and exaggeration. Our myth of the West is precious and not to be destroyed, but it needs to be balanced by the cooler scrutiny of fact and reality. We have had picture makers even from the early days who could supply those elements or, shall we say, had a reasonable balance of the two elements of imagination and clear-eyed scrutiny.

Certainly the first artists to penetrate the early West set out with great expectations and they found a scale, a grandeur, a complexity that made supreme demands upon their talents. None had faced such pictorial immensities before. And then there were the Indians. Almost all pictured the Indians with wonder, relish and admiration. The perpetually fierce and bloodthirsty Indian of later picture-making and prose had to await the overly dramatized future.

Those early artist-adventurers were a group with diverse accomplishments, backgrounds and outlooks. Fortunately a large proportion of their work is available to us in public collections and in reproduction. They range from the earliest men of modest talent, Samuel Seymour, Peter Rindisbacher and James Otto Lewis, to the gifted George Catlin and John Mix Stanley, the Swiss-born Karl Bodmer and Friedrich Kurz, the sumptuous landscapists Albert Bierstadt and the Moran brothers, and to the men of the frontier's last decades, Charles Schreyvogel, Charles M. Russell and Frederic Remington. Then came the many late-comers who had to be content with the still magnificent mountains and canyons, the city-dotted prairies, small, scattered cattle herds and Indians in reservations.

The dean of the real Western artists, the talented man who devoted his life to the study and recording of the life of the Indian tribes in their unspoiled primitive state, was George Catlin. Born in Wilkes-Barre, Pennsylvania in 1796, he left the practice of law to follow his inner urge to paint. He had encouragement from Thomas Sully, John Neagle and Rembrandt Peale. Seeing a delegation of skin-clad Indians from the West visiting Philadelphia moved him to decide upon his lifework—to celebrate the life of the Indian in picture form.

So began his long crisscross of travels throughout the West with easel and paint-box in hand. To provide himself with funds, he usually opened a studio in one of the Western cities to paint local portraits and then, with money in his pocket, started out in the spring for the Indian camps. He became a fast friend of many tribes, and was welcomed as were few whites to their dances, ceremonies and home life. He traveled by canoe, sail and steamer, on horseback and on foot. No other American artist has made such a complete record of the old Indian life.

He wrote a book about his work and adventures and, unable to find a publisher, finally saved enough of his own money to pay for publication. The *Notes of Eight Years Travel Amongst the North American Indians* was published in London in 1841. It was a two-volume work containing 400 engravings from his paintings. It is a great work of art and information and went through numerous editions. A few years later his *North American Indian*

Portfolio was printed in London with twenty-five colored lithographs—in later editions it was enlarged to thirty-two plates. In his later years he published several other books on tribal life.

Catlin even journeyed to South America, visiting native tribes from Tierra del Fuego to the Upper Amazon and from the coast of Brazil to Peru. Eventually he returned to the West and in later life traveled through little known parts of Alaska.

Although some of Catlin's work has been lost, books and portfolios of excellent reproductions of his work and a large collection of 450 of his paintings are in the National Collection of Fine Arts, Smithsonian Institution, Washington, D.C. Another large collection of 417 paintings is in the American Museum of Natural History in New York City and the New-York Historical Society has 221 drawings. These pictures are a priceless record of a vanished time and life.

The circumstances of army frontier life threw an American military man, with a gift for drawing, into an advantageous position to observe Indian life. Captain Seth Eastman, moving from one Western assignment to another, filled sketchbook after sketchbook with drawings of the various tribes he had an opportunity to study.

Married to a gifted writer, he illustrated her first book, *Dakotah, Life and Legends of the Sioux*, which was published in 1849. The success of this book encouraged them to spend much of their time accumulating Indian material for a published portfolio of Indian pictures, with text. Meanwhile Captain Eastman's reputation as an artist had been growing and he was selected to be one of the illustrators for a voluminous work on all the Indian tribes of the country. This six-volume work, authorized by Congress and almost ten years in preparation, was filled with many full-page plates from Eastman's paintings.

In 1853 the Eastmans published *The Romance of Indian Life*, with twelve color plates by the captain and text by his wife, and *The Aboriginal Port-Folio*, with twenty-six reproductions and text. These publications were soon followed by still another collaboration, *Chicora and Other Regions of the Conquered and the Unconquered*. Then came the Civil War and Eastman had to return to active duty. He retired at the war's end and was given a commission to execute paintings for committee rooms in the United States Capitol, where they still hang.

The fascination of the strange, new West reached across the Atlantic. Among those who came to it from the Old World was Alexander Philip Maximilian, Prince of Weid-Neuweid, a small royal state of Rhenish Prussia, accompanied by a young and talented artist, Karl Bodmer, a Swiss. They reached St. Louis in March of 1833 and followed Catlin's route of a year before. They went westward as far as Fort McKenzie, a new fortified outpost about a hundred miles from the Rockies, and here observed an attack of the Assinaboin and Cree tribes upon the Blackfeet. After their return to Europe, Bodmer reworked many of his sketches, and eighty-one of his pictures were reproduced in full-color in a folio that accompanied the two-volume text by the Prince. Bodmer's full-color illustrations have been considered among the best of their kind.

Even the young Felix Darley entered the Western scene at the beginning of his long creative career. In the early 1840's he made a sketching trip beyond the Mississippi. He wrote a story of the life of an Indian chief and accompanied that with a set of drawings in line; it was published as *Scenes in Indian Life*, in Philadelphia in 1843.

The West changed rapidly from the late 1830's to the Civil War. Would-be farmers, ranchers, miners, adventurers and drifters were swarming in. Where the early explorers and traders had traveled by canoe, now came the large, puffing, paddle-wheel riverboats. Where the half-breed traders with their pack-animals had broken the first trails, now came the long, lumbering wagon trains.

Then came the great Gold Rush to California in 1849 and the 1850's. This mad rush by many thousands was partly by ship through the Straits of Magellan or by portage across the Isthmus of Panama, but a great deal was by the endless prairie miles, over the mountains and deserts to the Promised Land. The West was never the same after that rush. But we find scarcely an artist who recorded it.

After the Civil War came the days of the cowboy. The railroads were pushed westward, the long drives of the herds from the range to the railheads were beginning. Here was a new chapter with great pictorial possibilities. Another new chapter was opening for the Indian troubles. The Indians, quieted by the slackening of white migration during the war years, were rising against the renewed push of tens of thousands of settlers. The bloodiest of the Indian wars were to take place.

The most prominent delineator of our Western regiments and the last years of warfare with the Indians was the New York-born Charles Schreyvogel. He was a poor boy who had to struggle for a living, but from his early days he seems to have set his hopes upon picturing the Army, the Indians and the West. With aid from generous friends he was enabled to study in Munich for three years and came back an accomplished draughtsman and painter. His first cowboy and Indian pictures were executed on the grounds of Buffalo Bill's Wild West Show. Colonel Cody became a helpful friend.

Only then did he make his first trip to the West. He drew and painted his chosen subject matter continuously, but for years faced a life of sharp poverty. It was not until after sending one of his pictures to the annual National Academy Exhibition that he was startled to learn it had been awarded the highest prize. That was a turning point. His pictures were eagerly bought; articles were written about him; President Theodore Roosevelt praised him and gave him the complete freedom of any military post in the country. Art prints were made of many of his paintings but in his lifetime there was no book of reproductions of his work.

There were two important portrayers of the final years of the old West. They were Charles M. Russell and Frederic Remington. Russell was born in the West and was of it, bone and sinew. He drew from his early days and was self-taught. At sixteen he set out for the cattle country, sketchbook in hand. For years he worked as a wrangler, rode with the herds, lived with the Indians and did odd jobs, but always drawing. He wrote too.

Some of his pictures were published in *Outing, Leslie's Magazine* and *Harper's Weekly* but he didn't take picture making very seriously until he married in 1896. His pictures have the authentic tang of that outdoor world and his book, *Trails Plowed Under,* carries one back to a time that is forever gone.

If there is a public image of the old West in the American mind it almost certainly contains more from the picture-making of Frederic Sackrider Remington than from any other artist. His pictures have had a wider circulation than others and have had a pronounced influence upon the work of those artists who came to the theme too late for first-hand experience. His works have been searched for information on types, costumes and backgrounds by the directors of the motion-picture, stage and television. He became the chief pictorial spokesman for the old West.

Remington came from the East, born in 1861 in Canton, near the banks of the St. Lawrence River in northern New York. His father was a newspaper owner and editor, who raised a squadron of cavalry and went to war, coming back a Lieutenant-Colonel at the war's end. Young Remington was sent to military school and then to Yale, but he was no student—he was interested only in sports and drawing. His father died at the end of young Remington's second year at Yale and that brought an end to his schooling. With a small inheritance he took off for the West.

He went with the idea of capturing a fortune and fell in love with the West. He was nineteen and already an expert horseman. He was tough, strong and daring. In little time he became an excellent shot and the equal of most with the lariat. He worked as a cowpuncher, rode with the troopers and dug for gold. His somewhat sudden determination to devote his life to drawing and painting the West that was vanishing under his eyes, was told in his own words in an article in *Collier's Weekly* some years later:

> Evening overtook me one night in Montana. I by good luck made the campfire of an old wagon freighter who shared his bacon with me. I was nineteen years of age and he was a very old man. Over the pipes it developed he…had gone West at an early age…During his lifetime he had followed the receding frontiers always further and further West.
>
> 'And now,' said he, 'there is no more West. In a few years the railroad will come along the Yellowstone…' I knew the wild riders and the vacant land were about to vanish forever—and the more I considered the subject, the bigger the *forever* loomed.
>
> Without knowing exactly how to do it, I began to record some facts around me…

So he committed himself to a lifetime of Western picture-making.

The large heritage of drawings, paintings and sculpture amassed by Remington over the years, was a great educational and inspirational storehouse for the would-be artists of the West who came later. It was not only the documentary content of his work that invited study and emulation, but its pace, ardor and inspirational spirit.

The old West has been one of America's giant themes. It has generated a great flood of prose, poetry and picture. Some of this has been inspired, some of it is trash and there is much between. The theme, the legend, the story is not likely to die; it is fast in our imaginations. The historian, the writer, the poet, the picture-maker will continue to work upon it—we will remake it to our purposes. The old West is already a land that never was.

George Catlin (1796–1872). *O-jib-be-ways.*
Hand-tinted lithograph, 12½″ x 16½″. Lent by Dr. and Mrs Robert H. Cox.

Chapter 5

Toward the Twentieth Century

Frederic Sackrider Remington (1861–1909). *Arrest of a Poacher in the Forest.*
Harper's New Monthly Magazine, April 1894.
Gouache, 21" x 29½". Lent by the Graham Gallery.

The years immediately following Appomattox were touchy, troubled years and naturally the illustration world reflected the times. Actually the day by day anxiety over the swing of battle results had stimulated the communication of information, both of word and picture. The whole mechanism of printing at the periodical level—daily newspaper, weekly and monthly magazines—was much improved. The reading public was larger and it had grown to expect a generous amount of picture material in its newspapers and magazines.

The answers to that need were forming slowly. There were now a number of thriving weekly and monthly magazines on the market and the book publishers were growing in numbers and size. Conspicuous in both fields was Harper Brothers. It was the largest publishing firm in the country, with a thriving book business and three popular magazines, *Harper's Weekly, Harper's Monthly* and *Harper's Young People*. Later *Harper's Bazaar* was added to the list.

The House of Harper was ensconced in two large buildings on Franklin Square in New York City, connected by an overhead bridge. Inadvertently these buildings became a prime school for the training of young illustrators. By the early 1870's here was assembled a redoubtable group of talents. At their head was Charles Parsons, the art editor, a remarkable man who was becoming a famous name in American publishing history. He was shrewd at discovering young talent, guiding it and watching it develop. In addition, on the mechanical side, he was alert to the newest methods and best equipment. Surrounding him in the two buildings were the personnel and machinery for the complete production of both books and magazines. There, an interested person could follow the journey of a drawing or manuscript from submission to finished appearance in a magazine or book. This was the ideal training ground for young artists of the time. This was a new conception in the land and Parsons was the organizing brain behind it. His task was not only finding young artists of promising talent, but he was looking for a combination of qualities—the ability to execute rapidly, to have resourceful creativity and at the same time have a feeling for their unseen audiences and an ability to communicate with them.

The group he gathered by the early Seventies was very remarkable. It was headed by Charles Stanley Reinhart, an excellent figurative draughtsman with an ability to handle with ease large and complex compositions. Next in ability was young Edwin Austin Abbey, short, chipper and jocund, whose remarkable pen style was just being formed. Soon his pen would be drawing the pictures that would make him famous, the drawings for *The Deserted Village* and *She Stoops to Conquer*, by Goldsmith, *Old Songs, The Comedies of William Shakespeare* and others. Then came an artist of a different flavor: Arthur B. Frost, a master of the homespun approach with his kindly and ingratiating humor. In the near future were his masterpiece pen pictures for Joel Chandler Harris' *Uncle Remus*.

There were others of more than average gifts in the Harper's group—W. T. Smedley, who had just come back from study in Paris, and J. W. Alexander, who considered Harper's an interesting way-station while he saved enough money to enroll in one of the Paris ateliers. There was A. R. Waud, now a veteran illustrator, who had been one of Harper's art correspondents in the Civil War years, and Frank Vincent DuMond, with great

Edwin Austin Abbey (1852–1911). *What Hap Had I to Marry a Shrew.*
Old Songs, Harper & Bros., 1888. Pen and ink, 17½″ x 13¾″. Lent by the Yale University Art Gallery.

Edwin Austin Abbey (1852–1911). *Harvest Home.*
Old Songs, Harper & Bros., 1888. Pen and ink, 13½" x 20½". Lent by Mr. and Mrs. Benjamin Eisenstat.

decorating dreams in his head, who was to become famous as a mural painter and teacher. The most famous of the Harper's artists was the grand old man, Thomas Nast, who worked at home but was a regular visitor.

These gifted men did a great deal for each other, just by association. A greater part of their creative work was done in the cluttered art room, quiet while the concentration of creation was working, often raucous when the pictured wood-block was on its way upstairs to their friendly enemies, the wood engravers. Sometimes they climbed the stairs to the engraving room. There was usually quiet, for engraving was a matter of great concentration. At their benches the engravers bent over their work, eyeshades over their brows, the short-shanked steel graving tool with its rounded wooden handle resting against a palm and the other hand changing the adjustment of the block from time to time. Slowly the gravers cut their nicks and delicate lines. One inaccurate cut in an important part of a design and the artist's intention was changed if not spoiled.

The artist regarded the engraver with mixed feelings. He was fearful of the engraver's mistakes or lack of skill, he always tried to have his picture cut by one of the most skilled of the craftsmen. On the other hand the engravers had their just complaints. They liked to cut the pictures that were executed with sharp black lines, but in the case of tonal drawing, the impossible was often expected. Any gray tone, light or dark, could only be simulated, not reproduced exactly as an even tone. The flat wash of pigment made by the artist, had to be translated into a network of nicks and delicate lines left by the cutting of the graver. The engravers of the late 1800's were highly skilled, some of the best in the world.

Howard Pyle found himself drawn into this group of artists as he began to do his first illustration assignments for the Harper's magazines, and the Harper's artists found themselves the nucleus of a larger company of congenial interests as more Americans returned from the schools of Europe. William Merritt Chase came back from Munich with a glowing reputation and soon he headed a coterie that gathered once a week at the Art Students League to draw and then retired to a hotel around the corner for beer and pretzels. The group had now grown to include Walter Shirlaw, Rufus Zogbaum, John Mitchell,

Charles S. Reinhart (1844–1896). *Title unknown.*
Pen and ink, 12⅝" x 18¼". Lent by Mrs. Thomas Wilcox.

Frederick Edwin Church and Julian Alden Weir. There were friendly relations with other nearby artists such as John LaFarge, George Inness, Louis Comfort Tiffany and Swain Gifford. These men had a feeling of common interests—there was no division between painters and illustrators—they were all picture-makers. The new arrivals from the European schools had much to give to the homestayers and also much to learn. Having been taught to see with a European point of view, many of them were rediscovering the vitality of a uniquely American attitude.

For the illustrator, the time had come when a mechanical invention would gradually work many improvements in the reproduction of his work—the development of the half-tone process. This was neither an overnight nor a one-man invention. For a number of years, many minds in both America and Europe had been working on the problem of developing a printing method that would quickly and mechanically reproduce the gradations of a tonal drawing.

When, after much trial and error, the new process became workable, it was a composite invention, completed by Americans. Photography played a key part. The artist's picture, with its gradations of gray, was photographed through a fine screen. The screen separated the picture into myriad dots—large ones for dark areas, smaller for light grays. The photographic negative with its picture image converted into thousands of dots was then transferred to a sensitized metal printing plate and acid etched. The plate now had its former surface etched away around the protected dots; the dots were now the only remaining part of the original surface. This plate was inked and impressions printed from it. With refinements, this process has continued to be used to the present. The screens which create the dots usually vary from 120 to 210 to the inch. Sometimes the screens for newspaper reproduction are as coarse as sixty to the inch—these can be seen with the naked eye, the finer screens only reveal themselves under a magnifying glass.

The perfection of the half-tone brought about a revolution in picture reproduction. Within a few years, the highly skilled wood engravers were forced to retire or seek other work. A small number were retained to sharpen up and retouch some of the new photo half-tone plates, for in those early years the plates were often muddy and lacking in sharp clarity.

The new process introduced in the late 1880's was a blessing to the publisher. Whereas a complicated block might require several days or even a week to complete, now it might be ready for the printer in an hour or two; and a full-page half-tone could now be processed for a fraction of the cost of a wood engraving.

Most of the illustrators were happy with the new process, except those whose favorite medium was pen and ink. The straightforward ink drawing was the easiest, cheapest and most likely to be accurately cut by the wood engraver. Theoretically he could make an exact replica of it on his block. Now, rather suddenly, the rage was for tonal reproduction. Often the brisk sparkle of the pen reproduction was replaced by the somewhat cloudy tonalities of the photo half-tone. Eventually quite a number of illustrators were forced to change their techniques.

As a result of the growing success of the photo half-tone method, the same principle of the drawing being photographed through a screen was applied to the making of plates for the reproduction of full color. By the end of the century full color printing was a partial success, but there were frequent failures.

Color reproduction is based upon the use of four plates, printing respectively red, yellow, blue and black impressions. Theoretically, color can be printed by using one, two or three of the primary color plates. Black is also necessary to produce tonal strength and grays.

Howard Pyle was the artist involved in one of the most important break-throughs. He had a naturally rich and sumptuous color sense, which had never found proper fulfillment. He had often talked to the Harper's editors of his eagerness to try the new methods and they were equally interested in having him use his talents to that end. The opportunity arrived when they planned to use an imaginative manuscript by Eric Bogh in the Christmas issue of *Harper's Monthly* for 1900. Pyle painted seven small panels in rich glowing color which were among his finest conceptions. We have no record of the unsatisfactory factor in the engraving department, but the attempt at full-color process was abandoned and Pyle produced new artwork for a different process of black line-cut plates over which a number of flat color plates could be printed. Although the full-color attempt was a failure, the new set for flat color was a triumph.

Before another year had passed, Pyle was given an opportunity to try another color set to illustrate one of his own manuscripts. This time he limited his color to the three primaries, leaving out black. The set came out handsomely. A year after this came another triumphant group and full-color photo-engraving was past its experimental stage.

Glancing backward from this point of technical success and artistic opportunity, we can see the broadening and deepening of the field. New magazines had come and were coming in steadily: *McClure's, The Saturday Evening Post, Ladies' Home Journal, Delineator, Everybody's, Woman's Home Companion, Pic-*

Frederick S. Church (1842–1924). *Xmas '88.*
Harper's Weekly, 1888. Oil, 15½″ x 10½″. Lent by Mrs. Thomas Wilcox.

William Thomas Smedley (1858–1920). *Each Letter Slowly Consumed to Ashes.*
Harper & Bros., 1915. Watercolor, 12″ x 8″. Lent by Mrs. Thomas Wilcox.

torial Review, Good Housekeeping, Outing, Cosmopolitan and others. Illustration was spreading among the advertisers and book publishers, particularly those for children. The period of great expansion was under way.

At the century's end had come the Spanish-American War, which received wide pictorial coverage in the magazines by artist war-correspondents at the front: Frank Schell, Frederic Remington, Henry Reuterdahl and William Glackens. Glackens, together with Frederick Gruger, Everett Shinn and John Sloan, had worked on the art staffs of the Philadelphia newspapers in earlier years when artists rather than photographers covered the dramatic events of day or night. They recorded riots, parades, fires, accidents, sporting events and elections. Probably nothing could equal that training—drawing incessantly on the spot from moving figures, in all kinds of light, against all kinds of background. Their later work showed the incredible facility drilled into them by that experience. As Glackens, Sloan, Shinn and George Luks fell under the spell of Robert Henri's teaching and philosophy, they became known as the famous 'Ash Can School' of painters and draughtsmen.

Most of the older men were still busy at their easels and drawing boards—Frost and Edward Kemble; Thomas Sullivant still pouring out his inimitably humorous pen and inks for *Judge* magazine; Abbey, gone to England to paint his murals and large historical canvases in the Cotswold village of Broadway, and Henry Hutt and Albert Wenzell busy creating their paintings of elegant life for the popular magazines. Elizabeth Shippen Green and Charlotte Harding were contributing to Harper's magazines, and Charles Dana Gibson was the most popular illustrator of the day.

The three fields of American illustration—magazine, book and advertising —were now in a pattern of rapidly accelerating growth. Fortunately the growth was not merely of size and numbers but of quality and diversity as well. After having learned so many lessons from the illustrations of Europe and elsewhere, American illustration could now indulge in its own teaching and enjoy the dubious pleasure of being imitated.

Chapter 6

Delineator for an Age

Howard Chandler Christy (1873–1952). *Women in Restaurant. 1923.*
Charcoal, 30" x 40". Lent by Mr. and Mrs. Alan Goffman.

The pen pictures of Charles Dana Gibson are now an important heritage of our past—not merely as a record of two decades or more of American life, but as a model which was emulated, and which formed a pattern for real life.

Those pictures are a social marvel. They were not merely a portrait of an age—the age was a portrait of them. Imagine a time when hundreds of thousands of women primped and posed, tried to look and act like a series of drawings—and that all this should be the product of one mind, and should have come out of an ink bottle!

In an age of the motion picture and television, mimicry on a national scale is no longer the phenomenon it was at the beginning of this century. It is safe to say that never before or since has any American picture-maker aroused such a large, steadfast and imitative audience, an audience that tried to model itself upon his pictures. His primary vehicle of communication was the new, lively, comic magazine *Life.* But from those pages the Gibson pen images multiplied in inventive ways—into the large horizontal Gibson albums on countless parlor tables, the Gibson girl faces and figures on china plates, tablecloths, screens, hangings, fans, pillowcovers and a score of other surfaces. Thousands of young and old would-be artists copied or tried to imitate the slashing Gibson pen style. There was even a Gibson wallpaper designed for bachelors' rooms and stereopticon slides of the Gibson repertoire for parties.

The craze for a series of pen drawings of a certain type of head and body was translated into the thoughts, the conversations, the acts and impulses of millions.

The source of all this pictorial power was a modest, earnest and enormously talented man—who simply exercised his natural gifts and found the most fruitful time for them. Young Gibson spent two hard-working years at the Art Students League at a time when the faculty list carried such outstanding names as Thomas Eakins, William Merritt Chase, Kenyon Cox, John Sartain, Walter Shirlaw, Julian Alden Weir and Edwin Blashfield. He began to be captivated by the pictorial possibilities of the pen line and he pored over the work of Edwin A. Abbey, A. B. Frost, Albert Sterner, and Charles S. Reinhart. He became aquainted with the young Frederic Remington, who was a fellow student at the League.

He had now become aware of the European pen artists too, particularly of the two men who were at the root of so much of the pen techniques of the period, the Spanish Parisian Daniel Vierge and the German painter and draughtsman Adolf Menzel. In addition, the British school appealed to him: George Cruickshank, John Leech, Charles Keene and George DuMaurier. Gibson learned from all these men and others, but it was not mere imitation—a sweep, a verve, a mastery was developing in his own work, and it was happening at a propitious time when the illustrator was being freed from his bondage to the wood engraver.

About this time young Gibson also became interested in the draftsmanship of the English artist Phil May, who endeavored to express his subjects in the fewest possible lines. It was a very spare technique of longer lines, very little tonality or texture. Gibson followed the principles of longer sweeping lines, more from the shoulder and elbow than the wrist, but he retained his delight in rich darks, dramatic shadows and full-bodied, scintillating expression.

Gibson developed a masterful technique that was new in the field and the world fell in love with it. The popular interest

Charles Dana Gibson (1867–1944). *At the Recital.* Pen and ink, 18" x 29". Lent by the Society of Illustrators.

always centered around his 'Gibson Girl,' with her companion, the 'Gibson Man,' in second place. They were a handsome, youthful pair, moving through life in a serenely competent, assured way, never stirred to excitement, perplexity or anger. Courteous and secure, they had an Anglo-Saxon attractiveness that seemed to protect them from annoyances and confrontations. They became the models for untold numbers of the young and not so young.

But Gibson's reach was deeper and broader than this. Interwoven with this compelling pair, and also apart from them, were a whole company of varied characters, some satirized, some delineated with compassion. Here was night life, home life, the American abroad, the social climber, the sport enthusiast, royalty, the bread line. Here was the cable car, the ninth inning, the fashionable funeral, the sidewalks of New York. He had a broad spectrum of interest and some penetrating and sympathetic comments to make, and he had the admiration of a giant audience to delineate its dreams. Is the power to delineate the dreams of a vast audience of trifling importance?

While Gibson's social vision had followers, his spectacular pen technique had more. Some were mere imitators, a few were creative artists in their own right, taking what was needed from the master to augment their own resources. Prominent among them were Howard Chandler Christy, James Montgomery Flagg

and Harrison Fisher. All these were gifted draughtsmen who adapted the recurring 'American Girl' theme to their particular outlook and techniques. Flagg, especially, carried on the Gibson type of pen technique, but even he was never able to match the urbane wit and insight that made Gibson the most perceptive interpreter of the post-Victorian era.

Charles Dana Gibson (1867–1944). *Her Heart Is in the Kitchen.*
Collier's Magazine, 1904. Pen and ink, 17" x 29". Lent by the Society of Illustrators.

Chapter 7

Howard Pyle and the Brandywine School

Howard Pyle (1853–1911).
. . . gazed and gazed until his heart melted away within him.
Twilight Land by Howard Pyle, Harper & Bros., 1895. Pen and ink, 6" x 9".
Lent by Mrs. Thomas Wilcox.

If any one man can be considered the father of American illustration, it is Howard Pyle. When he came to artistic maturity wood engraving was still the prevailing method of reproduction; within a decade photo-engraving was emancipating the illustrator from the wood engraver, so that he was in at the beginning of the era of modern illustration.

Pyle's overwhelming influence stems from two sources, either of which would have been enough to have established his preeminence. First, he was a superb illustrator, unequalled in power, imagination and scope ever since. Second, he was America's greatest teacher of illustration. His students have passed on his precepts to a third and fourth generation of illustrators and the inspiration of Pyle is still a strong part of the illustration mainstream.

He was a lover of history from his early boyhood and inevitably this crept into his later picture-making. His *Christmas Morning in old New York,* reproduced in the December 25th, 1880 number of *Harper's Weekly* seems to mark his professional entry into the field of historical illustration, which from then on occupied much of a life crammed with diverse activities. Pyle came from a long line of Quaker ancestors who had moved into the Brandywine valley when it was still Indian territory and lived within walking distance of the Revolutionary battlefield of the Brandywine, so it was natural that American history was a first love that expanded into a lifetime commitment for him.

Two of his largest and most important series of historical pictures were for Woodrow Wilson's *History of the American People* and James Truslow Adam's *History of the United States.* While working on the pictures for Woodrow Wilson's book he discovered several inaccuracies in the text. He wrote a friendly note to the author and received a reply full of friendliness and gratitude.

The New York editors had early estimated the possibilities of Pyle's dual talents of writing and picture-making and had encouraged him to strike out on his own for relevant material. The results were a number of illustrated articles for *Harper's New Monthly Magazine* through the early 1880's.

Although many of his pictures and books dealt with the Middle Ages, it was the history of his own country's Colonial, Revolutionary, Early Independence and Civil War periods that attracted him most. As a small boy he had watched the blue, freshly uniformed Federal troops move through Wilmington on their way to the Virginia front and saw the wounded and the ragged gray prisoners come back. His Civil War pictures probably reached their peak in the large canvas decoration of *The Battle of Nashville,* in the Governor's reception room in the Minnesota State Capitol in Minneapolis.

Over the years hundreds of Pyle's historical pictures appeared in print in magazines and books. They helped to imprint mental images in the minds of tens of thousands. Almost all of us have shared these pictures of the frontiersman, the pioneer homesteader, the pioneer wife, the ragged Revolutionary soldier, the redcoat, the Indian trader, the plantation owner, the slave. From the brain image they have passed to the theatre, to the motion picture set, to the television stage. This is the chain that has had more effect upon the public mind than the text of history books.

Pyle's natural aptitude for history was fortified by more than the study of history books—he had, like all excellent artists, developed the power of *identification.* This is the wisdom learned

Howard Pyle (1853–1911). *Hamilton Addressing the Mob.*
Harper's New Monthly Magazine, October 1884. Wash, 9¾″ x 7½″. Lent by the New-York Historical Society.

47

Howard Pyle (1853–1911). *The Spy. Harper's New Monthly Magazine, February 1905*. Oil, 24″ x 16″. Lent anonymously.

Howard Pyle (1853–1911). *The Trotting Match.*
The Autocrat of the Breakfast Table by Oliver Wendell Holmes, Riverside Press, 1894.
Oil, 12¼″ x 8″. Lent anonymously.

Howard Pyle (1853–1911). *A Reminiscence of the Marigold.*
The Autocrat of the Breakfast Table by Oliver Wendell Holmes, Riverside Press, 1894.
Oil, 12¼″ x 8″. Lent anonymously.

by the watchful eye, by the test of all the senses—not by the studious mind alone. This is the homely awareness that the same pair of legs, clad in moccasins, moves differently when it is wearing jack-boots; that a body in a farthingale sits differently from one in an Empire shift; that lace ruffles at a velveteen cuff dictate the gestures of a hand and arm so clothed.

This sense of identification was also expressed in an unusual ability to dramatize a given situation and present it with graphic immediacy. His pictures did not need explanation. They told their stories without reliance on a caption or text. Each character's role was conveyed by a telling gesture or attitude and heightened by compositional devices of placement, color or tone. Above all, he chose themes of importance; even in weak manuscripts he managed to find situations relating to the basic human motivations of the characters involved.

At a time when most artists were European trained or looked to Europe for artistic leadership, Pyle felt strongly that

illustration was a valid art form that should contribute to the development of an American art.

So Howard Pyle, with his years of practice and success behind him, brooded upon this condition, and felt impelled to help correct it. He reviewed the experiences of his own training: the strict and incessant drill in reporting the aspect of a posed figure and the need for the acquisition of this skill, but also the limitations of it for an imaginative, creative illustrator. There could be a long list of the usual limitations of academic training, not only the lack of experience with the multiple effects of outdoor light or the mysteries of artificial light indoors, the general lack of out-of-doors experience in picture-making, but also the disinclination to deal with movement, the body and expression of emotion, the need for imagination in general and in picture composition in particular, and practice in drawing and thinking beyond the posed model.

Pyle felt within himself the ability to supply these

Howard Pyle (1853–1911). *In the Valley of Delight.*
The Story of King Arthur and His Knights by Howard Pyle, Scribner's Sons & Co., 1903.
Pen and ink, 10″ x 7″. Lent anonymously.

deficiencies and began to act upon his conviction. There was no suitable center in his hometown of Wilmington but in nearby Philadelphia were three art schools. Conspicuously the oldest in the country was the Pennsylvania Academy of the Fine Arts. He offered his services, which were refused, but shortly after he was invited to join the faculty of the Drexel Institute of Art, Science and Industry. This he accepted and his Course in Practical Illustration was launched.

It was an instant success. There were many more applicants than could be accommodated—the first class had to be limited to thirty-nine. It was a new experience for Pyle, but he and his students quickly discovered that he was a natural teacher. The effect of his teaching was soon clearly apparent in the superior work of his students and Pyle realized that he was learning from them as well.

From the many would-be students he interviewed, he was able to make a canny selection of talent. In a very few years some of them were not only working successfully in the field but also forging impressive reputations. Names like Maxfield Parrish, Violet Oakley, Clyde DeLand, Jessie Wilcox Smith, Elizabeth Shippen Green, Charlotte Harding, Stanley Arthurs, Walter Everett and Frank Schoonover began to become familiar to the magazine and book reading public.

The success of his first year of teaching led to more and more applications for entrance and he was forced to find additional

time for this work, which began to encroach seriously upon his creative time in his studio. Then a new, innovative idea for his students led him into a fresh path of teaching that lasted until the final years of his life.

He was a lover of the out-of-doors and often felt that the four walls of a classroom could have cramping consequences. He and his family were spending their summers in Chadds Ford on the Brandywine River about twelve miles from his studio in Wilmington. He broached the idea of a summer class in the country to the president of Drexel and the project came into being. A thousand dollars was raised to be divided into ten one-hundred-dollar scholarships and awarded to his best pupils. This covered board, lodging, instruction, everything except supplies and personal expenses. Pyle received no salary.

The class began in the summer of 1898 and that first class and its successor the next year became treasured memories in the minds of all those fortunate enough to be a part of them. A great deal of the work was done in the open air and the students experienced the infinite moods and lighting of nature. These were memorable and enriching experiences.

Pyle's report on the 1899 summer session to Drexel's president read in part:

> Though the work done by the pupils during the past summer is perhaps not so great in number of examples finished for exhibition purposes, it is yet in many respects of the highest order achieved in our Institute. Each pupil has been working throughout the summer at a single composition made originally by the individual. These have been worked up into finished pictures in more or less full color. I had photographs taken of these examples of work and showed them to my friends at Harper & Brothers. These publishers were so pleased with the work that they have expressed a willingness to publish all or nearly all of the drawings made by the summer school in *Harper's Weekly,* and also others done through the season under the auspices of the Class of Illustration at the Institute . . . Besides these examples of full work, one of the pupils has made two illustrations for *McClure's Magazine,* and others have illustrated books for Houghton Mifflin & Company and Dodd, Mead & Company. This has, of course, consumed a part of the summer, but my chief instruction has been directed to the perfection of our Institute work, and those people who have been delayed in the finishing thereof because of these important books undertaken are remaining here at their own expense to complete the Drexel Institute Class work.*

This report contains a description of what became a steady practice through all Pyle's teaching days—his regular showing of the work of his advanced students to the New York art editors. Over the years, student after student was to enter the professional ranks through the recommendations of his teacher.

But the great success of the two summer sessions made Pyle very discontented with the winter classes. He had come to

*Philadelphia, Penna. Drexel Archives.

Howard Pyle (1853–1911). *'I am Captain John Mackra,' said I, and sat down on the gunwale of the boat. Harper's Weekly, 1887.* Sepia wash, 10″ x 16″. Lent anonymously.

realize that unless he had complete power to select his own students, he would waste too much of his energy with those who had no creative potential. The only solution was to build up a hand-picked student enclave, closely attuned to his eye and voice. So he drafted an explanatory letter of resignation to the head of Drexel Institute and worked out plans for forming his own class in illustration.

Pyle's own studio was on what was then the fringes of Wilmington; it stood on a sizable plot of land and there was room for a long, two-storied building he had built especially for classes. It was divided into three studio units, with bedrooms and facilities above. Here everything would be under his eye and only a few steps away. Any idle five or ten minute interval could be spent with his students. There was no tuition, only small prorated interest charges on his capital outlay. In 1902, for example it was $4.90 per month, per student. The whole mechanism of the class was held to a minimum, almost all of it handled by Pyle's secretary and his two student monitors, Stanley Arthurs and Frank Schoonover. There were no lists, no attendance records, no marks, no diplomas.

From the first formation of his own class Pyle was beseiged by applicants, over three hundred in one year alone. Only a few could be chosen. Vacancies occurred only rarely, since there were

There seems to have been a certain creative magic implanted by Pyle in his students which almost never failed, and for most lasted a lifetime. The greatest number of them moved into the busy world of illustration and carved out notable careers. None of them displayed, except in small degree, Pyle's dual talents of no graduations; in most cases it was a farewell with blessings to a student who had reached a professional level and was ready for independence.

Most of these students were young, around the twenty-year mark, like Newell Convers Wyeth, William Aylward, Philip Goodwin, George Harding. Thornton Oakley and Harvey Dunn. This type of student represented the core of his student body, but after a few years another group was added to the younger, developing core. In this group were older men and women, already practicing professionals, who were dissatisfied with their own work and who came hoping to be prodded into a higher level of attainment by this famous teacher. They sought out their own living and studio space nearby and worked independently of the younger students. These older students, among them Ernest Peixotto, Henry Soulen, Anton Otto Fischer, John Wolcott Adams, Douglas Duer and Edward Wilson, were usually given individual criticisms apart from the class.

51

Howard Pyle (1853–1911). *King and Jesters.* Pen and ink, 6″ x 9″. Lent by the Society of Illustrators.

picture-making and writing, but many of them taught. Violet Oakley held classes in decoration at the Pennsylvania Academy of the Fine Arts, Frank Schoonover and Stanley Arthurs had studio classes in later years and William Aylward taught at the Newark School of Art. But four former students gave a good deal of time to large classes over a long term of years. They were George Harding at the Pennsylvania Academy of the Fine Arts, Walter Everett at the Pennsylvania Museum School of Art and later the Spring Garden Institute in Philadelphia, Thornton Oakley at the Pennsylvania Museum School of Art and Harvey Dunn at his own school in Leonia, New Jersey and later at the Grand Central School of Art in New York City. All four were imbued with the ambition to transmit the creative fervor which Pyle had implanted in them, to a new generation of ambitious talents.

The personalities of all four were quite different and naturally their teaching reflected those differences. Pyle's teaching had not been a pat system or formula, and that would have been the last thing he would have desired to find in his former students. Harvey Dunn had the closest character resemblance to Pyle, both as an illustrator and as a teacher. He was a large, striking, athletic man with the magnetic qualities of the evangelist in his makeup, and his was the most fruitful in student inspiration. A large number of important talents developed under his eyes—among them were Dean Cornwell, Harold Von Schmidt, Saul Tepper, Mario Cooper, John Steuart Curry, Arthur D. Fuller and Albin Henning.

So the influence of the Brandywine days spread, even as these four retired. Harvey Dunn was succeeded by his pupil Dean Cornwell, George Harding at the Pennsylvania Academy of the Fine Arts by former student Edward Shenton and Thornton Oakley of the Pennsylvania Museum School by Henry Pitz. This was not the transfer of a tight and formulated doctrine, it was the passing on of a creative experience, a sense of social responsibility to one's audience, an impulse to project the multitudinous story of man and his world in pictorial terms.

Chapter 9
Pictures for Children

Rose O'Neill (1875–1944). *A Night with Little Sister.*
Harper's Bazar, July 1906. Pen and ink, 5" x 14½".
Lent by Mrs. Thomas Wilcox.

The early years of book illustration in the new Republic were necessarily tentative, as we have seen. The two dominating figures of those early days were Alexander Anderson, whose white-line wood engraving set in motion an increasingly skilled and spreading method of picture reproduction, and Felix Darley, whose talent was far above any others.

Some books for children were appearing, but almost all were dull and dreary productions, heavy with moralizing and devoid of fun and laughter. Often they were without pictures or illustrated with a stock of old, used wood-blocks with little or no relation to the text. When, a few days before Christmas of 1823, there appeared in a newspaper in Troy, New York, a Christmas ballad with the title *A Visit from St. Nicholas*, that obscure incident became a landmark. Here was established the endearing figure of the Dutch legendary saint with his Christmas Eve sleigh and reindeer. Here arrived love and merriment and imagination for American children, and an unforgettable figure in American mythology that would be endlessly depicted by illustrators in the future.

Things began to improve for the children of America in both text and picture. The *Tales of Peter Parley* appeared in 1827 and the first of Jacob Abbott's *Rollo* books was published a few years later. More and more often children's books began to contain illustrations as a matter of course, but too often the illustrator's name was not mentioned.

Felix Darley as a professional picture-maker did a great deal to correct that neglect. The superiority of his talent and popularity encouraged the publishers to advertise his name, and this practice eventually became accepted for other illustrators. Darley reached the high point of his career with his illustrations for Washington Irving's classics.

There also appeared at this time one of the great figures in American art, Winslow Homer. Homer's first book illustration in 1859 was a design for the title page of a series of children's books called *The Percy Family*. His first magazine drawing had appeared two years before in the *Pictorial Drawing Room Companion* and a little later his finest work appeared in *Harper's Weekly* and *Every Saturday*.

Illustrated magazines for children were now coming into being, one upon the heels of another. The publishers of the *Atlantic Monthly* introduced the first number of *Our Young Folks* in

Newell Convers Wyeth (1882–1945). *The Cowboy's Life.*
The World of Music Series: Adventure, 1938. Tempera, 36″ x 26″. Lent by Ginn and Company.

Newell Convers Wveth (1882–1945). *A Gypsy Sings to his Pony.*
The World of Music Series: Discovery, 1937. Tempera, 36″ x 26″. Lent by Ginn and Company.

Peter S. Newell (1862–1924). *A Careless Father.*
Harper's Bazar, March 25, 1899. Pen and ink and gouache, 7¾" x 6⅞".
Lent by Robert J. Mehlman.

1865. *The Riverside Magazine for Young People* appeared in 1867 using artists like John LaFarge, Winslow Homer, Thomas Nast, E. B. Bensell, H. L. Stephens and Darley. Harper and Brothers entered the field of children's magazines in 1879 with their *Harper's Young People,* which later changed its name to *Harper's Round Table* (it ceased publication in 1899).

Our Young Folks and *The Riverside Magazine for Young People* were absorbed into America's longest lived and most important magazine for children, *St. Nicholas.* Under the editorship of the famous Mary Mapes Dodge and her successor, William Fayal Clark, its files, running through more than a half century, are now an important source for the study of earlier American illustration for children. The work of A. B. Frost, Howard Pyle and Reginald Birch are on some of the earlier pages, that of Maurice Bower, Henry Pitz and John Steuart Curry on some of the later ones. There has been a parade of children's magazines over the years: *Boys' Life, American Boy* and *American Girl, Story Parade, Jack and Jill, Boys Today, American Junior Red Cross News* and others. Norman Rockwell was the first Art Director of *Boys' Life* magazine, published by the Boy Scouts of America. During the early years of this century there was wide distribution of eight-page illustrated story papers to the children's Sunday school classes of various churches, notably the Presbyterian, Methodist, Baptist and Lutheran.

In short, the late years of the nineteenth century and the opening years of the twentieth were witnessing a great change and expansion in the writing and illustration for children. A landmark event was the publication of *Huckleberry Finn* in 1885. Mark Twain had made the brilliant choice of E. W. Kemble for his illustrator and the combination was ideal. Here was the breezy, zestful heart of America in prose and picture.

Two years earlier Howard Pyle's *The Merry Adventures of Robin Hood* had appeared. There was an English as well as an American edition and the British reviews were kind. Pyle was delighted to hear that the great William Morris had been puzzled that such an excellent achievement, worthy of a Briton, could have come out of America.

It was a fertile time for Pyle. He was painting and drawing regularly for adult magazines, but at the same time writing and illustrating a series of books for children. In the five years after the publication of *Robin Hood,* he had brought out three more exceptional books, crammed with pictures and engaging in text—*Pepper and Salt, The Wonder Clock* and *Otto of the Silver Hand. The Wonder Clock* can be bracketed with its two predecessors, a triumvirate of delightful masterpieces.

The fourth and last book, *Otto of the Silver Hand,* was both like and different from the other three. It was neither a collection of separate tales and verses, nor a retelling of an old legend—it was fiction, a story of medieval life in old Germany. It was a bold book—it dealt straightforwardly but touchingly with the reality of the Middle Ages. Pyle did not veer away from its harshness and brutalities or ignore its beauty and nobility. The book is as moving today as when it appeared, against a lingering background of Victorian inhibitions.

The pictures in these books are bold and rich, straightforward in draughtsmanship, convincing in characterization, refreshingly different in design—a handsome combination of word and picture. Throughout his work, the strong, confident drawing of Pyle's illustrations, their rich humanity and stimulating design, created a new pictorial world for the young.

Pyle's work represents the new, a break with the old. Reginald Birch was a bridge, a Victorian galvanized by the new. His most famous creation, *Little Lord Fauntleroy,* was trying to move toward the twentieth century decked out in velvet suit, broad lace collar and long curls. But under that costume was a real youngster and his portrayer was an excellent technician.

A complete contrast to Pyle and Birch was Palmer Cox, who created the Brownies, those delightful inhabitants of a never-never world outside the boundaries of normal time. To place Pyle, Birch and Cox side by side may seem incongruous but it gives an indication of the width of reach of illustration for children.

Waiting in the wings, as American illustration moved across the dividing line of the centuries, was a host of young talents. Few could have suspected the rich and varied abilities of the new, eager generation of magazine and book illustrators, who sensed the opportunities of the beginning century.

The material conditions for expansion were present or shaping themselves: greater wealth, population explosion and the spreading growth and wider use of educational facilities. Our multiplying population was attuned to the accessibility of the

Henry C. Pitz (1895–1976). *Title unknown. The Saturday Evening Post.* Pen and ink, 13" x 16½". Lent by the artist.

printed word and picture. One of the most inviting fields was that of illustrating for children. The stringent years of World War I put a temporary halt to the rising tide, but by the second quarter of the century it was running strongly again.

Naturally, not every talent was adaptable to the children's audience. Some of the most gifted artists seem to have given all their attention to adults.

On the other hand, there were delightful picture-makers who spoke directly to children, like Harrison Cady, Oliver Herford, Alice Barber Stevens, Peter Newell and Rose O'Neill. Harrison Cady created a pictorial world of absurd bug life, crammed with incident and nonsense detail, that enticed the eye to linger, explore and enjoy. Rose O'Neill invented the Kewpies, who entertained both children and their mothers by their charming antics. Ernest Thompson Seton's books about animals, like *The Trail of the Sandhill Stag, Lives of the Hunted* and *Biography of a Grizzly,* are still in demand; and Seton and Dan

Beard, who were two of the founders of the Boy Scout movement in this country, each wrote and pictured a series of other children's books.

Within a few years the author-artist combination was to become a much more customary figure in the field of children's books. Many an illustrator, reviewing the work of his copiously pictured book and the few, scanty lines of two-syllable text supplied by the author, said to himself, 'I could do this!' and sometimes succeeded. Presently the works from the hands of the twin-talented formed a very important section of children's books: the creations of Wanda Gag, Lois Lenski, Peggy Bacon, Ludwig Bemelmans, James Daugherty, Hugh Lofting, Dorothy Lathrop and many others.

Some of Howard Pyle's gifted students were entering the field, notably N. C. Wyeth, who had embarked on his long series of classics, illustrated with full-color pages, jackets and limited-color end-leaves. He gave a new note of rousing color, athletic rhythms and general exhilaration to old favorites like *The Legends of Charlemagne*, *Robinson Crusoe*, Malory's *King Arthur*, Cooper's *The Last of the Mohicans* and *The Deerslayer*, Stevenson's *Treasure Island* and *Kidnapped* and many others. Frank Schoonover, too, used the same method in his pictures for *Roland, the Warrior,* as did Jessie Wilcox Smith for *Little Women* and *Old Fashioned Girl,* Thornton Oakley in Kingsley's *Westward Ho* and Maxfield Parrish in *The Arabian Nights* and *The Golden Treasury of Songs and Lyrics.* This type of book makeup, for older children, with its full-color plates printed on glossy paper and inserted at intervals between the pages of text, set a pattern for many years.

Into the field of book illustration, which was rapidly altering by the end of the first quarter of the century, came a large group of greatly varied and gifted illustrators: Warren Chappell, Willy Pogany, Edward Shenton, Henry Pitz, James Daugherty, Charles Falls, Lynd Ward, Robert Lawson and many others.

This was a time when a great many forces were working to widen, deepen and improve the entire American book publishing field and that of children's books in particular. There were more art schools offering courses in illustration, and more competent and experienced illustrators were devoting part of their time to teaching.

The growth of the audiences for children's illustration and of the company of artists to provide it coincided with a series of mechanical innovations in the printing industry leading to the perfection of offset lithography. Now type and picture could be printed as a unit. Now line and tone could be used together or in combination and the illustrative shapes could follow any inventive compositional urge. The illustrator felt a sense of increased control and children's books, in particular, changed rapidly. Now the illustrator often had the opportunity to design the whole book.

Looking back over the years for the first rooting of that renaissance, we might select the moment in 1919 when the MacMillan Company in New York City created a children's book department and named Louise Seaman as its first editor. Three years later, May Massee was appointed to the same position at Doubleday, Doran and Company and shortly after, Lillian Bragdon at Alfred Knopf. These women of exceptional energy, taste and enterprise led many publishers to follow the same example. Today the now enlarged body of children's book editors is remarkably astute and aware. They have not only been receptive to budding American talents but have also combed Europe and other countries.

In a field studded with personalities Bertha E. Mahony is important. The opening of her Bookshop for Boys and Girls in Boston in 1916 led to a chain of accomplishments. Her first book catalogs were so informative and popular that they became an annual and then a semi-annual review, which turned into the now well known *Horn Book.* From that sprang the 'who's who' of children's illustrators, *Contemporary Illustrators of Children's Books,* in 1930, followed by expanded volumes, *Illustrators of Children's Books,* in the Forties.

The name of Anne Carroll Moore stands high on the list of

Newell Convers Wyeth (1882–1945). *Queen Astrid Comes no More. The World of Music Series: Treasure, 1938.* Tempera, 36″ x 26″. Lent by Ginn and Company.

those who have played a major part in championing excellence in children's books. She edited the first children's book page in the *New York Herald Tribune* and her *Three Owls* was one of the first books to deal with American art and writing for children. Children's book columns are no longer uncommon in our newspapers and magazines.

Many other activities have multiplied around the theme of books for children. In 1918, the first Children's Book Week was launched by New York librarians and editors, and that soon grew into an annual event of great importance. At the crowded annual conventions of the American Library Association, a goodly portion of the time and activities was devoted to the interests of children, and here the important awards of the Newberry Medal for distinguished writing in the children's field and the Caldecott Medal for outstanding book illustration were given.

The first Caldecott award was given in 1938 to Dorothy P. Lathrop and in succeeding years to Thomas Hanforth, Ingri and Edgar Parin d'Aulaire, Robert Lawson, Robert McCloskey, Virginia Lee Burton, Maud and Miska Petersham, Leonard Weisgard, Leo Politi, Katherine Milhous, Nicholas Mordvenoff,

Newell Convers Wyeth (1882–1945). *The Prince.*
The World of Music Series: Discovery, 1937. Tempera, 36″ x 26″.
Lent by Ginn and Company.

Charles Buckles Falls (1874–1960). *God Rest You Merry, Gentlemen.*
Everybody's Magazine, December 1905. Pen and ink and gouache, 13″ x 7½″.
Lent by Robert J. Mehlman.

Lynd Ward, Ludwig Bemelmans, Feodor Rojankovsky and many others.

The list of names, which could be much longer, also indicates the cosmopolitan background of our American illustrators, which at least partly accounts for the wide diversity of our pictorial expression. Our artists speak with many voices, to the largest audiences the world has known.

To survey the vast upsurge in children's illustrated books in the past thirty-five to forty-five years is to be overwhelmed by numbers as well as diversity. The globe has been ransacked for material and known and unknown planets are being catalogued. The earth's surface has been searched, yard by yard, and the waters beneath. Innumerable little boys and girls from every race, tribe and clan have been put through their paces. The animal kingdom has been a happy hunting ground for every beastie which can be made to talk and reveal its inner thoughts. Every compartment in the natural world has been pried open, described and pictured.

And every size, shape, format, page arrangement and binding has been tried. Many books still open in the old traditional way but others pull apart, unfold, pop in one's face, make noises or pull out like an accordion. American inventiveness has not been overstated. There are sometimes areas of synthetic fur for fingers to stroke. Instead of surprise endings, many of these books have surprise openings. The American passion for variety has been very fruitful but it can and sometimes has become a scamper after mere novelty.

No one knows if there is a saturation point for children's books. For years there has been mushroom growth in the field, slowed recently by a recession in the economic tide—perhaps a temporary interlude; perhaps a warning of creative relaxation or exhaustion.

Chapter 10

History As Illustration—Illustration Is History!

Irving Nurick (1894–1963). *Armistice Day—World War I.*
Collier's Magazine, November 13, 1937. Watercolor, 9¾″ x 13″.
Lent by Mrs. Dorothy Nurick.

From our early days, American illustrators have dealt with historical subject matter. History has been one of the important themes of their picture-making and a number of our most gifted illustrators have built reputations upon their deep knowledge of and interest in past times and events. Other illustrators have been busy with favorite themes of everyday life, the rich and the poor, the world of childhood, of the genial eye, the critical eye, itemized fact, fantasy, fiction, of almost anything—all unconscious that they have been picturing history, for illustration is history and like a mirror—faulty or faithful, truthful or fanciful—illustration is a historical fragment.

Perhaps we might be arbitrary and divide all illustration into conscious and unconscious history. Unconscious history has little or no standing, but what a way to savor the flavor of a time, through the recording eye! The history of our own times, through the multitudinous proliferation of the picture, will have a different cast from that of older times. Our descendants will find it easier to don our garments, walk our streets and copy our antics in their imaginations—we have spent much time revealing ourselves to the future.

Most illustrators—those we have just tagged with the title of 'unconscious historians'—will go about their daily picture-making unmindful of the fact that perhaps some day, their work may be plundered by some note-taking history student of the future. Let us have a few things to say about the illustrator of historical themes, who must catch the flavor and fact of a given time, place and event. Usually he finds that there is no scarcity of texts that may be consulted, and if he has some experience behind him, he can immediately predict their limitations. Those texts will probably be rich in descriptions of events and persons, but poverty-stricken in the description of the appearance of places and things. He craves pictures of things, but most of all—the real thing. He will gloat over an actual rapier of Roundhead days or a curled wig of the mid-eighteenth century. The real thing is best, a picture next best, a paragraph of print comes last.

But he has imagination, he is something of an actor. An unseen eavesdropper in his studio might think him a bit unhinged. He is wrinkling his brow in a strange way and stomping about the studio in an unheard of manner. He is just conscious of the heavy sweat trickling down from the brow band of his wig and getting the feel of the weight and clumsiness of his imaginary jackboots. He will be his normal self as soon as he gets back to his picture. Strangely enough, his picture will probably be helped by all this seeming nonsense. That Civil War jacket: it

Albin Henning (1886–1943). *To the Living and the Rest of Them. The Saturday Evening Post, June 2, 1928.* Oil, 27" x 54". Lent by Dr. Terry W. Slaughter.

has been in the field for months, there will be worn spots on the shoulders where the rifle has been carried—the left elbow may be frayed where it has rested on the ground or a rock when firing, the sleeves may be short or long.

Howard Pyle's immense pictorial contribution to the recreation of historical subjects has already been described. He passed on this interest to his students, a number of whom found creative nourishment in historical material; particularly Stanley Arthurs, many of whose carefully researched canvases were later reproduced in a handsome volume, *The American Historical Scene.* In his later years Edward Wilson worked largely in the book field, illustrating such classics as *The Last of the Mohicans, Two Years Before the Mast, Man Without a Country* and *Westward Ho.* Clifford Ashley and William Aylward were both lovers of the sea and in each case it was their chief subject matter. Ashley painted many pictures of whaling and fishing subjects and wrote and illustrated several nautical books, including the *Yankee Whaler* and *The Ashley Book of Knots.* Aylward painted many brilliant water colors of early seafights, including a rousing depiction of Perry's hastily built flotilla and the heavier British fleet in their Lake Champlain engagement during the War of 1812. John Wolcott Adams was producing his long series of vignetted pen drawings of early American life. N. C. Wyeth, in great demand like other popular illustrators to furnish pictures for the classics for the teenage group, had to do his share of research for the costumes and backgrounds of such books as *The Deerslayer, The Last of the Mohicans, Robin Hood, Black Arrow, Scottish Chiefs* and *The White Company.* Clyde DeLand gave most of his time to painting pictures of America's past.

Pyle's women students were in general less involved with the historical, although Violet Oakley's brilliant series of mural panels in the Pennsylvania State Capitol at Harrisburg depicting the life of William Penn is an important exception. Jessie Wilcox Smith in her color illustrations for Louisa May Alcott's *Little Women,* and Elizabeth Shippen Green, Sarah Stilwell Weber and the Betts Sisters in many of their magazine illustrations, depicted the domestic side of mid- and later Victorian life.

In reflecting upon the vast tide of historical material that has poured from the pencils and brushes of the illustrators, it is interesting to note the extremes of this material. At one extreme, we may choose Charles Dana Gibson. He was not a researcher; his pictures were not of the past; he recorded history for a decade of his own time. At the other extreme is the quiet, industrious life of Henry Alexander Ogden. At seventeen he began as an artist for *Frank Leslie's Illustrated Weekly* and shortly thereafter embarked upon his hobby, the study and depiction of the uniforms of the American Army. That was his major project until his retirement at the age of eventy-six.

Most illustrators have worked between the two extremes, responding to historical assignments as they came. Many of these assignments, such as those to accompany a magazine story or article, would require a limited amount of time for research and execution. A book assignment would usually involve more study and time. Then there were the long-term commissions to accompany the troops or warships in our various wars. We have told about the correspondents of the Civil War but by the time of our Spanish American War operations in Cuba and the Philippines, our periodicals were more advanced

Gayle Porter Hoskins (1887–1962). *Battle of Little Big Horn.*
Brown and Bigelow Company, 1930. Oil, 11″ x 17¾″. Lent by Peggy and Harold Samuels.

and better organized. The war was very well covered both at the fronts and the home bases and at least four accomplished artists were on the scene: Frederic Remington, William Glackens, Frank Schell and Henry Reuterdahl. Remington and Glackens served with the Army in Cuba and Schell and Reuterdahl sailed with the Navy. A decade and a half later Reuterdahl would be assigned to the Navy in World War I.

In that great world-wide war, not only was there heavy coverage by the press, but several illustrators were sent overseas, to the front, to record the fighting. A Division of Pictorial Publicity established under the Federal Committee of Public Information was headed by Charles Dana Gibson as President of the Society of Illustrators. Many artists were involved in creating pictorial publicity for the war effort; James Montgomery Flagg's *I Want You* was produced for that agency. A considerable number of pictures were produced, a great many of them portraying ruined villages and bombed-out towns. Notable was the work of George Harding, Harvey Dunn, Wallace Morgan, Kerr Eby and Harry Townsend, who pressed up to the front and caught the mingled drama and monotony of the trapped endurance in the curling trench lines from the sea to the Alps, and the rotting bones of No-Man's Land. This record is among the archives in the Smithsonian Institution in Washington, D.C.

By the time of our entry into World War II we had prepared for the widest coverage of warfare in history. The camera had taken over much of the work of pictorial recording, but not all. Illustrators served in various capacities, both in and out of the Armed Services. Some, like Floyd Davis, Harold Von Schmidt, Gilbert Bundy, Joseph Hirsch, Robert Benney, Fred Freeman, John Groth and Tom Lea were war correspondents who went on special assignments to one of the war theaters for news services or magazines. Others were part of the Armed Services assigned to specific duties: Tom Lovell and John Clymer were with the Marines' *Leatherneck*, Ed Vebell and Bill Mauldin were with *Stars and Stripes*, Howard Brodie with *Yank* magazine; McClelland Barclay, Kerr Eby (covering his second war), Griffith Bailey Coale, Mitchell Jamieson, John Falter and Jon Whitcomb served with the Navy. (Barclay went down with a torpedoed LST in the Pacific.) Anton Otto Fischer and John J. Floherty, Jr. were assigned to the Coast Guard. Many others were enlisted men who, as combat artists, simply recorded what they saw. Notable were Albert Gold with the Army, John McDermott with the Marines, and John Pike, who with Steve Kidd recorded the occupation of Korea for the O.W.I. Clayton Knight, with flying battle experience with the U.S. Army Air Service in France in World War I, was combat historian for the 8th, 11th and 20th Air Forces in the Pacific and Alaska areas. Noel Sickles was engaged by the War and Navy Departments to do highly confidential

68

illustration. And not to be overlooked was the important contribution of Norman Rockwell, whose self-assigned paintings of the 'Four Freedoms' provided a visualization of the war aims for the home front. Others on the home front, such as Al Parker, C. C. Beall and Lyman Anderson, visited hospitals to do portraits of wounded servicemen, a boost to the morale of both the men and their families who were the eventual recipients.

During the Korean War, William A. Smith and Ward Brackett were among many illustrators who were sent to Korea and Japan by the U.S.O. to do portrait sketches in hospitals, rest centers and artillery bunkers in the field.

The New York, Los Angeles and San Francisco Societies of Illustrators have had a continuing relationship with the U.S. Air Force. Artists of the caliber of Bob McCall, Robert Geissmann, Neil Boyle and Al Pimsler have travelled to the far reaches of the world to cover such subjects as the Berlin air lift, the care of the wounded, and natural disasters. This large chronicle of historic art can now be seen in the Pentagon, at the Wright Patterson Air Force Museum, in the new air and space wing of the Smithsonian, and in travelling exhibits all over the country.

Our war in Vietnam had a first-class picture-reporter in Charles Waterhouse. In 1967 he roughed it through the Mekong Delta with sketchbooks, flew on helicopter missions against the Viet Cong and motored on river-boat patrols. From a large group of almost 500 drawings which are a part of the Combat Art Collections of the U.S.N. and U.S.M.C., a selection has been reproduced in paperback, entitled *Vietnam Sketchbook—Drawings from Delta to DMZ*. These are on-the-spot sketches, done with great fluency and command.

The use of artists on the spot to record historical events as they are being enacted goes back to our Civil War, as we have seen, but in more recent years the United States Government has been alert to the depicting of the great scientific adventure of our age, the N.A.S.A. space program.

The program of illustration was planned by two knowledgeable and competent men, Hereward Lester Cooke, Curator of Painting at the National Gallery, Washington, and his N.A.S.A. collaborator, James D. Dean. They made a selection of a wide variety of artists, particularly those gifted with ability to make rapid sketch notes on the spot, and invited them to the Space Center at Cape Kennedy, Florida, and the Space Headquarters at Houston, Texas. They were free to roam the highly restricted areas and select any aspects that interested them. Later they had an opportunity to flesh out any of their sketch notes in their own studios. Among those participating were Paul Calle, Franklin McMahon, Mario Cooper, Norman Rockwell and John Pike. A thick volume, *Eyewitness to Space*, containing 258 paintings and sketches, was published as an artists' record of one of the world's greatest scientific events.

Very few illustrators have had the opportunity to record the dramatic episodes of history on the spot—it is usually a problem of revitalizing a past event through the use of research plus imagination. This is a combination that is not too common, but some with special talents have built reputations in that field.

Lyle Justis had a lifelong obsession with the early history of

James Montgomery Flagg (1877–1960).
I Want You. 1917.
Poster, 41″ x 30½″. Lent by Louis Cowan.

his country and his roving pen line recorded hundreds of episodes of Colonial and Revolutionary days, often for sheer pleasure. Norman Price, Rufus Zogbaum and Benjamin Clinedinst, through their long, active lives, were concerned largely with historical subject matter. James Daugherty, illustrator of many books, dealt mostly with historical material in his *Abraham Lincoln*, *Daniel Boone* and Parkman's *Oregon Trail*, as did Henry Pitz in his book illustrations for the medieval *Froissart's Chronicles*, and the *Indian History for Young Folks*. Donald Teague and Harold Von Schmidt are two masterly painters whose subjects have often dealt with the old West that has vanished.

The whole story of the American illustrator's involvement in the elucidation of history is an extensive one, and we can do no more than sketch in the story. The length and depth of that story can be given some point by mentioning contributor Rudolph Zallinger, who has painted a series of murals which reconstructs the age of dinosaurs for the Peabody Museum. So the span of the involvement of our illustrators in the story of history, ranges from long before the advent of man on earth to the present moment.

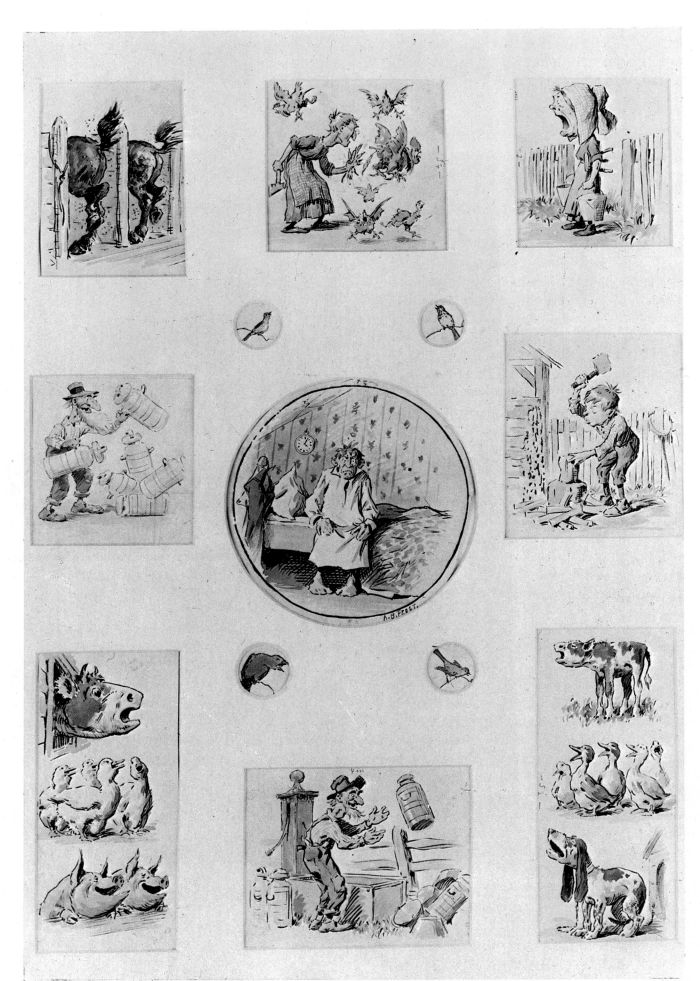

Arthur Burdett Frost (1851–1928). *He Went to the Country for Some Peace and Quiet.*
Watercolor, 19½″ x 14″. Lent by the Graham Gallery.

Chapter 11

Humor In The Printed Picture

Mike Ramus (b. 1917). *The Populist Bandwagon. American Heritage, June 1972.*
Watercolor and pencil, 14" x 24½".
Lent by the American Heritage Publishing Company.

American humor isn't what it used to be. It is more grown-up. It has learned new inflections in the past few decades. It has acquired a large wardrobe of costume changes and has mastered the art of make-up. But that fine, healthy, pink complexion is in danger of disappearing year by year. It is reaching the age when it might find itself looking better by artificial light.

The smell of the deep woods and the barnyard is almost gone: in its place are the odors of close living, shot with whiffs of perfume. The thinking and language of humor are urban and sub-urban now. It has become very complicated and sophisticated —aware of many things that were formerly ignored and ignoring many things of which it was formerly aware.

Humor had a crude and rambunctious youth but perhaps our guffaws then were louder and easier to come by. The old humor was so gutsy and hearty that there was no mistaking the gamey American tang; but America has changed and with the changes have come a hundred and one new and exotic flavors. The sap from the tree and the juice from the apple are now spiked with synthetics.

Humor moves into American picture-making by way of the back-woods. There are some early woodcuts that we have been told are funny, but we find it difficult to respond. But when A. B. Frost, E. B. Kemble, T. S. Sullivant and Will Crawford's works arrive upon the scene we do respond. They are very comfortable, the intervening years are no barrier.

They speak from a scene that is almost a century old—the old village general store, the rutted dirt road, the homemade fishing pole, the horse and buggy. Here are Br'er Fox and Br'er Rabbit and The Tar Baby, Huckleberry Finn and Pudd'nhead

Wilson and the old plantation bellringer. Somehow the exaggerations or distortions of Sullivant and Crawford, Kemble and Frost seem inevitable, never forced. There they are, snug in our mythology, safe for the years, a picture record of a way of dealing with life.

Yes, there they are snug and safe because they have descendants. This kind of humor happens to be the ingredient that stirs a whole cycle of feeling, a feeling that defies sharp definition. It has to do with our awakening to the society in which we find our roots, our sense of belonging, our accumulating memories, our sense of comforting attachments. This is a mingled emotion that is deeper and wider than what we attempt to cover by the single word, humor.

This quality is alive, thriving and beloved today and has been for many years, in the widely circulated works of one man, Norman Rockwell. He is America's best known and best loved illustrator. His work touched his audience immediately and has held it ever since, over a half century of time. His work has appeared in many magazines, books, posters and advertising pages, but for many years his looked-for vehicle was the weekly cover of *The Saturday Evening Post.*

Here is an unrivaled portrait of America—a natural and unforced portrait, whose humor is not a spotlighted element, but a permeating spirit, springing from the little everyday involvements of everyday people. Most illustrators have been very sensitive to the setting of the times, and Rockwell has too, but always with a knowing, general eye, never with a loss of proportion. His message is not couched with the spectacular, it is conveyed in the steady heartbeat of the American pulse. Leafing through the collections of his work which are now available in

Russell Patterson (1896–1977). *Helpful Janitor.* Watercolor, 14½″ x 13″. Lent by Mr. and Mrs. Benjamin Eisenstat.

Norman Rockwell (b. 1894). *John Chew in the Rumble Seat. The Saturday Evening Post, July 13, 1935.* Oil, 21" x 17¼". Lent by the Chemist's Club.

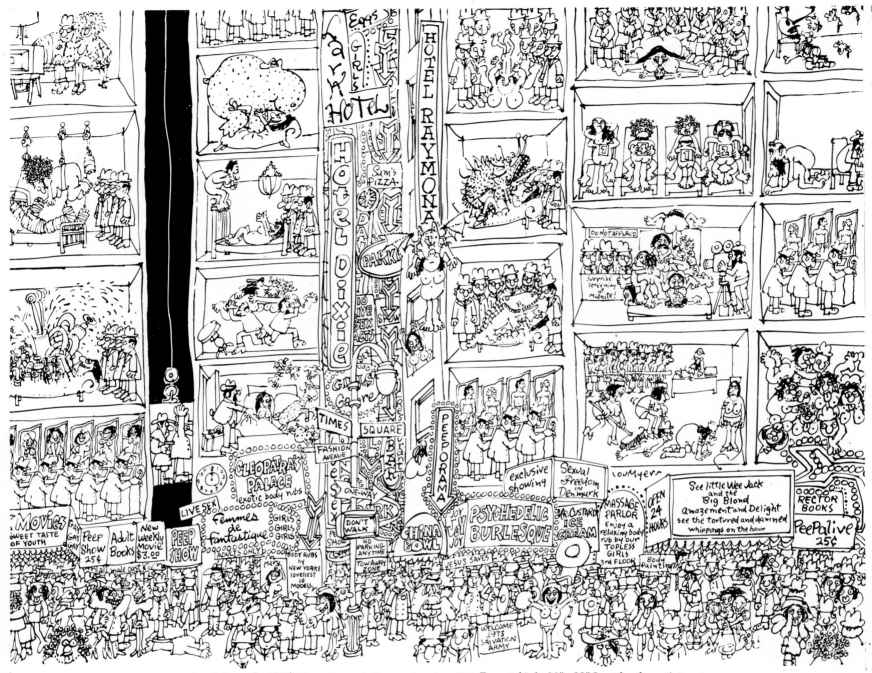

Lou Myers (b. 1915). *Times Square. Self-promotion piece, 1976.* Pen and ink, 28″ x 22″. Lent by the artist.

book form, one is aware of the even tenor of the message—the human story passes through changes of dress and background but shining through are the unchanging problems of mankind.

If Rockwell has passed through changes of popular fashion without missing a step, others have stumbled. The flapper age of the Twenties galvanized a number of gifted satirists, notably John Held Jr. and Russell Patterson. Looking back over their lively drawings, we catch the spirit of a brief and bizarre interval, but the styles of these two responsive artists could not survive beyond the period that brought them acclaim.

It must be a matter of course that a certain amount of a nation's humor is fated to be of its moment—perishable, quickly forgotten. Its power of survival is relatively brief. It has served its moment. America has had a congregation of momentary voices

and still the torrent of humor sweeps on, refusing any prim boundaries, singing high, singing low—harsh, polished, subtle, crude—defying neat summaries.

We can scan one of our great concentrations of American humor in our avowed humorous magazines, from the old *Life*, *Puck* and *Judge* to *The New Yorker*, but a similar review of our multitudinous newspaper comic strips through the years will leave a different taste. We can jump from Alajalov to Dick Tracy, from Charles Dana Gibson to Horrible Hagar. We can sweep from the 'Katzenjammer Kids' to Walt Disney, from *The Wonder Clock* to 'Krazy Kat' and 'Donald Duck', and from Palmer Cox and Peter Newell to Al Hirschfeld, Sandy Huffaker, David Levine, Carol Anthony and R. Crumb, without straying beyond the bounds of American humor. In fact, what are its bounds?

Chapter 12

Magazine Covers and Posters

Maxfield Parrish (1870–1966). *Collier's.*
Collier's Magazine. Pencil and wash, 15½" x 20".
Lent by Haverford College.

The last years of the nineteenth century and the earlier years of the present one were times of rapid growth and change for American magazines, which had their own look, their own content, in picture as well as in prose. They were growing in the size of their market, and this was creating new problems and new opportunities.

The older, smaller size magazines had been prone to use their cover pages for titles and content listings. A few, like *Scribner's,* had been tempted into pictorial covers, with interesting results. But the larger cover page cried out for the picture and so developed a distinctive brand of American illustration, the full color cover painting with typical American subject matter. Here, on the average magazine cover page, had piled up, week by week and month by month, a vast portrait gallery of American life. This was not America as it was, but America as we would like to believe it was. This is the way Americans wanted to see themselves. Artists responded to that urge.

Naturally, the editors of each magazine tried to establish a general style that would be recognizable to its readers, and that resulted in the use of the same group of artists repeatedly. This was not particularly easy, especially in the case of the weeklies with the burden of fifty-two issues a year. But in a rough and ready way, editors and artists sorted themselves out, and readers began to expect the work of the same group, in the same place, week after week or month after month. Many artists were signed to exclusive, long-term contracts.

The Saturday Evening Post established an early cover tradition, to be dominated by J. C. Leyendecker and Norman Rockwell, and supplemented by other able artists practicing a slightly decorative vein of realism and everyday native subject matter. The contributions vary from John Falter's long series of street scenes from many American cities and of home life in the Western farm belt, to Neysa McMein's pretty young girls and Mead Schaeffer's dramatic war and Western paintings. In the long list of *Post* cover illustrators are Harrison Fisher, Anna Feind, Steve Dohanos, Paul Bransom, John Atherton and Amos Sewell. It constitutes a long and revealing gallery of American interests and tastes.

Collier's, a rival weekly, followed a somewhat different pattern, leaning toward the more simplified statements of poster art. Edward Penfield's work represents this at its best, with able contributions by Frederic Dorr Steele, Walter Appleton Clark, Herbert Paus, Earl Oliver Hurst, and others. These two general types of magazine covers flourished side by side on the news-stands for years. It is likely that if a group of artists were collecting old covers, the majority would choose among the *Collier* assortment. If the choice were made by Mr. and Mrs. Average American, the odds would favor their choosing the *Post* variety, that interesting and sometimes revealing pageant of American life.

The feminine influence upon our magazines has, of course, been massive. *Woman's Home Companion, Ladies' Home Journal, Pictorial Review, Good Housekeeping, Delineator, Harper's Bazaar, Woman's Day, Vogue, Vanity Fair* and others give a detailed report not only of women's fashions, but of their household concerns, their family life, their hopes, their aversions—the whole story. Again the cover policy of each publication gives important signs of its viewpoint and contents. *Good Housekeeping* established a conservative, well-contented note through years of Jessie Wilcox

Joseph Christian Leyendecker (1874–1951). *Arrow Collar Ad. Cluett, Peabody and Company, 1913.* Oil. Lent by Michael Schau.

Norman Rockwell (b. 1894). *Ever Onward. 50th Anniversary of the Boy Scouts, 1960.* Oil, 47" x 38". Lent by the Boy Scouts of America.

Smith's cozy, family life paintings, with their flavor faintly reminiscent of late Victorian days. Later a somewhat different note was struck with Coles Phillips' compromise between realistic and poster techniques—a patrician-faced beauty with realistically modelled face and hands with a flat poster-like treatment of dress, accessories and background. *Vogue* and *Harper's Bazaar* naturally emphasized the latest and often most extreme of women's fashions, often with a Parisian flair and sometimes by Parisian artists. *Vanity Fair* radiated its wit and sophistication.

For the young readers, *American Boy* and *Boys' Life* tended to follow a kind of junior *Saturday Evening Post* trend but those for younger ages like *Story Parade, Jack and Jill* and *Junior Red Cross News* tended to have more lighthearted and inventive covers. *Reader's Digest,* the smallest of the 'big' magazines, probably because of its restricted format, follows the older practice of using the covers for a list of contents. But in order not to deprive a picture-hungry public of its usual fare, it uses the back cover for painted scenes, usually of landscape or wildlife subjects. Reader's Digest is a major purchaser of illustrations today, not only for the magazine, but also for books.

We haven't completed the span of American magazines by any means, but let us conclude with one that can claim to be unique, *The New Yorker*. Recently there was an exhibition of

original paintings for *The New Yorker* covers. What a delight. What invention, what seemingly effortless appeal—without any strain, struggle or stereotype.

The American poster entered the field of the magazine cover in a rather glancing way, but it was an influence. In its own domain as a large placard upon fence, wall, news-stall, train platform or other display suface, its best days were earlier in the century when Edward Penfield was in his productive years and was supported by some able designers like Will Bradley, Maxfield Parrish, Charles B. Falls, Louis Fancher, Jules Guerin, S. N. Abbott, James Preston and J. C. Leyendecker.

Many fine things were being done then, like Penfield's long series of news-stand placards for *Harper's Magazine* and a similar series for Scribner's by Jules Guerin, Louis Fancher and J. C. Leyendecker. Naturally the two world wars stimulated poster design and produced excellent examples from such differing talents as Charles B. Falls, J. C. Leyendecker, F. G. Cooper, Joseph Pennell, James Montgomery Flagg, Herbert Paus, Adolph Treidler, Walter Everett and Howard Chandler Christy for World War I, and Treidler again, Ervine Metzel and John Atherton for World War II.

In those earlier years we had developed a poster art of considerable variety, and of a level of design often approaching those of Europe. Today's posters are also exciting, yet we are prone to associate poster art in terms of the unending miles of billboards that line our highways rather than the vast assortment of work done for museums, record album companies and independently by the artists themselves, such as Peter Max and Ivan Chermayeff.

John Held, Jr. (1889–1958). *Sitting Pretty. Life*
March 31, 1927. Watercolor, 14½″ x 11½″
Lent by Walt Reed.

Peter Arno (1904–1968). *The Last Leaf.*
The New Yorker, October 29, 1938. Watercolor and ink,
21⅞″ x 13⅜″. Lent by the Brooklyn Museum.

Courtesy of CBS Records.

Robert Zoell (b. 1940). *Flamin' Groovies.*
Columbia Record Cover. Print, 12" x 12". Lent by CBS Records.

The whole world knows of the giant empire of American business, and of the mammoth voice of its advertising. Its message, in word and picture, is heard and seen in every nook and corner of the world. The Art Directors Club was organized in 1920 and its first exhibition was held in the Spring of 1921. It was an overwhelming success. Earnest Elmo Calkins in *Printers' Ink Monthly* said of it, 'Here is practically a new art, a new metier, that scarcely existed twenty years ago.' And of that first show, Richard J. Walsh said, 'Art directing has become a recognized profession...The day will come when a set of these volumes *Annuals of Advertising Art* will be of distinct service to the historian writing of our time.'

Presumably these volumes contain the cream of the crop, but we all have some favorites that were never displayed—perhaps because they were not entered. Making allowances for some of the good things that were not shown, it is a huge, remarkable diversified and unprecedented collection—without counterpart in the world. If there seem to be some diminishing trends of late, that may be a passing wave or a sign of the future

It was not only the widespread increase in our reading public that ignited the growth of the American magazines; it was American business buying up the advertising pages. Since the fiction and article pages were largely illustrated by our realistic illustrators, it was natural that they should have the advertising pages turned over to them also. The American audience has unmistakably shown its preference for realism in its pictures.

In those earlier days it was commonplace to find the same artist in several of the fiction pages and also in an advertising page or two at the back...J. C. Leyendecker's art could be found on the cover and also on a full-page ad for Interwoven Socks...Frederick Gruger divided his skill between fiction and Yuban Coffee. Today this practice is highly unlikely—the fiction has dwindled, the advertising is largly in the hands of the photographer.

Highlights of those long series of advertising pictures would include the Steinway and Sons color paintings, such as Ernest L. Blumenschein's *Indian Suite*, N. C. Wyeth's *Beethoven and Nature* and Harvey Dunn's *Schubert Composing 'The Earlking'* and the *Fantastic Symphony by Berlioz.* There was Franklin Booth's handsome series for the Estey Organ Company and Rene Clark's sensitive compositions for Crane's papers. That great draughtsman, Henry Raleigh, did some of his finest drawings for a long series for Maxwell House Coffee, Robert Riggs' paintings and lithographs distinguished the advertising campaigns of many clients.

Not all these long-term campaigns were presented in terms of the realistic picture. One of the most noted sets of designs was that prepared for the Westvaco booklets of the West Virginia Pulp and Paper Company. Some of the country's best designer-illustrators were enlisted, such as T. M. Cleland, Edward A. Wilson and C. B. Falls.

The great spate of advertising pictures and designs flooded the country in an infinite variety of forms; booklets, leaflets, folders, cuecards, posters and billboards, catalogs, annual reports, postcards, circulars, cutouts for window displays and all sizes and shapes of packages. Constant change and experimentation were routine practice in almost all of it. A great portion of it is forgotten.

The enormous flood of material, increasingly of photographic orgin, was given some cohesion and summing up by the work of the Art Directors Clubs judges and organizers of the annual exhibitions. They did the first sorting out...time will do the rest.

Robert M. Cunningham (b. 1924). *Big, Bold, Beautiful—Big A. New York Racing Association Poster, 1965.* Acrylic, 11½″ x 20″. Lent by the artist.

Peter Helck (b. 1893). *This is My Birthright.*
Caterpillar Tractor Company, 1945. Tempera, 30″ x 30″. Lent by Louis B. Neumiller.

Robert Benney (b. 1904). *Harvesting Sugar Cane. Amstar Annual Report, 1953.* Oil, 30″ x 50″. Lent by the Amstar Corporation.

Ken Dallison (b. 1933). *June Bug.*
Scott Paper Corporation, Inc. Pen and ink and watercolor, 17½″ x 16½″. Lent by the artist.

Chapter 14

Mid-Century and On

© 1964, Time, Inc.

Robert Weaver (b. 1924). *The Blue Room Bar, Green Bay, Wisconsin.*
Sports Illustrated, November 2, 1964. Acrylic, 19¼" x 30". Lent by Sports Illustrated.

As the illustration world rolled up to and past mid-twentieth century, the tide of expansion began to send out signals. The size, number and diversity of our magazines were unmatched as were the methods, variety, and resourcefulness of advertising communication. The American magazine was at its peak for size, stuffed with pictures and bloated with advertising pages. Feeding its picture appetite was the largest and most gifted corps of illustrative talent the world had ever seen.

Just to list some of the names that have gilded this period is to call up images of superior and widespread talent, great resourcefulness and unmatched technical competence. Headed by Norman Rockwell is a splendid roll-call of names: Henry Raleigh, N. C. Wyeth, Robert Fawcett, Harvey Dunn, Frederic Gruger, Rockwell Kent, Floyd Davis, Harold Von Schmidt, Peter Helck, Robert Riggs, Al Parker, Walter Biggs, Mead Schaeffer, Coles Phillips, John Gannam, Martha Sawyers, Herbert M. Stoops. Then Noel Sickles, Donald Teague, Austin Briggs, Carl Erickson, John LaGatta, Frank Hoffman, Maginel Wright Barney, Gordon Grant, Stevan Dohanos, Maud Tousey Fangel and Tom Lovell. Moving toward the present day – Bruce Bomberger, Joe DeMers, Stanley Meltzoff, William A. Smith, Morton Roberts, Robert Peak, Denver Gillen, Bernard Fuchs, Mark English, Robert Andrew Parker, Murray Tinkelman, Robert Weaver, David Levine and Brad Holland.

Lists such as the above can only be a most elementary step in calling attention to America's astonishing outburst of pictorial talent. It has been there, under our very eyes, for a long time. It has been taken as a matter of course—the time has now come for it to become history. The pictures themselves are the premier source material—so many are now gone or are hidden in some closet. In earlier years, it was not customary to return original paintings and drawings to the artists. Many art editors had choice collections culled from the pictures they had ordered and used. Sometimes the larger publishers amassed large piles of original art and some sold it off for small amounts or house cleaned it at intervals into the waste receptacle. Later it became more customary for the illustrator to demand his picture back after it had been reproduced. Some large collections of this kind have come to light when estates were settled and quite certainly more treasures will be found.

The actual work of the illustrator's hand is the prime material, of course, but that should be supplemented by the written word, by evaluation, criticism and interchange of ideas. In view of the size and importance of the subject, that has been remarkably small. The first comprehensive exhibition of American illustration by the Society of Illustrators was not held until 1959. The exhibition was a large and notable one, and a large and well designed book reproducing the show's contents was issued. This exhibition now has become an annual event approaching its third decade. There is no other exhibition or book to rival these as an impetus to developing interest in illustration as a profession. The annual, recording the show, is now an important source book, for it registers an awareness of change in the field. There is an attempt to grapple with exploring the use of the illustrator in the television world and with giving full recognition to the inventiveness of design in children's books.

In his introduction to the section 'Book Illustration,' Lynd Ward has this to say: 'The first thing that must be noted about book illustration in America today is that it is predominantly work for children. The number of books published for adults that utilize the work of artists, anywhere other than in the exterior packaging, is small—some limited editions, some reprints of classics, a few books of travel or humor, a handful of others. In contrast to this, children's books invariably regard pictures as an integral part of their total identity, and since the end of World War II it is in the field of work for children, that book illustration has come full harvest.'

Too long the average magazine and advertising illustrator and art director had been unmindful of pictures in books, and now there was the new instrument of television stealing the audiences. The annuals issued since, added to those of the New York Art Directors' series reaching back to 1921, present a panorama of the illustrator's art through its most prolific period. Another indispensable source is *The Illustrator in America— 1900-1960's,* compiled by Walt Reed, presenting a comprehensive group of our prominent illustrators, with short biographies and examples of their work.

For many years *American Artist* magazine has given generous space to richly illustrated articles about illustrators and their art, and usually emphasis is given to the illustrator's explanation of how he plans and goes about the execution of his work. Other magazines that have deep interest in the field of illustration are *C A Magazine, Print, North Light* and *Today's Art.*

The literature on illustration has grown rapidly in recent years. There have been large, richly illustrated volumes on the work of men like J. C. Leyendecker, A. B. Frost, John Held Jr., Maxfield Parrish, Norman Rockwell, Howard Pyle, Harvey Dunn, Frederic Remington, Charles Russell, Charles Dana Gibson, Harold Von Schmidt, N. C. Wyeth, and James Montgomery Flagg. Two important editions on the illustration of books, by Diana Klemin, are *The Illustrated Book, Its Art and Craft* and *The Art of Art For Children's Books.*

The art museums, with few exceptions, have shown an almost complete lack of interest in the work of the illustrator, except perhaps in the cases of Audubon or Catlin. The exceptions are the splendid collection of American illustration in The New Britain Museum of American Art in New Britain, Connecticut, the finest collection of the work of Howard Pyle and of his studens in the Delaware Art Museum in Wilmington, Delaware and the growing groups of illustrative work in the Brandywine River Museum in Chadds Ford, Pennsylvania.

However, the tide of interest is swelling. There have been a number of retrospective exhibitions of illustration during the past few years, notably the *Century of American Illustration* at the Brooklyn Musuem in 1972. The most comprehensive exhibition to date, *200 Years of American Illustration* at the New-York Historical Society Museum, forms the basis for this book. For years, there have been growing collections pertaining to book illustration in the libraries of three of our large universities, those of Oregon, Minnesota and Southern Mississippi. These collections include not only original art, but also proofs, manuscripts, correspondence, anything involved in the creation of the illustrated book, chiefly the children's book.

The interest has come, the material of the past is accumulating. The illustrator has been, with a few exceptions, too bent upon his own immediate work to raise his eyes to the sweep and depth of his own profession. It was all too easy to think of making pictures for the passing day. But pictorial records of the passing day are now history and are rapidly becoming today one of America's most exciting art forms, sought by museums and collectors alike.

Tomi Ungerer (b. 1931). *How to Survive in a French Restaurant. PLAYBOY Magazine, October 1970.* Watercolor, 18" x 48". Lent by Playboy Enterprises.

Philip Hays (b. 1940). *A Confrontation in a Circle Ruled by a Tiger . . . Sports Illustrated, December 20, 1965.* Watercolor, 15½″ x 22½″. Lent by Sports Illustrated.

Norman Rockwell (b. 1894). *Al Kooper and Mike Bloomfield.*
The Adventures of Al Kooper and Mike Bloomfield, Columbia Record Cover, 1968. Oil, 14″ x 14″.
Lent by CBS Records.

Bob Peak (b. 1928). *Rollerball. 1975.* Oil and tempera, 39¼″ x 29″. Lent by Smollen, Smith and Connoly, Inc.

1800's

Currier & Ives. *Trolling for Bluefish. Artist—Frances F. Palmer (1812–1876), published 1866.* Lithograph, 20½″ x 29″. Lent by the Museum of the City of New York.

Arthur Burdett Frost (1851–1928). *Black Bass Fishing.*
Harper's Weekly, 1882.
Wood engraving, 9″ x 13½″. Lent by Bob Crozier.

Currier & Ives. *The Grand Drive, Central Park. Artist—Thomas Worth (1834–1917), published 1869.* Lithograph, 19½″ x 28″. Lent by the Museum of the City of New York.

Will H. Low (1853–1932). *1899.* Watercolor, 5⅞″ x 9⅜″.
Lent by Robert J. Mehlman.

Frederick Catherwood (1799–1854). *New York Taken from the North West Angle of Fort Columbus, Governors Island. Published by Henry J. Megarey, 1846.*
Print, 16½″ x 26¾″. Lent by the New-York Historical Society.

William R. Miller (1818–1893). *Cromwell Farmhouse, Bronx, New York. 1855.*
Watercolor, 11¾″ x 16¼″. Lent by the New-York Historical Society.

Arthur Burdett Frost (1851–1928). *In Luck. Harper's Weekly, December 1884.* Wood engraving, 13½" x 9". Lent by Bob Crozier.

Charles Marion Russell (1864–1926). *Bronc in Cow Camp. 1897.* Oil, 31¼″ x 20⅛″. Lent by the Amon Carter Museum of Western Art.

Thomas Nast (1840–1902). *The Tammany Tiger.*
Harper's Weekly, November 1871.
Woodcut engraving, 17⅛″ x 24⅜″. Lent by the New-York Historical Society.

Charles Marion Russell (1864–1926). *Indians Attacking. 1895*. Oil, 19¾″ x 13⅞″. Lent by the Amon Carter Museum of Western Art.

Walter Granville-Smith (1870–1938). *Turkey Shooting. 1894*.
Watercolor, 15½″ x 25¾″. Lent by the Graham Gallery.

Frances Flora Palmer (1812–1876). *Engagement between the Monitor and the Merrimac.
Currier & Ives, Co., 1862*.
Watercolor, 15″ x 22½″. Lent by the New-York Historical Society.

Winslow Homer (1836–1910). *Gathering Berries. Harper's Weekly, July 1874.* Wood engraving, 9″ x 13½″. Lent by Bob Crozier.

Winslow Homer (1836–1910). *The Last Days of Harvest.*
Harper's Weekly, December 1873.
Wood engraving, 9″ x 13½″. Lent by Bob Crozier.

Winslow Homer (1836–1910). *Making Hay.*
Harper's Weekly, July 1872.
Wood engraving, 9″ x 13½″. Lent by Bob Crozier.

Winslow Homer (1836–1910). *Skating on the Ladies' Skating Pond in Central Park. Harper's Weekly, January 28, 1860.* Wood engraving, 13¾" x 20⅛". Lent by the Brooklyn Museum.

Winslow Homer (1836–1910). *The Battle of Bunker Hill. Harper's Weekly, June 1875.*
Wood engraving, 9" x 13½". Lent by Bob Crozier.

George Harvey (1801–1878). *A Broken Axletree|American Wood Scene near Thornville, Ohio. Scenes of the Primitive Forest of America, 1841.* Watercolor, 13⅞″ x 10⅜″. Lent by the New-York Historical Society.

Howard Pyle (1853–1911). *The Prince and the Priest. Harper's New Monthly Magazine.* Oil, 24″ x 16″. Lent by Walt Reed.

William H. Bartlett (1809–1854). *American Scenery. 1839.* Watercolor, 4⅞″ x 7⅜″. Lent by the New-York Historical Society

Howard Pyle (1853–1911). *Suspicious Strangers. Unpublished.* Watercolor, 19¾″ x 29½″. Lent anonymously

Joseph Pennell (1860–1926). *Lichfield Cathedral. Century Magazine, July 1888.*
Ink wash, 12⅛″ x 18″. Lent by the New Britain Museum of American Art.

William Thomas Smedley (1858–1920). *Three Folks in Rockers.* 1890. Opaque wash, 8″ x 11″. Lent by the Society of Illustrators.

Joseph Pennell (1860–1926). *The Gacherel. 1890.*
Pen and ink, 14″ x 18¾″. Lent by Bob Crozier.

98

Will Ladd Taylor (1854–1926). *Lady with Two Gentlemen. 1895.* Watercolor, 13″ x 21½″. Lent by Walt Reed.

Nicolino Calyo (1799–1884). *Broadway. 1840–44.*
Watercolor, 10″ x 12½″. Lent by the Museum of the City of New York.

Frederic Sackrider Remington (1861–1909). *Cavalryman's Breakfast on the Plains.*
Soldiering in the Southwest by Frederic S. Remington, 1890. Oil, 22" x 32⅛". Lent by the Amon Carter Museum of Western Art.

Joseph Keppler, Jr. (1838–1890). *Indian Encampment. 1889.* Watercolor, 9⅞″ x 13⅛″. Lent by the New-York Historical Society.

Frederick S. Church (1842–1924). *Little Girl Converses with a Rabbit.* Oil, 7½″ x 11½″. Lent by Mrs. Thomas Wilcox.

Charles R. Knight (1874–1953). *Rabbits. 1888.*
Pencil, 7¼″ x 7½″. Lent by the Graham Gallery.

Frederick S. Church (1842–1924).
Dog Howling While a Turtle Looks On.
Pen and ink, 11½″ x 7½″. Lent by Mrs. Thomas Wilcox.

Violet Oakley (1874–1961). *Lenten Cover. Collier's Magazine, 1899*. Charcoal, 17″ x 14½″. Lent by Mr. and Mrs. Benjamin Eisenstat.

Edwin Austin Abbey (1852–1911). *Thou Shalt Have Charge and Sovereign Trust Herein.*
Harper's New Monthly Magazine, March 1906. Oil, 36″ x 24″. Lent by the Yale University Art Gallery.

Edwin Austin Abbey (1852–1911). *Friar Thomas and the Duke.*
The Comedies of William Shakespeare (Measure for Measure), Harper & Bros., 1899.
Oil, 17⅛″ x 12⅜″. Lent by the Yale University Art Gallery.

E. Percy Moran (1862–1935). *Title unknown. 1882.*
Scratchboard, 10″ x 7⅝″. Lent by Peggy and Harold Samuels.

Artist Unknown. *Fashion Illustration. Godey's Fashion Book, c. 1868.*
Reprint, 10″ x 8″. Lent by Janet and Arthur Weithas.

Frank Craig (1874–1918). *At the Queen's Drawing-Room. Harper's Bazar, May 20, 1899.* Tempera, 14⅛″ x 17⅛″. Lent by Mrs. Thomas Wilcox.

Reginald Bathurst Birch (1856–1943). *Title unknown.*
Pen and ink and gouache, 16½″ x 12″. Lent by Robert J. Mehlman.

Wesley P. Snyder. *Hard-A-Lee.*
Harper & Bros., 1899. Gouache, 15¼″ x 12½″. Lent by the Graham Gallery.

George Hayward (1834–1872). *View of Brooklyn Heights, New York, 1841.*
Manual of the Common Council of the City of Brooklyn, 1865.
Watercolor, 6″ x 9″. Lent by the New-York Historical Society.

Arthur Burdett Frost (1851–1928). *Quail Shooting—An Unexpected Bevy. Harper's Weekly, November 1882.* Wood engraving, 9″ x 13½″. Lent by Bob Crozier.

Palmer Cox (1840–1924). *The Brownies at Archery.*
Another Brownie Book by Palmer Cox, Century Publishing Company, 1890.
Pen and ink, 9⅛″ x 7⅝″. Lent by the Brooklyn Museum.

C. D. Weldon. *Carrying Water from the Spring.*
Gouache, 14¾" x 10". Lent by Walt Reed.

Arthur Burdett Frost (1851–1928). *The Winner of the Rifle Match.*
Harper's Weekly, February 1882. Wood engraving, 13½" x 9". Lent by Bob Crozier.

C. D. Weldon. *The Happiest Christmas.*
Watercolor, 8½" x 12½". Lent by Mrs. Thomas Wilcox.

Joseph Clement Coll (1881–1921). *The Casket Scene. The Merchant of Venice.* Pen and ink, 6¾″ x 10½″. Lent by Walt Reed.

Michaelangelo Woolf (d. 1899). *Waifs.*
Pen and ink, 13½″ x 18″. Lent by the Graham Gallery.

Edward Potthast (1857–1927). *Brother Lazarus, des er minute fo' yer fling dat line. The Century Magazine, July, 1899.* Ink wash, 16¾" x 22¼". Lent by Mr. and Mrs. Alan Goffman.

William Allen Rogers (1854–1931). *A Holiday in a Logging Camp.*
Harper's Weekly, January 8, 1898.
Wash drawing, 14" x 22". Lent by Peggy and Harold Samuels.

113

John Hill (1770–1850). *Passage of the Juniata through Warrior Mountain. Lucas's Progressive Drawing Book, 1828.*
Print, 7″ x 9¾″. Lent by the New-York Historical Society.

Rufus Zogbaum (1849–1925).
Skirmishers in Pursuit. 1883.
Gouache, 11¾″ x 9¾″.
Lent by Robert J. Mehlman.

Louis Loeb (1866–1909). *The Kinds that Cured. 1894.* Gouache, 11½″ x 17⅝″. Lent by the New Britain Museum of American Art.

COMPENSATION NOT REQUIRED.

AGENT:- "If I give you the position of janitor, Uncle, what remunerative compensation will you require?"
UNCLE:- Oh, I wont need none ob dem flings, boss— I got mah own brush an' mop an' pail!"

J. Foeller, Jr. *Compensation not Required. 1895.*
Watercolor, 5½″ x 5¼″. Lent by Mrs. Thomas Wilcox.

Charles Dana Gibson (1867–1944). *In the Rue de la Paix: Before leaving Paris, Mr. Pipp, at the suggestion of his daughters, makes a few purchases.*
The Education of Mr. Pipp by Charles Dana Gibson, Russell Publishing Company, 1899. Pen and ink, 20½″ x 28¼″. Lent by Mort Künstler.

Charles Dana Gibson (1867–1944). *I Got the Letter.*
Rupert of Hentzau by Anthony Hope,
Henry Holt and Company, 1898. Charcoal, 21″ x 15″.
Lent by Mrs. Thomas Wilcox.

1900's

James Montgomery Flagg (1877–1960). *I've Been Abroad.*
Watercolor, 27¾″ x 19¼″. Lent by the New Britain Museum of American Art.

James Montgomery Flagg (1877–1960). *Mr. Simpson Directs.*
Ink wash, 16″ x 30″. Lent by the Society of Illustrators.

James Montgomery Flagg (1877–1960). *Marriage Request.*
Pen and ink, 21¼″ x 27½″. Lent by the New Britain Museum of American Art.

Walter Appleton Clark (1876–1906). *The Party Clown.* Watercolor, 18″ x 15″. Lent by the Society of Illustrators.

C. Clyde Squires (1883–1970). *The Kiss. Life, 1909.* Oil, 24″ x 36″. Lent by Showcase Antiques.

Thomas King Hanna (1872–1952).
*The Hell-Hounds of the System Had Overtaken Their
Maimed and Hunted Victim.*
Everybody's Magazine, March 1907.
Watercolor, 17″ x 11½″. Lent by Mrs. Thomas Wilcox.

William Thomas Smedley (1858–1920). *At the Piano.*
Life and Character, 1899. Gouache, 13¾″ x 10″.
Lent by Walt Reed.

Frederic Sackrider Remington (1861–1909). *His First Lesson. Collier's Magazine, September 26, 1903.* Oil, 27¼" x 40". Lent by the Amon Carter Museum of Western Art.

Walter Appleton Clark (1876–1906). *Girl at the Piano, 1903*.
Watercolor, 17½″ x 11½″. Lent by Walt Reed.

Frank Craig (1874–1918). Tempera, 16″ x 8″. Lent by the Society of Illustrators.

Fred Pegram. *Kissing Couple.* Watercolor, 11¼″ x 12⅜″. Lent by Walt Reed.

Edward Penfield (1866–1925). *Young Lady on Veranda.* Watercolor, 12½″ x 11½″. Lent by Walt Reed.

Edward Penfield (1866–1925). *Harper's March.*
Harper's New Monthly Magazine. Poster, 16¾" x 11". Lent by Louis Cowan.

Edward Penfield (1866–1925). *European Bridge.*
Watercolor, 10½" x 9". Lent by the Society of Illustrators.

James Montgomery Flagg (1877–1960).
Annual Show—Society of Illustrators.
Print, 21" x 15".
Lent by Beverly and Ray Sacks,
The Art Couple.

Harrison Fisher (1875–1934). *Man and Woman. 1910.*
Watercolor, 25½″ x 19″. Lent by the Society of Illustrators.

Harrison Fisher (1875–1934). *Woman's Head.*
Pastel, 20″ x 14½″. Lent by Sam Tomlin.

Gordon Hope Grant (1875–1962). *Man and Cupid.*
Puck, 1907. Pen and ink, 16″ x 19″. Lent by the Graham Gallery.

Frederic Rodrigo Gruger (1871–1953). *The Editor's Office.*
Mixed media, 9″ x 12⅝″. Lent by Mort Künstler.

Frederic Rodrigo Gruger (1871–1953). *The Magic of Mohammed Din.*
Redbook, August 1918. Charcoal, 14″ x 18″. Lent by the Graham Gallery.

Frederic Rodrigo Gruger (1871–1953). *The Meeting.*
Wolff pencil and wash, 14¼″ x 13½″. Lent by Walt Reed.

Edward Penfield (1866–1925). *Harper's November. Harper's New Monthly Magazine.* Poster, 11″ x 18¼″. Lent by Louis Cowan.

Edward Penfield (1866–1925). *Post Rider—1780.*
Watercolor, 8½″ x 11½″. Lent by Mrs. Thomas Wilcox.

Harrison Fisher (1875–1934). *A Winter Promenade. The Harrison Fisher Book,*
Scribner's Sons & Co., 1907. Pastel, 37" x 22". Lent by Mr. and Mrs. Alan Goffman.

Arthur William Brown (1881–1966). *Title unknown.*
Charcoal, 13¾″ x 21½″. Lent by the Society of Illustrators.

B. Cory Kilvert (1881–1946). *Man and Children. 1904.*
Watercolor and ink, 21½″ x 13⅜″. Lent by the Graham Gallery.

William Allen Rogers (1854–1931). *It Was a Merry Jest.*
Harper's, 1907. Pen and ink, 13½″ x 10½″.
Lent by the Graham Gallery.

Joseph Clement Coll (1881–1921).
The Garden of Fate by Roy Norton, Watt & Co., 1910.
Pen and ink, 13″ x 12″. Lent by Mrs. Thomas Wilcox.

Horace Taylor (b. 1881). *Under the Spreading Chestnut Tree.*
Everybody's Magazine, 1906.
Pen and ink, 6½″ x 15″. Lent by Robert J. Mehlman.

Arthur William Brown (1881–1966). *For Your Boy.* YWCA War Work Council, 1918.
Watercolor, 12″ x 11″. Lent by Mr. and Mrs. Alan Goffman.

Frederick Coffay Yohn (1875–1933). *Inch by inch he fought his way along his dizzy perch.*
Gouache, 19¾″ x 13½″. Lent by Peggy and Harold Samuels.

Frederick Coffay Yohn (1875–1933). *Story of the War '98.*
Collier's Weekly. Oil, 20″ x 30″. Lent by Peggy and Harold Samuels.

Anna Nordstrom Feind. *Portrait of Girl.*
Watercolor, 18″ x 8½″. Lent by Walt Reed.

Harrison Fisher (1875–1934). *At the Opera.*
Collier's Magazine, 1901. Watercolor and gouache, 27″ x 19″.
Lent by Beverly and Ray Sacks, The Art Couple.

Harrison Fisher (1875–1934). *Red Cross Nurse.*
American Red Cross, 1918. Poster, 24″ x 28″. Lent by Gustav Krell.

Jessie Wilcox Smith (1863–1935). *Mother and Child. 1908.* Mixed media, 24″ x 18″. Lent by Mr. and Mrs. Benjamin Eisenstat.

Arthur Burdett Frost (1851–1928).
And the Sheriff and Canada Center were squeezing themselves through the gate.
Tioba by Arthur Colton, The Century Magazine, November 1900.
Gouache, 19½″ x 15″. Lent by the New Britain Museum of American Art.

Arthur Burdett Frost (1851–1928).
I Feel Lak I Gwine Ter Sleep.
Everybody's Magazine, 1902.
Wash drawing, 14″ x 11½″. Lent by the New Britain Museum of American Art.

Arthur Burdett Frost (1851–1928). *All Paint and No Engine.*
Watercolor, 12″ x 9¼″. Lent by Mrs. Thomas Wilcox.

Arthur Burdett Frost (1851–1928). *Large Ferocious Cat.*
Pen and ink, 14¼″ x 13¼″. Lent by Mrs. Thomas Wilcox.

Philip R. Goodwin (1882–1935). *Travel on the Wells Fargo. 1906.* Oil, 19½″ x 25½″. Lent by Mort Künstler.

Reginald Bathurst Birch (1856–1943). *Title unknown.*
Pen and ink, 14″ x 18″. Lent by Mrs. Thomas Wilcox.

Reginald Bathurst Birch (1856–1943). *Title unknown. St. Nicholas Magazine, September 1902.*
Pen and ink, 14¼″ x 18″. Lent by Mrs. Thomas Wilcox.

"Over-the-Top"

Joseph Christian Leyendecker (1874–1951). *Over the Top. House of Kuppenheimer.*
Oil, 38¼″ x 19¾″. Lent by Mort Künstler.

Joseph Christian Leyendecker (1874–1951). *Arrow Collar Man.*
Cluett, Peabody and Company. Oil, 23½″ x 17½″. Lent by Mort Künstler.

Joseph Christian Leyendecker (1874–1951). *Antony and Cleopatra. 1904.*
Gouache, 24½″ x 15″. Lent by Beverly and Ray Sacks, The Art Couple.

Francis Xavier Leyendecker (1877–1924). *The Blacksmith. 1904.*
Gouache, 18½″ x 15″. Lent by Peggy and Harold Samuels.

Francis Xavier Leyendecker (1877–1924). *Football Players.*
Oil, 25″ x 16″. Lent by the Graham Gallery.

Boardman Robinson (1876–1952).
Peer Gynt. 1905.
Pen and ink, 10″ x 7½″.
Lent by Robert J. Mehlman.

Harvey T. Dunn (1884–1952). *Bastille. 1919.* Oil, 25½″ x 39½″. Lent by the Society of Illustrators.

Walter Granville-Smith (1870–1938). *The Story of the Spanish War.*
St. Nicholas Magazine. Watercolor, 15¾″ x 11¾″.
Lent by the New Britain Museum of American Art.

Henry Patrick Raleigh (1880–1944). *The Boyfriend. The Saturday Evening Post, January 30, 1915.* Charcoal, 10½″ x 10½″. Lent by Mrs. Thomas Wilcox.

Harrison Fisher (1875–1934). *Couple Fishing.*
Watercolor, 32" x 24". Lent by Walt Reed.

Edwin Howland Blashfield (1848–1936). *Figure Study.*
Charcoal, 28" x 17". Lent by the Graham Gallery.

Frank Walter Taylor (1874–1921). *Ode.*
Charcoal, 21" x 26". Lent by Walt Reed.

Frank Walter Taylor (1874–1921). *I calkilate this'll fetch her in about a week.*
McClure's Magazine, May 1906. Charcoal, 15" x 21". Lent by Mrs. Thomas Wilcox.

Worth Brehm (1883–1928).
The Circus Tom Sawyer by Mark Twain, 1911.
Charcoal, 22″ x 14¾″. Lent by Walt Reed.

Thornton Oakley (1881–1955).
Miner on Railroad Ties. Hrdlika by Maximillian Foster, Everybody's Magazine, June 1906.
Charcoal, 29″ x 19″. Lent by Walt Reed.

Everett Shinn (1876–1953). *Ichabod Crane. The Legend of Sleepy Hollow by Washington Irving.*
Pen and ink, 9″ x 15″. Lent by the Graham Gallery.

Daniel Carter Beard (1850–1941). *A King and His Court.*
Pen and ink, 20″ x 27″. Lent by Mr. and Mrs. Alan Goffman.

John Scott Williams (1877–1976). *Man and Lion. Associated Sunday Magazine, 1906.*
Pencil, 6¼″ x 5½″. Lent by Walt Reed.

Albert E. Sterner (1863–1946). *Title unknown. Jugend Magazine.*
Colored crayon, 17″ x 12¾″. Lent by the Graham Gallery.

Florence Scovel Shinn (1869–1940).
Our Prosperity is Based on Lobsters and Boarders. The Century Magazine, October 1902.
Pen and ink, 10½″ x 13½″. Lent by Mrs. Thomas Wilcox.

S. D. Ehrhart, *Little Dog Barking at Foppish Man Calling on Girl.*
Pen and ink, 14½″ x 18″. Lent by Mrs. Thomas Wilcox.

Howard Pyle (1853–1911). *A Dream of Young Summer.*
Harper's Monthly, June 1901. Oil.
Lent anonymously.

Artist Unknown. *John Deere Advertisement, c. 1914.* Print, 13″ x 20″. Lent by the John Deere Company.

Tony Sarg (1882–1942). *Inspecting Antiquities. 1912.*
Pen and ink and gouache, 8½″ x 12″. Lent by Robert J. Mehlman.

Peter S. Newell (1862–1924). *Title unkown*.
Opaque wash, 14" x 11". Lent by the Society of Illustrators.

Walt Kuhn (1880–1949).
Absolutely No Trouble Travelling Incognito, When One is an Extinct Bird Like Myself. 1906.
Watercolor and pen and ink, 7" x 9¾". Lent by the Graham Gallery.

Peter S. Newell (1862–1924). *The Walrus and the Oyster.*
The Hunting of the Snark and Other Poems by Lewis Carroll, Harper & Bros., 1903.
Watercolor, 9" x 13". Lent by Mrs. Thomas Wilcox.

John Conacher (1876–1947). *He Paused and Eyed them Wistfully.*
Everybody's Magazine, November 1906. Pen and ink, 11" x 15½".
Lent by Mrs. Thomas Wilcox.

Daniel Carter Beard (1850–1941). *Dancing Couple.*
Pen and ink, 6¼″ x 5¾″. Lent by Walt Reed.

Thomas Fogarty (1873–1938).
When a Wheeled-Chair Came Around the Corner, Pushed by a Half-Grown Girl.
Everybody's Magazine, July 1906.
Watercolor and charcoal, 16″ x 14″. Lent by Mrs. Thomas Wilcox.

William J. Glackens (1870–1938). *E. Pluribus Jones.*
Scribner's Magazine. Pencil and wash, 7¼″ x 8½″. Lent by the Graham Gallery.

John Scott Williams (1877–1976).
A Single Light from the Chandelier Fell Full on Her Delicate Face.
Collier's Magazine, October 26, 1912. Conti crayon, 8″ x 9″.
Lent by Mrs. Thomas Wilcox.

Elizabeth Shippen Green (1871–1954). *Aunt Olivia! Aunt Olivia! she cried.*
The Return of Rebecca Mary, Harper's, October 1905. Charcoal, 24″ x 14½″.
Lent by Mr. and Mrs. Benjamin Eisenstat.

Elizabeth Shippen Green (1871–1954). *The Eyes of Gold.*
The Treasure by F. Isham, Harper's, 1910. Oil, 24″ x 15¼″. Lent by the Graham Gallery.

Norman Mills Price (1877–1951). *Beatrice and Benedict.*
Tales from Shakespeare, 1905. Gouache, 10¼″ x 8⅜″. Lent by Mort Künstler.

Rose O'Neill (1875–1944). *I Sat Down to Think.*
Harper's Bazar, 1906. Pen and ink, 14″ x 20″. Lent by the Graham Gallery.

Arthur Ignatius Keller (1866–1925). *Man and Boy on a Wagon. 1912*. Charcoal wash, 20″ x 28″. Lent by the Society of Illustrators.

Vernon Howe Bailey (1874–1953). *Madison Avenue, New York. 1905*.
Pen and ink, 21¾″ x 20¾″. Lent by the New-York Historical Society.

150

Arthur Ignatius Keller (1866–1925). *Two Belles In Paris.*
Her Letter by Bret Harte, 1906. Watercolor, 20¾″ x 14″. Lent by Walt Reed.

Arthur Ignatius Keller (1866–1925). *Title unknown.*
Oil wash, 20″ x 24″. Lent by Frank Willbright.

G. Patrick Nelson. *Young Woman in Church. 1904.*
Pen and ink, 14″ x 8¼″. Lent by Walt Reed.

151

Jessie Wilcox Smith (1863–1935). *Peter, Peter, Pumpkin Eater. The Little Mother Goose, Dodd & Co., 1912.* Mixed media, 18½″ x 23″. Lent by Mr. and Mrs. Benjamin Eisenstat.

Philip R. Goodwin (1882–1935). *Two Men in a Canoe Shooting Through White Water.*
Oil, 25″ x 36″. Lent by Mrs. Thomas Wilcox.

Harvey T. Dunn (1884–1952). *Buffalo Bones Plowed Under.* Oil, 24″ x 40″. Lent by Harold Von Schmidt.

Harvey T. Dunn (1884–1952). *The Football Squad. 1911.*
Oil, 15″ x 36″. Lent by Peggy and Harold Samuels.

Martin Justice (1892–1960).
The Heights of Art. Everybody's Magazine, April 1906.
Gouache, 19¼" x 16". Lent by Robert J. Mehlman.

Edward Windsor Kemble (1861–1933). *Three Negroes in Church.*
Pen and ink, 6" x 6". Lent by Mrs. Thomas Wilcox.

John Wolcott Adams (1874–1925).
The Paper Lady's Lodger.
Everybody's Magazine, May 1906.
Gouache, 6¼" x 11".
Lent by Robert J. Mehlman.

Walter Appleton Clark (1876–1906).
'Why it's old Charlie Channing,' he exclaimed drowsily.
Scribner's Magazine, August 1901.
Gouache, 14" x 8".
Lent by Robert J. Mehlman.

Walter H. Everett. *Family at the Bedside of a Sick Girl.*
Collier's Magazine, 1901. Charcoal, 17″ x 10″. Lent by Walt Reed.

Violet Oakley (1874–1961). *Study of Jessie Wilcox Smith.*
Mixed media, 22″ x 9″. Lent by Mr. and Mrs. Benjamin Eisenstat.

Maxfield Parrish (1870–1966). *The Prospector. Collier's Magazine, February 4, 1911.* Oil, 15¼" x 14¼". Lent by George Schriever.

Howard Chandler Christy (1873–1952). *Portrait of Nancy Christy—The Christy Girl. 1926.*
Oil, 40″ x 30″. Lent by Mr. and Mrs. Alan Goffman.

Howard Chandler Christy (1873–1952). *Girl Wearing Tiara.*
Watercolor, 14″ x 11″. Lent by Walt Reed.

Elmer Boyd Smith (1860–1943). *King Philip's War—1675.*
Story of Our Country by E. Boyd Smith, 1920.
Gouache, 9″ x 12″.   Lent by Peggy and Howard Samuels.

Elmer Boyd Smith (1860–1943). *The First Railroad Across the Plains—1869.*
Story of Our Country by E. Boyd Smith, 1920.
Gouache, 9″ x 12″.   Lent by Peggy and Howard Samuels.

Henry Patrick Raleigh (1880–1944). *All Eyes on Her. Harper's Bazaar, 1922.*
Pen and ink, 16½″ x 13¾″. Lent by the New Britain Museum of American Art.

Henry Patrick Raleigh (1880–1944). *Interior with Figures. Curtis Publications. 1922.*
Watercolor and pen and ink, 12½″ x 14½″. Lent by Mr. and Mrs. Benjamin Eisenstat.

Louis Rhead (1857–1926).
The Pathfinder by James Fenimore Cooper, 1912.
Pen and ink, 13½″ x 9″. Lent by Robert J. Mehlman.

166

Charles Dana Gibson (1867–1944). *'Advice to Radio Beginners—Do not become discouraged at static trouble. It may not be static at all, but merely trouble in the receiving set.'*
Life, February 7, 1924. Pen and ink, 16" x 26". Lent by Mort Künstler.

William Andrew Loomis (1892–1959). *Portrait of a Little Girl.*
McCall's Magazine. Oil, 24" x 20". Lent by Walt Reed.

Dean Cornwell (1892–1960). *Dozens of People Debarking from a Liner.* 1920–30. Oil, 35½″ x 22½″. Lent by Mrs. Thomas Wilcox.

Dean Cornwell (1892–1960). *Title unknown. 1922.* Oil, 36″ x 27¾″. Lent by Mort Künstler.

Norman Mills Price (1877–1951). *Revolutionary War, Wagons and Soldiers.* Oil, 17″ x 28″. Lent by the Society of Illustrators.

Norman Mills Price (1877–1951). *The Reluctant Bride.*
Woman's Home Companion. Watercolor, 14½″ x 19¾″. Lent by Walt Reed.

Norman Mills Price (1877–1951). *Waiting to Report.*
Pen and ink, 5½″ x 8½″. Lent by Mort Künstler.

Clara Elsene Peck (b. 1883). *Lunette. Delineator Magazine.* Gouache, 12″ x 24″. Lent by Mr. and Mrs. Benjamin Eisenstat.

Clara Elsene Peck (b. 1883). *Youth is all around us: ardent lovely youth.*
Pencil and crayon, 12″ x 14½″. Lent by Mrs. Thomas Wilcox.

Rose O'Neill (1875–1944). *The Very Little Person.*
Pen and ink, 14½″ x 20″. Lent by Walt Reed.

171

Norman Mills Price (1877–1951). *Introducing the Fiancé. The Rake and the Hussy by Robert W. Chambers.* Gouache, 11⅛″ x 12½″. Lent by Mort Künstler.

Mead Schaeffer (b. 1898). *Interrogating the Prisoner by Howard Vance, McCall's Magazine, 1926.* Oil, 26″ x 50″. Lent by Dr. Robert Denby.

Charles Shepard Chapman (1879–1962). *Title unknown.*
Watercolor, 9½″ x 11″. Lent by Robert J. Mehlman.

Charles Buckles Falls (1874–1960). *Haitian Girl.*
Unpublished. Watercolor, 9″ x 12″. Lent by Walt Reed.

Jay Hambidge (1867–1924). *Chinese Laundry.*
Litho pencil, 26″ x 22″. Lent by Walt Reed.

Thornton Oakley (1881–1955).
Burning Seaweed—Brittany. The Century Magazine.
Charcoal, 26½″ x 16½″. Lent by Walt Reed.

C. Clyde Squires (1883–1970). *The Cow Poke.*
Charcoal, 17¾″ x 10″.
Lent by Peggy and Harold Samuels.

Edward Windsor Kemble (1861–1933).
Cold Weather at the Zoo.
Pen and ink, 14¼″ x 11″.
Lent by Mr. and Mrs. Benjamin Eisenstat.

William de la Montagne Cary (1840–1922). *High Toss.* Wash drawing, 15½″ x 19½″. Lent by Peggy and Harold Samuels.

Raeburn Van Buren (b. 1891). *Prize Fighters.*
The Saturday Evening Post, 1928. Charcoal, 12″ x 20″. Lent by the artist.

Edmund F. Ward (b. 1892). *We Mean Business. April, 1923.* Oil, 30" x 27". Lent by Peggy and Harold Samuels.

176

Frank Earle Schoonover (1877–1922). *Wheat. The Country Gentleman, 1924.* Oil, 33″ x 30″. Lent by M. Knoedler & Co., Inc.

Sarah Stilwell-Weber (1878–1939). *Happy Days by Sarah S. Stilwell.*
Pen and ink, 9½″ x 8″. Lent by Mrs. Thomas Wilcox.

Clara Elsene Peck (b. 1883). *Berry Pickers.*
Watercolor, 16″ x 14″. Lent by Mrs. Thomas Wilcox.

Charles Nicolas Sarka (1879–1960). *The Speed Demons.*
Pen and ink, 12″ x 18″. Lent by Walt Reed.

John Held, Jr. (1889–1958). *George Washington.*
Pen and ink, 6″ x 9″. Lent by Mrs. Thomas Wilcox.

Harold Brett (b. 1882). *Anti-aircraft Gunners in World War I.*
Oil, 26" x 19". Lent by Carl Sciortino.

Orson Byron Lowell (1871–1956). *Officers Pushing Auto.*
Watercolor, 27" x 21". Lent by Walt Reed.

André Castaigne *Fiddler and Dance.*
Oil, 21¾" x 31". Lent by the New Britain Museum of American Art.

Newell Convers Wyeth (1882–1945). *Miles Standish. The Courtship of Miles Standish by Henry Wadsworth Longfellow, Houghton Mifflin Co., 1920.* Oil, 28¾" x 26¾". Lent by Mort Künstler.

Herbert Morton Stoops (1888–1948). *Monica Found Herself Alone on Bogus Again.*
Cosmopolitan, August 1926. Oil, 44″ x 32″. Lent by Peggy and Harold Samuels.

George Harding (1882–1959). *South Sea Traders.*
Watercolor, 16″ x 11″. Lent by the Society of Illustrators.

Herbert Morton Stoops (1888–1948). *The Interrupted Supper. 1924.*
Oil, 30″ x 44″. Lent by the New Britain Museum of American Art.

Herbert Morton Stoops (1888–1948). *Youth Rides West. Youth Rides West, April 1924.* Oil, 26″ x 40″. Lent by Peggy and Harold Samuels.

Worth Brehm (1883–1928). *Loafers at the Stable.*
Woman's Home Companion. Charcoal, 17¼″ x 25½″. Lent by Walt Reed.

Edmund F. Ward (b. 1892). *The Prairie Child.* 1921.
Oil, 24″ x 34½″. Lent by Peggy and Harold Samuels.

Russell Patterson (1896–1977). *Windy Day on the Pier.*
Watercolor, 10½″ x 11″. Lent by the Graham Gallery.

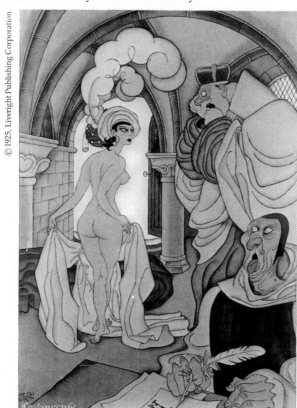

Ralph Barton (1891–1931). *Le Succube.*
Droll Stories by Honoré de Balzac, Boni & Liveright Co., 1925.
Gouache, 14″ x 10″. Lent by the Graham Gallery.

John Held, Jr. (1889–1958). *The American Girl. 1925.*
Pen and ink and watercolor, 9¾″ x 5¾″. Lent by the Graham Gallery.

Dean Cornwell (1892–1960). *Purdie, Hallie, and Gail. Cosmopolitan, October 1924.* Oil, 30″ x 48″. Lent by Mort Künstler.

Frank Earle Schoonover (1877–1922). *In the South Seas.*
The Popular Magazine, February 18, 1928. Oil, 33″ x 30″. Lent by M. Knoedler & Co., Inc.

Thomas Fogarty (1873–1938). *The Country Store. Unpublished, 1925.* Watercolor. Lent by Thomas Fogarty, Jr.

Thomas Fogarty (1873–1938). *The Blacksmith Shop.*
Unpublished, 1925. Watercolor. Lent by Thomas Fogarty, Jr.

185

Arthur Ignatius Keller (1866–1925). *The Marrakech Market*. Oil, 25″ x 40″. Lent by the Society of Illustrators.

William Meade Prince (1893–1951). *Circus Scene*. 1922.
Oil, 16″ x 32″. Lent by the Society of Illustrators.

Wallace Morgan (1873–1948). *At the Seashore.*
Charcoal and wash, 15½″ x 26½″. Lent by Mort Künstler.

Pruett A. Carter (1891–1955). *The Past Hunters. McCall's Magazine, October, 1929.* Oil, 37″ x 31″. Lent by Walt Reed.

Dan Content (b. 1902). *Ladies at Leisure. 1929.*
Oil, 30" x 24". Lent by the Graham Gallery.

Rolf Armstrong. *Title unknown.*
Pastel, 25" x 19". Lent by Beverly and Ray Sacks, The Art Couple.

Rolf Armstrong. *Title unknown. Shrine Magazine, March 1928.*
Pastel, 22" x 19". Lent by Beverly and Ray Sacks, The Art Couple.

Pruett A. Carter (1891–1955). *Lincoln's War Cabinet. 1929.* Oil, 22″ x 48″. Lent by Mort Künstler.

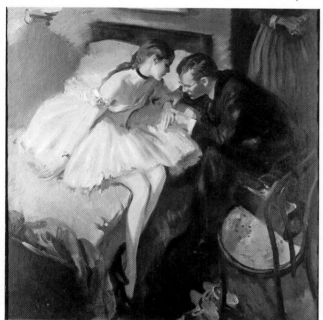

Pruett A. Carter (1891–1955). *Ballerina.*
McCall's Magazine, October, 1929.
Oil, 39″ x 38″. Lent by the Society of Illustrators.

Orson Byron Lowell (1871–1956). *Angels. 1925.*
Oil, 27″ x 22″. Lent by Robert J. Mehlman.

Herman Pfeifer (b. 1879). *Frontier Wedding.*
Pastel, 18″ x 14″. Lent by the Society of Illustrators.

Charles Davis Mitchell (1887–1940). *Costume Party.*
Wolff pencil, 21″ x 17″. Lent by Walt Reed.

Saul Tepper (b. 1899). *At the Masquerade.*
Liggett & Meyers, Corp., 1928. Oil, 32″ x 37″. Lent by the artist.

Albin Henning (1886–1943). *Stretcher Bearers. The Saturday Evening Post, 1929.* Oil, 23¼" x 40". Lent by Fritz Henning.

Saul Tepper (b. 1899). *View from the Bridge.* Oil, 19¾" x 34¾". Lent by the artist.

Saul Tepper (b. 1899). *Title unknown.* Oil, 19¾" x 34¾". Lent by Joseph T. Mendola.

191

Anton Otto Fischer (1882–1962). *To the Rescue. The Saturday Evening Post.* Oil, 24″ x 35″. Lent by the New Britain Museum of American Art.

Gardner Rea (1892–1966).
She's Funny That Way. Judge, May 18, 1929.
Watercolor, 14″ x 10¾″.
Lent by the Graham Gallery.

Anna Whelan Betts.
Girl with a Valentine.
Oil, 13⅛″ x 21⅛″.
Lent by the New Britain Museum
of American Art.

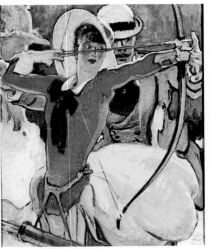

Samuel Nelson Abbott (1874–1953).
The Archery Lesson.
The Saturday Evening Post, 1920–1925.
Gouache, 11″ x 9½″.
Lent by Marshall Berland.

It had the irresponsibility of a cyclone

Wallace Morgan (1873–1948). *Title unknown.* Pen and ink and watercolor, 24″ x 30″. Lent by Frank Willbright.

Wallace Morgan (1873–1948). *A Dog's Life.*
Brush and ink, 12½″ x 9″. Lent by Walt Reed.

Arthur William Brown (1881–1966). *Untitled. 1927.*
Pencil and wash, 14″ x 12½″. Lent by Robert Greenhalgh.

Gardner Rea (1892–1966). *The New Yorker, August, 1929.*
Lent by the Museum of the City of New York.

James W. Williamson (b. 1899). *Three Drawings.*
Watercolor, 10½″ x 18″. Lent by the Society of Illustrators.

194

Raeburn Van Buren (b. 1891). *Bill Collector.*
The Saturday Evening Post, 1925. Wolff pencil, 12″ x 18¼″. Lent by Walt Reed.

Peggy Bacon (b. 1895). *Frenzied Effort.*
The New Masses, October 1926.
Drypoint, 5¾″ x 9″. Lent by the Brooklyn Museum.

Frank Earle Schoonover (1877–1922). *In the South Seas.*
Endpaper for Yankee Ships in Pirate Waters by Rupert S. Holland, Macrae Smith Co., 1931.
Pen and ink, 11″ x 15″. Lent by Walt Reed.

Arthur D. Fuller (b. 1889). *Which Would You Rather Be? 1925.*
Charcoal, 11¼″ x 15″. Lent by Mrs. Thomas Wilcox.

Paul Bransom (b. 1885). *Always ahead that calling cry rang through the white dimness.*
The Love of 'Little Feet' by Vingie E. Roe; McCall's Magazine, May 1929.
Watercolor and charcoal, 15″ x 27″. Lent by the Graham Gallery.

Clarence William Anderson (b. 1891). *Pants to Match Your Coat and Vest.*
Life. Watercolor, 17″ x 13″. Lent by the Graham Gallery.

Guy Hoff (1889–1962). *Girl in the Green Hat. Smart Set.*
Pastel, 20″ x 17″. Lent by Walt Reed.

Francis Xavier Leyendecker (1877–1924).
Girl in Spanish Shawl. Vogue.
Watercolor, 10¼″ x 7″. Lent by Mrs. Thomas Wilcox.

Orson Byron Lowell (1871–1956). *Lo Gwendolyn.*
Harper's Bazar, July. Monochrome oil, 24″ x 16½″. Lent by Mrs. Thomas Wilcox.

William Hatherell. *News Dealer.*
Opaque wash, 15″ x 9″. Lent by the Society of Illustrators.

Artist Unknown. *Aucassin and Nicolette.*
Oil, 15″ x 23″. Lent by Beverly and Ray Sacks, The Art Couple.

Frederic Rodrigo Gruger (1871–1953).
Urdaneta entrenched himself for many weeks with my daughter in the governor's mansion.
When her leg was shattered by a bullet, she loaded the rifles. The Virgin Warrior by Blasco Ibaniez,
Cosmopolitan, October 1926.
Charcoal, 13⅜″ x 12⅛″. Lent by the New Britain Museum of American Art.

Walter Biggs (1886–1968). *Family Circle.*
Oil, 42″ x 34″. Lent by Walt Reed.

William Meade Prince (1893–1951). *Pioneer Family.*
Opaque wash, 16″ x 20″. Lent by the Society of Illustrators.

Frederick Coffay Yohn (1875–1933). *The Last Ounce.*
American Boy, 1921. Gouache, 15½″ x 20¼″. Lent by Peggy and Harold Samuels.

Wallace Morgan (1873–1948). *Black Night Club. 1929.* Charcoal, 17″ x 28″. Lent by the Society of Illustrators.

Malcolm Fraser (1869–1949). *Tea on the Lawn.*
Wash drawing, 18⅞″ x 21⅞″. Lent by the New Britain Museum of American Art.

Henry Patrick Raleigh (1880–1944). *The Star. 1930.*
Pencil and wash, 17″ x 19¼″. Lent by Mort Künstler.

William J. Glackens (1870–1938). *Title unknown*. Charcoal, 13″ x 20″. Lent by the Society of Illustrators.

Earle B. Winslow (1884–1969). *The Woodstock Bus.*
Bingville Bugle, 1921. Lithograph, 14″ x 18″. Lent by Mrs. Marsden London.

Henry McCarter (1865–1943). *New England Beach. Scribner's Magazine.*
Gouache, 20″ x 12½″. Lent by Mr. and Mrs. Benjamin Eisenstat.

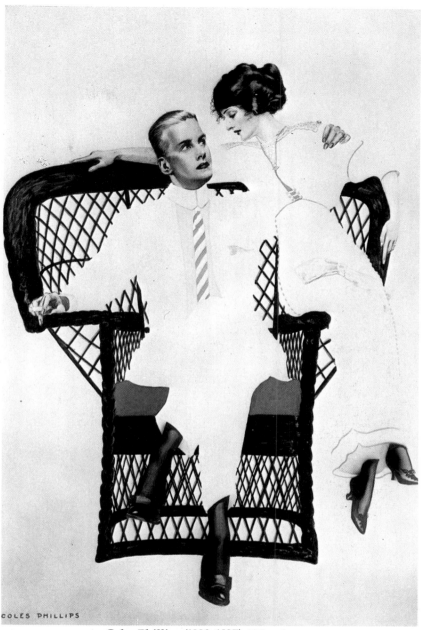

Coles Phillips (1880–1927). *Title unknown.*
Watercolor, 25″ x 16½″. Lent by Sam Tomlin.

Frank Godwin (b. 1889). *Naked Lady Meeting Naked Couple in Woods.*
Pen and ink and watercolor, 14″ x 24″. Lent by Mrs. Thomas Wilcox.

Robert L. Lambdin (b. 1886). *Soldiers and Fallen Horse.*
Kansas City Star. Pen and ink, 11″ x 12½″. Lent by Walt Reed.

René Clarke (b. 1886). *Homeward Bound.*
Watercolor, 9″ x 12″. Lent by Walt Reed.

Arthur Burdett Frost (1851–1928). *Hunter, Kangaroo, Snake.*
Pen and ink, each 5½″ x 7″. Lent by Mrs. Thomas Wilcox.

1930's

Constantin Alajalov (b. 1900). *Title unknown. The New Yorker, June 1930.*
Watercolor, 18″ x 13″. Lent by the Museum of the City of New York.

Richard Decker (b. 1907). *Department Store at Christmas. The New Yorker, December 1934.*
Watercolor, 13¼″ x 10″. Lent by the Museum of the City of New York.

Earl Oliver Hurst (1895–1958).
Old Snake in the Grass. Collier's Magazine.
Colored ink,
31″ x 19½″. Lent by Mrs. Earl Oliver Hurst.

Leonard Dove (d. 1964). *Gallery 14. The New Yorker.*
Watercolor, 12¼″ x 9″. Lent by Walt Reed.

Matt Clark (b. 1903). *Circus Capture. American Magazine, 1934.* Oil, 30½″ x 34½″. Lent by the New Britain Museum of American Art.

Steven R. Kidd (b. 1911). *True Lover's Knot.*
New York Sunday News, 1936. Pen and ink, 12″ x 12½″. Lent by the artist.

Steven R. Kidd (b. 1911). *True Lover's Knot,*
New York Sunday News, 1936. Pen and ink, 21″ x 12½″. Lent by the artist.

Steven R. Kidd (b. 1911). *True Lover's Knot.*
New York Sunday News, 1936. Pen and ink,
12″ x 12½″. Lent by the artist.

Garrett Price (b. 1896). *Smorgasbord.*
The New Yorker. Watercolor, 12¾″ x 8⅝″.
Lent by Walt Reed.

Franklin Booth (1874–1948). *Title unknown.* Watercolor, 6″ x 14″. Lent by the Graham Gallery.

Lu Kimmel (1908–1973). *Man Reading.*
Oil, 34″ x 34″. Lent by Walt Reed.

Lu Kimmel (1908–1973). *Girl in Front of the Mirror.*
Oil, 37″ x 32″. Lent by Alice Kimmel.

Harry Beckhoff (b. 1901). *Town Meeting. Collier's Magazine.* Watercolor, 11½" x 27½". Lent by the artist.

Neysa Moran McMein (1890–1948). *Portrait of a Lady.*
McCall's Magazine. Oil, 28" x 24". Lent by the Society of Illustrators.

Bradshaw Crandell (1896–1966). *Title unknown. Cosmopolitan.*
Pastel, 25" x 19". Lent by Walt Reed.

Norman Rockwell (b. 1894). *The Dover Coach*. Oil, 31″ x 74″. Lent by the Society of Illustrators.

Norman Rockwell (b. 1894). *Woman's Portrait*.
Pencil, 19″ x 16″. Lent by the Society of Illustrators.

209

Mead Schaeffer (b. 1898). *Indian Allies. Everybody's Washington, Dodd, Mead and Company, 1931.* Oil, 32" x 26". Lent by Dr. Robert Denby.

Mario Cooper (b. 1905).
He felt a pang as he watched her go up the stairs with the thieving monkey.
Brownstone Front by P. D. Augsburg, Woman's Home Companion, October 1932.
Colored inks, 21″ x 14¾″. Lent by the artist.

Herbert Paus (1880–1946). *Title unknown.*
American Magazine, Cover, January 1934.
Watercolor, 25″ x 21″. Lent by Mrs. Robert Bugg.

Herbert Paus (1880–1946). *The Balloonist.*
Watercolor, 4¼″ x 3½″. Lent by Walt Reed.

Theodore Geisel (Dr. Seuss) (b. 1904).
Good Gracious, Matilda—You Too?
Judge, December 26, 1931. Pen and ink, 20¼″ x 15¼″.
Lent by Mrs. Thomas Wilcox.

211

Harold Von Schmidt (b. 1893). *Horse Race. 1933.* Oil, 30″ x 50″. Lent by the Society of Illustrators.

Rockwell Kent (1882–1971). *LX Chapter Heading. Moby Dick by Herman Melville,*
Lakeside Press, 1930. Pen and ink, 3¼″ x 7″. Lent by the Weyhe Gallery.

Rockwell Kent (1882–1971). *XXXVIII Chapter Heading. Moby Dick by Herman Melville,*
Lakeside Press, 1930. Pen and ink, 2¾″ x 7″. Lent by the Weyhe Gallery.

Harold Von Schmidt (b. 1893). *Spike Team. The Saturday Evening Post, 1947.* Oil, 27″ x 43″. Lent by the artist.

Rockwell Kent (1882–1971). *LXXIX Chapter Heading. Moby Dick by Herman Melville,*
Lakeside Press, 1930. Pen and ink, $4\frac{1}{8}$″ x $7\frac{1}{8}$″. Lent by the Weyhe Gallery.

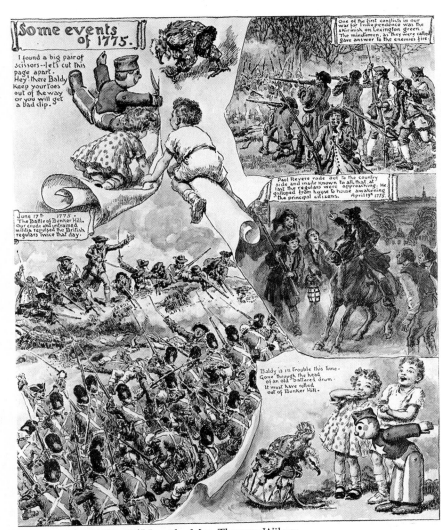

F. Luis Mora (1874–1940). *Some Events of 1775.* Watercolor and pen and ink, 19½" x 15½". Lent by Mrs. Thomas Wilcox.

Herbert Paus (1880–1946). *Title unknown. Collier's Magazine, June 1931.* Watercolor, 28" x 21½". Lent by Mrs. Robert Bugg.

Henry C. Pitz (1895–1976). *Title unknown. 1938.*
Pen and ink, 19½" x 24¾". Lent by the artist.

214

Saul Tepper (b. 1899). *Hitch Four Widows to a Plow in the Dead of the Night! Lysol Division of Sterling Drug Company, 1931.* Oil, 26″ x 40″. Lent by the artist.

Henry C. Pitz (1895–1976). *Sea Battle.*
Limited Editions Club. Ink and charcoal, 16″ x 21″. Lent by the artist.

Jean Dupas (1882–1964). *Saks Fifth Avenue, Inc. 1930*. Pen and ink and watercolor, 22″ x 16″. Lent by Beverly and Ray Sacks, The Art Couple.

Joseph Christian Leyendecker (1874–1951). *Easter. The Saturday Evening Post, March 31, 1934*. Oil, 32″ x 24″. Lent by the Society of Illustrators.

Floyd M. Davis (1896–1966). *Title unknown*. Tempera, 30″ x 40″. Lent by Frank Willbright.

Floyd M. Davis (1896–1966). *Last Act, Last Scene. The Saturday Evening Post, 1939.* Oil, 27½″ x 31½″. Lent by the New Britain Museum of American Art.

Harvey T. Dunn (1884–1952). *Outside the Hacienda.*
Oil, 20″ x 30″. Lent by Harry Greenstein.

Will Crawford (1869–1944). *Title unknown.*
Pen and ink, 16¼″ x 10″. Lent by Peggy and Harold Samuels.

Mario Cooper (b. 1905). *Stick Up.*
Collier's Magazine, 1933. Wash, 17″ x 10″. Lent by the Society of Illustrators.

Maurice Bower (b. 1889). *Stalking Indians.*
McCall's Magazine. Pastel and charcoal, 23″ x 24½″. Lent by Walt Reed.

Dudley Gloyne Summers (1892–1975). *Boarding Party.*
Maclean's Magazine, 1940. Watercolor and charcoal, 20¾″ x 20″.
Lent by the New Britain Museum of American Art.

George Howe (1896–1941).
'Roth Edmonds sold him,' the old Negress said.
She swayed back and forth. 'Sold my Benjamin.'
Go Down, Moses by William Faulkner, Collier's Magazine,
January 25, 1941. Watercolor, 16½″ x 13½″. Lent by Walt Reed.

Percy Crosby (1891–1964).
Janitor, Will You Tell Me if the Sun is Shining? I Want to Take the Baby Out.
Watercolor, 16½″ x 13¼″. Lent by Mrs. Thomas Wilcox.

Wladyslaw T. Benda (1873–1948). *Survivors of the Flood*. Watercolor, 24" x 18". Lent by the Society of Illustrators.

Ludwig Bemelmans (1898–1962). *Plaza Independencia—Quito, Ecuador. Vogue, April 1, 1938.* Watercolor, 17″ x 23½″. Lent by Mr. and Mrs. Benjamin Eisenstat.

James Williamson (b. 1899). *Family Scene with Candelabra.*
Tempera, 16¼" x 13¾". Lent by the New Britain Museum of American Art.

Walter Biggs (1886–1968). *Of the two it was he who clung, she who sustained.*
Peter Ashley by DuBose Heyward, Woman's Home Companion, December 1932.
Watercolor, 26¼" x 19½". Lent by the New Britain Museum of American Art.

Henry J. Soulen (1888–1965). *The Conversation.*
Oil, 23" x 27". Lent by Peggy and Harold Samuels.

Reginald Marsh (1898–1954). *Travelers Insurance Company.*
Pen and ink, 12" x 9". Lent by the Graham Gallery.

Robert Wesley Amick (b. 1879). *Tiger in the Grass.*
Adventure Magazine, November 15, 1931. Oil, 24" x 20½". Lent by Beverly and Ray Sacks,
The Art Couple.

William Andrew Pogany (1882–1955). *The Merman.*
Gouache, 19½" x 15¾". Lent by Peggy and Harold Samuels.

Lowell Leroy Balcom (1887–1938). *Logging.*
American Legion Magazine, December, 1930.
Tinted linoleum block, 15½" x 13½". Lent by Walt Reed.

223

John Held, Jr. (1889–1958). *Page Miss Glory. Poster for play, 'Page Miss Glory', 1935.* Pen and ink and watercolor, 13" x 22". Lent by Beverly and Ray Sacks, The Art Couple.

John Held, Jr. (1889–1958). *The Hobble Skirt. 1931.*
Scratchboard, 9½" x 12½". Lent by Mrs. John Held, Jr.

224

Mead Schaeffer (b. 1898). *Highwaymen*. Oil, 31″ x 45″. Lent by the Society of Illustrators.

Lawrence Fellows (1885–1964). *Mounted Captain*.
Pen and ink, 9½″ x 13″. Lent by Walt Reed.

Floyd M. Davis (1896–1966).
We lifted him clean off the ground, holding him, or trying to. 'Stop it, Jackson,' I says.
Tomorrow by William Faulkner, The Saturday Evening Post, November 16, 1940.
Ink wash, 30½" x 23¼". Lent by the New Britain Museum of American Art.

Earle B. Winslow (1884–1969). *Turning Wheels. 1931.*
Half-tone wash, 16¾" x 13". Lent by Mrs. Marsden London.

Paul Rabut (b. 1914). *The Return of Daniel Boone.*
American Girl, April 1941. Ink wash, 12¾" x 23¼". Lent by Lent by the artist.

Leonard T. Holton (b. 1906). *The Floating Population.*
Judge, August 2, 1930. Watercolor, 13″ x 10½″. Lent by the Graham Gallery.

Tony Sarg (1880–1942). *Lion on Hind Legs, Laughing.* 1930.
Pen and ink and watercolor, 19½″ x 14½″. Lent by Mrs. Thomas Wilcox.

Alfred J. Frueh (1880–1968). *Bicycle Race. Life.*
Watercolor and ink, 20½″ x 15″. Lent by the Graham Gallery.

Harry Beckhoff (b. 1901). *Irate Customer. Collier's Magazine.* Watercolor, 13½" x 18". Lent by Walt Reed.

George Brehm (1878–1966).
There used to be a gang of kids around these parts. And what they didn't swipe they couldn't carry.
The Saturday Evening Post, October 12, 1935.
Charcoal, 9" x 30". Lent by Walt Reed.

George Brehm (1878–1966). *Cowboys and Indians.*
Oil, 27″ x 22″. Lent by Walt Reed.

Henry Patrick Raleigh (1880–1944). *Incident at a Formal Affair. Curtis Publications, 1933.*
Watercolor and ink, 17″ x 14″. Lent by Mr. and Mrs. Benjamin Eisenstat.

W. Emerton Heitland (b. 1893). *Girl in Top Hat.*
Watercolor, 27″ x 22½″. Lent by Walt Reed.

Herbert Morton Stoops (1888–1948).
Now is the Time for Help. American Legion Magazine, December 1931.
Charcoal, 19″ x 14″. Lent by Mrs. Thomas Wilcox.

Maud Tousey Fangel. *The Curse of Drink.*
Watercolor and charcoal, 13½″ x 10½″. Lent by Murray Tinkelman.

Nicholas F. Riley (1900–1944). *But Love the Sinner.*
The Saturday Evening Post, November 18, 1939. Watercolor, 19½″ x 16½″. Lent by Walt Reed.

Ruth Grafstrom (b. 1905). *A Woman's Head.* 1937.
Pastel, 14″ x 11″. Lent by Janet and Arthur Weithas.

1940's

Peter Helck (b. 1893). *The Brighton 24 Hour (Quick tire change for Al Poole's Simplex). 'Roman Holiday at Brighton Beach' by John Leathers, Esquire, April 1946.*
Tempera, 31″ x 41″. Lent by the National Art Museum of Sport.

Albert Dorne (1904–1965). *Unfamiliar Spirit. The Saturday Evening Post.* Oil, 8¾″ x 27″. Lent by the New Britain Museum of American Art.

Lyman Anderson (b. 1907). *In breathless words I told her my dreams. The Blue Cloak by Temple Bailey, Woman's Home Companion, December 1940.*
Oil, 41" x 32' Lent by the Society of Illustrators.

Gilbert Bundy (1911–1955). *Horse Policeman.* Watercolor, 16″ x 18¾″. Lent by the Society of Illustrators.

Lyle Justis (1892–1960). *Colonial Figures. Unpublished, 1948.*
Pen and ink, 10″ x 11½″. Lent by Walt Reed.

Lyle Justis (1892–1960). *Seafaring Characters. Unpublished.*
Pen and ink, 8¼″ x 8⅝″. Lent by Walt Reed.

Mary Petty (1899–1976). *Cover. The New Yorker, April 1943.*
Watercolor, 16½″ x 12 1/16″. Lent by the Museum of the City of New York.

Leo Rackow (b. 1901). *Modern Packaging Catalogue. Packaging Annual, 1940–41.* Tempera, 19⅜″ x 32⅜″. Lent by David Enoch.

Nicholas F. Riley (1900–1944). *A Man's Mother by Gladys Hasty Carroll.*
The Saturday Evening Post, September 19, 1940. Watercolor, 17½″ x 19½″.
Lent by Mrs. Nicholas F. Riley.

Robert Fawcett (1903–1967). *Medieval.* Watercolor, 18″ x 28″. Lent by the New Britain Museum of American Art.

Amos Sewell (b. 1901). *Big Joe returned to the house.*
'Was it a ghost, Pop?' Babe called anxiously. Especially Babe by Ross Annett,
The Saturday Evening Post, December 14, 1940.
Charcoal, 29″ x 29″. Lent by the Society of Illustrators.

Benjamin Albert Stahl (b. 1910). *Morro Castle Disaster. The Saturday Evening Post, 1945.* Tempera and oil, 14½″ x 20½″. Lent by the New Britain Museum of American Art.

Steven Kidd (b. 1911). *4th Infantry—Replacement Depot, The Philippines.*
Watercolor and charcoal, 14½″ x 25″. Lent by the artist.

Howard Brodie (b. 1916). *GI's Marching.*
Yank Magazine, 1944. Print, 24″ x 18″. Lent by the artist.

Howard Brodie (b. 1916). *GI in Combat.*
Yank Magazine, 1944. Pen and ink and print, 24″ x 18″. Lent by the artist.

Kerr Eby (1889–1946). *Jungle Fighter.*
Charcoal, 20″ x 22½″. Lent by the United States Navy.
Courtesy of the United States Navy Combat Art Collection.

239

John LaGatta (1894–1977). *Couple on Balcony. Cosmopolitan, August 1949.* Mixed media, 29″ x 21″. Lent by the Society of Illustrators.

Benjamin Albert Stahl (b. 1910). *Title unknown*. Oil, 23½" x 24½". Lent by Joseph T. Mendola.

Zolzislaw Czermanski (1900–1970). *John L. Lewis.*
Fortune Magazine, 1949. Lent by Mrs. J. Czermanski.

Zolzislaw Czermanski (1900–1970). *Hitler in Winter.*
Fortune Magazine, 1949. Lent by Mrs. J. Czermanski.

Al Parker (b. 1906). *The Bouquet. Ladies' Home Journal.*
Gouache, 14″ x 20½″. Lent by Albert Gold.

242

Carl O. A. Erickson (1891–1958). *Title unknown. Vogue.* Gouache, 12″ x 9″. Lent by Janet and Arthur Weithas.

Floyd M. Davis (1896–1966). *Air Raid on Hamburg*. Oil, 30″ x 36″. Lent by the United States Army Center of Military History.

John Philip Falter (b. 1910). *Boys and Kites. The Saturday Evening Post.* Oil, 30" x 24". Lent by the New Britain Museum of American Art.

Benjamin Albert Stahl (b. 1910). *Cavalryman.*
Oil, 14″ x 16″. Lent by the New Britain Museum of American Art.

Saul Tepper (b. 1899). *Talk's Cheap! Life Isn't!*
Stetson and Company, 1944. Oil, 28″ x 33″. Lent by the artist.

McClelland Barclay (1891–1943). *Pacific War-Attack on a Battleship.* 1943.
Oil, 30″ x 40″. Lent by Walt Reed.

Boris Artzybasheff (1899–1965). *Wickwire. Life, July 24, 1942.*
Pen and ink, 12″ x 18¼″. Lent by Peggy and Harold Samuels.

Griffith B. Coale (1890–1950). *Pearl Harbor.* Paston on fabric, 21" x 72". Lent by the United States Navy.
Courtesy of the United States Navy Combat Art Collection.

Carl O. A. Erickson (1891–1958). *The Servicemen's Lounge—Grand Central Station.*
Vogue, April 15, 1944. Watercolor, 25" x 18". Lent anonymously.

Robert G. Harris (b. 1911). *There, in the far corner, was Pandora. Wedding Present by Newlin Wildes, Ladies' Home Journal, September 1948.* Oil, 21″ x 29″. Lent by the artist.

Alex Ross (b. 1908). *Arlene.*
Good Housekeeping, January 1948.
Gouache, 13″ x 10¼″.
Lent by the artist.

Edwin Georgi (1896–1964). *She stepped out of her dress. She was pitifully young and frightened to death. Date With Death by Leslie Ford, The Saturday Evening Post, January 25, 1949.*
Watercolor, 23″ x 18″. Lent by Mr. and Mrs. Benjamin Eisenstat.

Amos Sewell (b. 1901). *Leading Away the Pony. The Saturday Evening Post.* Watercolor, 23½″ x 35″. Lent by Walt Reed.

William Meade Prince (1893–1951). *The Sin-Splitter.*
Collier's Magazine, April 13, 1943. Gouache and pencil, 14″ x 17½″. Lent by Walt Reed.

250

Walter DuBois Richards (b. 1907). *Some of my Friends. Argosy.* Crayon, 13½″ x 20″. Lent by the New Britain Museum of American Art.

Perry Peterson (1908–1958). *Woman Holding Barbed Wire.*
Cauldron Folly. The Saturday Evening Post. Watercolor, 14¼″ x 19″.

Tom Lea (b. 1907). *Going In*. Oil, 22″ x 42″. Lent by the United States Army Center of Military History.

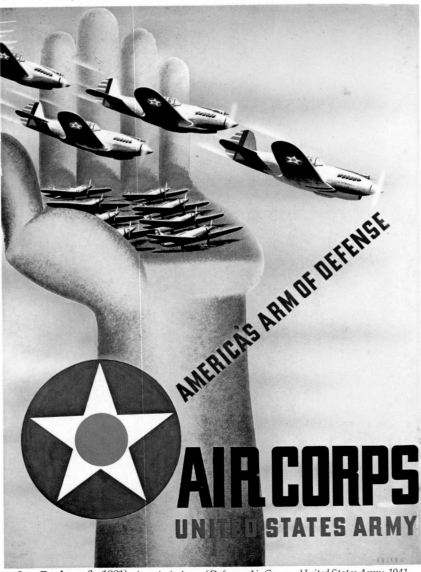

Leo Rackow (b. 1901). *America's Arm of Defense. Air Corps—United States Army, 1941.*
Tempera, 30″ x 28″. Lent by David Enoch.

Stevan Dohanos (b. 1907). *Penny Candy.*
The Saturday Evening Post, September 23, 1944. Watercolor and tempera, 26½″ x 22″.
Lent by the artist.

Robert G. Harris (b. 1911).
Suddenly, without a vestige of warning, you find out what this woman has just now found out.
What would the shock do to you—would you want to face tomorrow?
Gavin by John van Druten, Good Housekeeping, May, 1945. Oil, 26¾″ x 20¼″. Lent by the artist.

Tran James Mawicke (b. 1911). *Family Back Porch.*
Collier's Magazine. Tempera, 17″ x 26″. Lent by the Society of Illustrators.

James Thurber (1894–1961). *Spot.*
The New Yorker, October 1945. Crayon, 17¾″ x 11¼″. Lent by Peggy and Harold Samuels.

Paul Rabut (b. 1914). *Forest Interlude.*
The Saturday Evening Post, July 1945. Ink wash, 20¾″ x 15½″. Lent by the artist.

Stevan Dohanos (b. 1907). *Heartbroken. The Saturday Evening Post, 1944.* Watercolor, 15½″ x 35″. Lent by the New Britain Museum of American Art.

Carl O. A. Erickson (1891–1958). *Roosevelt Press Conference.*
Vogue, 1944. Watercolor, 13″ x 13″. Lent by Mrs. Jane Strong.

John LaGatta (1894–1977). *Girl in Black Negligee.*
Oil, 30″ x 26″. Lent by Walt Reed.

Frank Street (1893–1944). *Some Were Brave. Collier's Magazine, 1940.* Oil, 21″ x 29″. Lent by the Society of Illustrators.

Winold Reiss (1888–1953). *Crow Chief.*
Lent by Burlington Northern.

257

Winold Reiss (1888–1953). *Big Bull.*
Lent by the Riveredge Foundation.

Winold Reiss (1888–1953). *Chief Wades-In-The-Water.*
Lent by Burlington Northern.

Harold Von Schmidt (b. 1893). *The Watcher.*
The Saturday Evening Post, 1942.
Oil, 30″ x 50″. Lent by the New Britain Museum of American Art.

John Richard Flanagan (1895–1964). *The Duel. Bluebook, 1945.* Pen and ink, 11″ x 16″. Lent by Walt Reed.

Arthur William Brown (1881–1966). *Mr. Tutt.*
The Saturday Evening Post, 1943.
Pen and ink, 14″ x 20¾″. Lent by the New Britain Museum of American Art.

Earl Oliver Hurst (1895–1958). *'Pshaw now!' was Cully's fust words.*
Happiest Man in the World by Frederick H. Brennan, Collier's Magazine, March 30, 1940.
Colored inks, 24½″ x 35¾″. Lent by Mrs. Earl Oliver Hurst.

Robert Fawcett (1903–1967). *Old Man and Servant. The Saturday Evening Post.* Watercolor and ink, 18½″ x 14½″. Lent by Walt Reed.

Earl Blossom (1891–1970). *Ox Power. Collier's Magazine, February 24, 1942.* Tempera, 11½″ x 22″. Lent by the New Britain Museum of American Art.

R. John Holmgren (1897–1963). *Widow's Weeds.*
Watercolor, 18″ x 15″. Lent by the Graham Gallery.

René Bouché (1906–1963). *Soak up the sunshine . . . out where the blue begins.*
Elizabeth Arden Ideal Suntan Oil, Vogue, July 1944.
Watercolor, 18″ x 12″. Lent by Margaret J. Doherty.

John Atherton (1900–1952). *Bridge Construction.*
Watercolor, 21″ x 15½″. Lent by Walt Reed.

Zolzislaw Czermanski (1900–1970). *Uncle Sam & Stalin.*
Fortune Magazine, 1949. Lent by Mrs. Z. Czermanski.

Harry O. Diamond (b. 1913). *Title unknown. Holiday, 1949.* Ink wash, 20″ x 15″. Lent by the artist.

Robert Fawcett (1903–1967). *Military Visits Civilian Home. 1945.* Ink and color wash, 14″ x 17″. Lent by the Society of Illustrators.

Hardie Gramatky (b. 1907). *Tree Lined Street.*
Watercolor, 15″ x 25″. Lent by the Society of Illustrators.

Mario Cooper (b. 1905). *The Distances of the World. Collier's Magazine, 1942.* Colored inks, 14½″ x 16½″. Lent by the artist.

Leslie Saalburg (1902–1975). *Faro in the West in the '80's.*
Esquire. Watercolor, 12″ x 10″. Lent by Mrs. Jane Strong.

John Gannam (1907–1965).
Softly you move to the crib to make certain that all is well with the most precious thing in your life.
The Saturday Evening Post, February 19, 1949. Watercolor, 21″ x 18″. Lent by Walt Reed.

Albert Gold (b. 1916). *Ne pas Faire le Posit.* 1945.
Watercolor, 13½″ x 20¾″. Lent by the New Britain Museum of American Art.

1950's

Stevan Dohanos (b. 1907). *Ice Cream Break. The Saturday Evening Post, September 22, 1951.* Tempera, 36″ x 28″. Lent by the artist.

Peter Helck (b. 1893). *Briarcliff Trophy Race—1908. Automobile Quarterly,* 1952. Tempera, 13¾" x 18". Lent by the New Britain Museum of American Art.

Fred Ludekens (b. 1900). *Bank Robbery.*
The Saturday Evening Post, 1953.
Gouache, 17½″ x 13¾″. Lent by the New Britain Museum of American Art.

Fred Ludekens (b. 1900).
Sandy Anderson dismounted, and so did the others—not a minute too soon.
A bullet whined over them, and it was followed by a fusillade.
Killer's Canyon by Bennett Foster, The Saturday Evening Post, September 29, 1951.
Tempera, 19″ x 19″. Lent by the New Britain Museum of American Art.

William A. Smith (b. 1916). *Murder. True Magazine, June 1954.*
Oil, 17″ x 20¾″. Lent by the New Britain Museum of American Art.

John Gannam (1907–1965). *Cowboys and Steers*. Watercolor, 14″ x 26″. Lent by the Society of Illustrators.

Harold Von Schmidt (b. 1893). *Departure of the Stage*.
The Saturday Evening Post, 1950. Oil, 29½″ x 39½″. Lent by Frank Willbright.

Jon Whitcomb (b. 1906). *A Girl to Marry. Redbook, December 1958*. Watercolor, 20″ x 15″. Lent by Walt Reed.

John Gannam (1907–1965). *Comic Pages*. Watercolor, 20″ x 14½″. Lent by Walt Reed.

Walter DuBois Richards (b.1907). *Tipped off by a bearded informer, Iranian troops move in to raid building containing printing plant for Communist propaganda. Life, November 21, 1955.*
Litho pencil on gesso, 10⅜" x 27¾". Lent by the artist.

John Groth (b.1908). *The Battle of the Bulge.*
Collier's Magazine, December 23, 1955. Pen and ink wash, 21" x 29". Lent by the artist.

Mitchell Jamieson (b. 1915). *Dawn of D-Day.*
Oil, 39½" x 29½". Lent by the United States Navy.

Gustav Rehberger (b. 1910). *Crucifixion. Everywoman's Magazine, April 1957.*
Casein, 48″ x 36″. Lent by Adele Osonitsch Lucrezia.

Rudolph F. Zallinger (b. 1919). *The Muralist. Life, December 12, 1955.*
Egg tempera, 17″ x 14½″. Lent by the artist.

Ray Prohaska (b. 1901).
Life-Time-Fortune, 1958. Fisherman.
Oil, 50″ x 30″. Lent by Leonard Starr.

275

Jon Whitcomb (b. 1906). *Dancing Couple.*
Redbook, October 1956. Watercolor, 16¾″ x 12¼″. Lent by Walt Reed.

John LaGatta (1894–1977). *Girl with Palette.*
Oil, 36″ x 28″. Lent by Mr. and Mrs. Benjamin Eisenstat.

Alex Ross (b. 1908). *Blandings Builds his Dream House.*
Cosmopolitan, 1950. Gouache, 17″ x 24½″. Lent by the artist.

Alex Ross (b. 1908). *The Hours Apart.*
McCall's Magazine, May 1951. Gouache, 18″ x 17″. Lent by the artist.

Tom Lovell (b. 1909). *Laying the Atlantic Cable. True Magazine, 1956. Oil, 29″ x 30″. Lent by the artist.*

Harry O. Diamond (b. 1913). *Title unknown. Westways, 1950.*
Ink wash, 13″ x 10″. Lent by the artist.

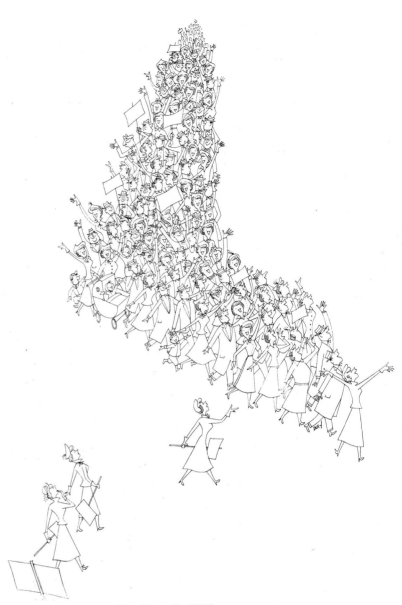

Roy Doty (b. 1922). *Protest Marchers.*
Pen and ink, 16″ x 10½″. Lent by Peggy and Harold Samuels.

Gordon Grant (1875–1962). *The Westing Sun.*
Oil, 23¼″ x 29″. Lent by Dr. L. R. Cowan.

Austin Briggs (1909–1973). *Posing the Model.*
Oil, 14″ x 11¾″. Lent by the New Britain Museum of American Art.

Al Parker (b. 1906). *Dad and Daughter.*
American Weekly, 1957. Gouache, 14″ x 12⅜″. Lent by the artist.

Frederick Trench Chapman (b. 1887). *Free and Easy. 1951.*
Pen and ink, 4½″ x 5″. Lent by Peggy and Harold Samuels.

Steven Kidd (b. 1911). *The Teamstress.*
New York Sunday News, 1951. Pen and ink, 19½″ x 20½″. Lent by the artist.

Morton Roberts (1927–1964). *Lenin Addressing Troops.*
Life, 1959. Oil, 30″ x 26″. Lent by Walt Reed.

Gerald McConnell (b. 1931). *Base Camp for Albert Eggler and the Swiss Assault on Mount Everest, 1956*. Acrylic, 20″ x 16″. Lent by the Society of Illustrators.

Stanley W. Galli (b. 1912). *Mink.*
The Saturday Evening Post, February 1955. Gouache, 12½″ x 15½″. Lent by the artist.

Norman Rockwell (b. 1894). *Weighing In. The Saturday Evening Post, June 28, 1958.* Oil, 33″ x 31″. Lent by the New Britain Museum of American Art.

Edward Arthur Wilson (1886–1970). *Naval Battle*. Tempera, 17" x 25". Lent by the Society of Illustrators.

Fred Zimmer (b. 1923). *Stuyvesant Town, New York.*
Ford Times, November 1956. Tempera, 12" x 16".
Lent by the Ford Motor Company.

Paul Sample (1896–1974). *Ford Times, July 1953*.
Watercolor, 10½" x 15½". Lent by the Ford Motor Company.

1960's

Jon Whitcomb (b. 1906). *Woman's Head.*
Good Housekeeping. Watercolor and acrylic, 12″ x 9″. Lent by the artist.

Paul Davis (b. 1938). *Time, Inc.*
Promotion Booklet, c. 1968. Lent by the artist.

Originally appeared in PLAYBOY Magazine, © 1963, by Playboy.

Robert Weaver (b. 1924). *On Her Majesty's Secret Service.*
PLAYBOY Magazine, April 1963. Tempera, 19″ x 20″. Lent by Playboy Enterprises.

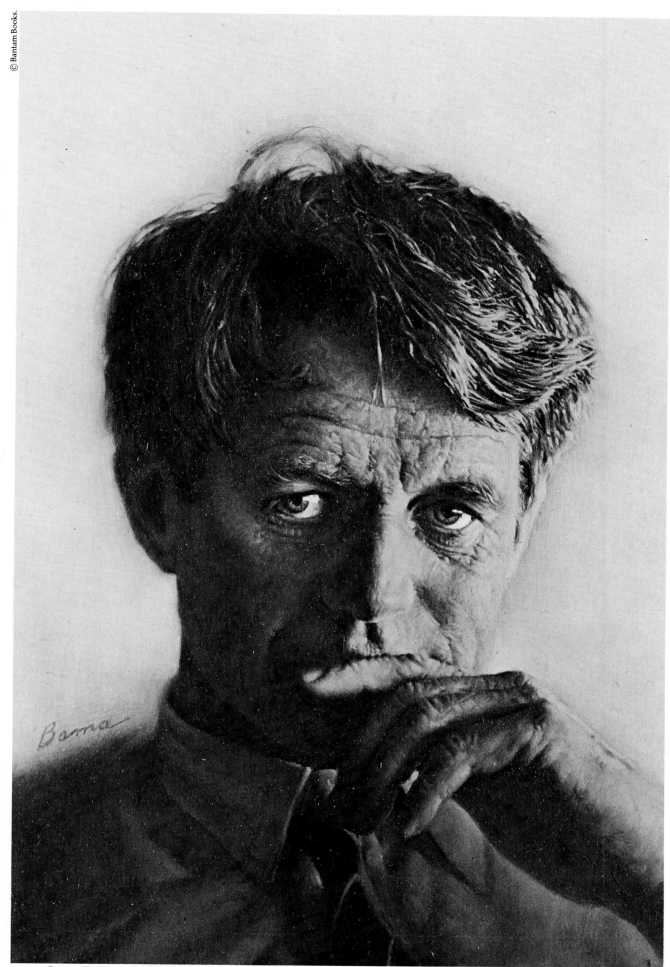

James E. Bama (b. 1926). *Robert Kennedy. Robert Kennedy: A Memoir by Jack Newfield, Bantam Books, April 1968*. Oil, 14″ x 8¼″.
Lent by Bantam Books.

Edward Gorey (b. 1929). *Les Roses Zinzolines L'Arrivée.* Watercolor and pen and ink, 5¼" x 7½". Lent by the Graham Gallery.

Edward Gorey (b. 1929). *The Abduction of Elsie Thrudd on August the 6th, 1907.*
Pen and ink, 5½" x 3½". Lent by the Graham Gallery.

Gerry Gersten (b. 1927). *Lindsay.*
Self-promotion piece, 1968. Pencil, 19" x 19". Lent by the artist.

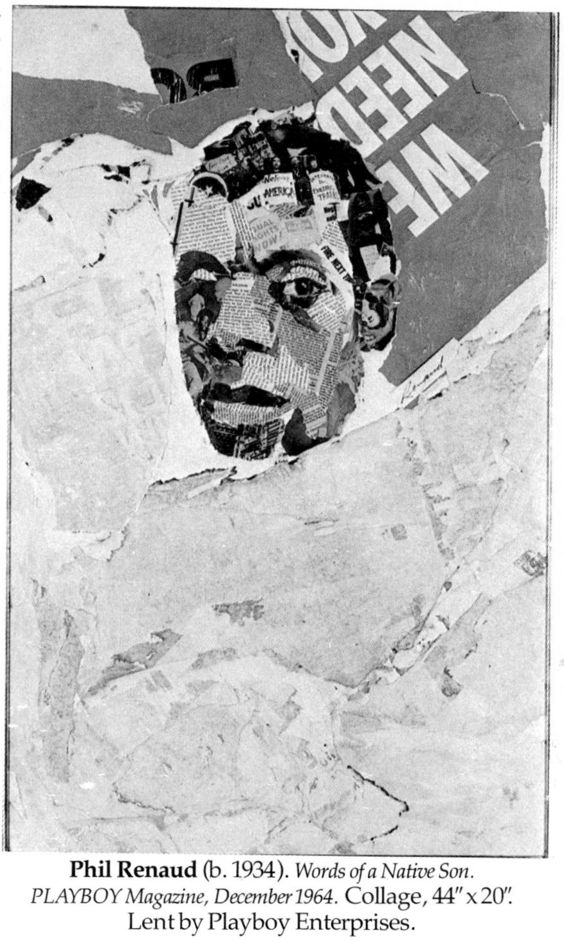

Originally appeared in PLAYBOY Magazine, © 1964, by Playboy.

Phil Renaud (b. 1934). *Words of a Native Son.*
PLAYBOY Magazine, December 1964. Collage, 44" x 20".
Lent by Playboy Enterprises.

Antonio Frasconi (b. 1919). *The Face of Edgar Allen Poe.*
Woodcut, 6" x $3\frac{1}{2}$". Lent by Bob Crozier.

Al Parker (b. 1906). *The Trellis.*
McCall's Magazine, 1966. Gouache, 21¼″ x 20¾″. Lent by the artist.

Al Parker (b. 1906). *Siamese Cats on Wicker Chair.*
Lithopinion. Crayon, 21½″ x 17″. Lent by the artist.

Robert Patterson (b. 1898). *Couple Poolside.*
Watercolor, 21″ x 22½″. Lent by Walt Reed.

James Lewicki (b. 1917). *The Mission of Johnny Appleseed.*
Life, April 11, 1960. Egg oil, 22½″ x 25″. Lent by the artist.

288

Al Parker (b. 1906).
What do you say when a very nice man looks you straight in the eye, smiles, and offers you one million dollars for your very own, just to become, among other good things, his wife?
A Matter of Convenience by Nancy Ferard, McCall's Magazine, June 1961. Oil, 17¾" x 27". Lent by the artist.

Marvin Friedman (b. 1930). *An Irish Hunt.*
Boys' Life, 1969. Mixed media, 29½" x 43". Lent by the artist.

Lucille Corcos (1908–1973).
Father, Dear Father, Come Home with me Now.
Songs of the Gilded Age, 1961. Gouache, 12″ x 8¾″.
Lent by David C. Levy.

Art Seiden (b. 1923). *Beowulf and the Dragon.*
Stories of Gods and Heroes, Grosset and Dunlap, 1960. Tempera, 12¾″ x 15″.
Lent by the artist.

Jack Unruh (b. 1935). *It's a Great Country, But You Can't Live in it for Nothing.*
Calendar series for The Houston Post, 1969. Acrylic, 11″ x 20½″. Lent by the artist.

Ezra Jack Keats (b. 1916). *One winter morning Peter woke up and looked out the window.*
The Snowy Day by Ezra Jack Keats, Viking Press, 1962. Paper cutout, 8″ x 18″.
Lent by the artist.

James Lewicki (b. 1917). *The Blacksmith of Brandywine.*
Life, January 25, 1960. Egg oil, 28½″ x 23″. Lent by the artist.

Jim Jonson (b. 1928). *Broad Jumper.*
Sports Illustrated, May 23, 1966. Tempera, 11″ x 8″. Lent by Sports Illustrated.

Stanley W. Galli (b. 1912). *Doctor Blanket's First Command.*
The Saturday Evening Post, July 1961. Watercolor and pencil, 15″ x 23½″. Lent by the artist.

Joe DeMers (b. 1910). *Two Girls with Still Life. The Saturday Evening Post, 1963.* Oil, 26¼" x 28". Lent by the New Britain Museum of American Art.

Bernard D'Andrea (b. 1923). *The Old Dog. 1969.* Oil and pencil and collage, 36″ x 36″. Lent by Bob Crozier.

Thomas Sgouros (b. 1927). *When You Tie the Can to a Union Man.*
Allandale Annual Report, 1965. Gouache, 30" x 22". Lent by the artist.

Alvin J. Pimsler (b. 1918). *Title unknown.*
Esquire, 1960. Watercolor and pencil, 21" x 16¼". Lent by the artist.

Chas B. Slackman (b. 1934). *The Preposterous Pathfinder.*
American Heritage, December 1967. Pen and ink,
9" x 6½". Lent by American Heritage Publishing Company.

Sanford Kossin (b. 1926). *Bay of Pigs. Life, May 10, 1963.* Ink on gesso, 16" x 30". Lent by the Society of Illustrators.

Jean Leon Huens (b. 1921). *Robin Hood. Reader's Digest Best Loved Books, 1966.*
Watercolor, 8½" x 6¼". Lent by Reader's Digest.

Jerome Snyder (1916–1976). *Title unknown The Lamp, Winter 1966.* Acrylic, 18″ x 14″. Lent by Exxon Corporation.

Thomas B. Allen (b. 1928). *A Snook Hunt Along the Shores of the Spanish Main.*
Sports Illustrated, January 3, 1966. Oil, 28¼" x 21¼". Lent by Sports Illustrated.

Vin Giuliani (1930-1976) and **Roger Hane** (1943–1975). *Computer Head.*
The Lamp, Summer 1969. Wood, metal, canvas construction, 25" x 19".
Lent by Exxon Corporation.

Robert Andrew Parker (b. 1927).
*A spring downpour casts a mellow patina over the bright colors of umbrellas that shelter a cluster
of dampened spectators.*
Sports Illustrated, April 2, 1962. Watercolor, 17¼" x 24". Lent by Sports Illustrated.

Frank Bozzo (b. 1937). *Robin Hood.*
Caedmon Record Cover, 1963. Acrylic, 13½″ x 13¼″.
Lent by the artist.

© From the cover of the Caedmon Record, The Ballad of Robin Hood (TC 1177).

Irving Nurick (1894–1963). *Title unknown.*
The Saturday Evening Post. Pen and ink, 8½″ x 13″.
Lent by Mrs. Dorothy Nurick.

William H. Whittingham (b. 1932).
One Day in the Life of Ivan Denisovich.
The Saturday Evening Post, February 1963. Ink wash, 23″ x 17″.
Lent by the artist.

Robert T. McCall (b. 1919). *Saigon, Vietnam. 1967.* Pen and ink and watercolor, 17½″ x 23″. Lent by the United States Air Force.

Courtesy of United States Air Force.

Ben Shahn (1898–1969). *Nazi and Victim. Poster with quote from Isaiah 5:20, 1966.* Egg tempera, 10″ x 15½″. Lent by Arnnold Roston.

Roy Schnackenberg (b. 1934). *Orient Express.*
PLAYBOY Magazine, February 1969. Oil, 24″ x 35″. Lent by Playboy Enterprises.

Frank Mullins (b. 1924). *Jenny is a Big Girl Now. The Lamp, Fall 1966.* Designer colors, 29″ x 19″. Lent by Exxon Corporation.

Wesley McKeown (1927–1975). *. . . And In The Beginning. 1967.*
Acrylic, 12″ x 20″. Lent by the Society of Illustrators.

Bob Peak (b. 1928). *My Fair Lady. 1966.*
Watercolor and tempera, 38½″ x 28″. Lent by Bill Gold Advertising.

Daniel Schwartz (b. 1929). *Village Girl.*
Fortune Magazine, January 1969. Oil, 26″ x 22″. Lent by Kathy Rommelmann.

Jerome Martin (b. 1926). *Car on the Mountain.*
PLAYBOY Magazine, August 1963. Watercolor, 18″ x 20″. Lent by Playboy Enterprises.

Joe Bowler (b. 1928). *Girl Looking in the Mirror. Legacy by Ethel E. Gordon, McCall's Magazine, April 1966.* Acrylic, 18" x 22". Lent by Murray Tinkelman.

Bill Charmatz (b. 1925). *Life on the Seine.*
The Lamp, Fall 1966. Acrylic, 26″ x 40″. Lent by Exxon Corporation.

Tom Lovell (b. 1909). *Wounded Man in Doorway.*
Cosmopolitan. Oil, 39″ x 26″. Lent by the Society of Illustrators.

Gustav Rehberger (b. 1910). *Telemachus in Search of Odysseus.*
Reader's Digest Best Loved Books, 1969. Casein, 17⅝″ x 27″. Lent by Reader's Digest.

Al Parker (b. 1906). *Woman at Window. Ladies' Home Journal.* Oil, 23¾″ x 23½″. Lent by the artist.

Clifford Condak (b. 1930). *Guerre-lieder. Columbia Record Cover.* Oil and pencil, 16½″ x 28½″. Lent by CBS Records.

Mitchell Hooks (b.1923). *A Separate Peace by*
John Knowles, Bantam Books, 1969. Gouache, 21″ x 17″. Lent by the Society of Illustrators.

Bernard Fuchs (b. 1932). *The March. Redbook, March 1967*. Pencil and acrylic, 24″ x 29″. Lent by the Society of Illustrators.

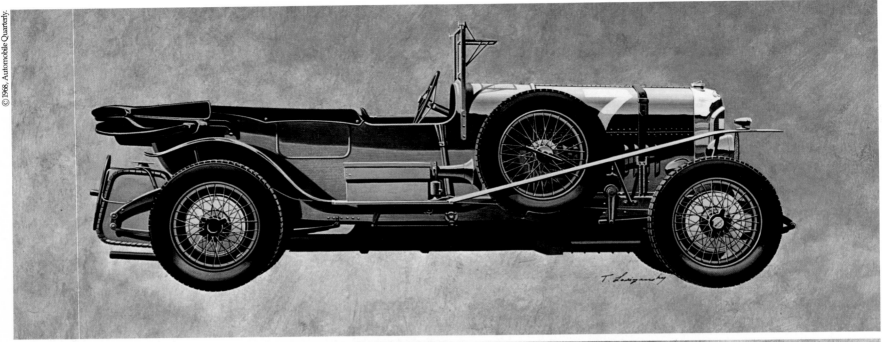

Theodore Lodigensky (b. 1930). *Title unknown. Automobile Quarterly, 1968.* Tempera, 36″ x 28″. Lent by the artist.

Fred Ludekens (b. 1900). *Treed Puma.*
True Magazine. Watercolor, 25″ x 19″. Lent by Walt Reed.

George Hughes (b. 1907). *Company Arrives Early.*
Oil, 25½″ x 23½″. Lent by the New Britain Museum of American Art.

Doris Rodewig (b. 1927). *Fruit Still Life.*
Unpublished, 1965. Oil, 30″ x 36″. Lent by the Society of Illustrators.

Marvin Friedman (b. 1930). *Woman in Red Interior. Unpublished for Ladies' Home Journal, 1964.* Mixed media, 24" x 26". Lent by the artist.

Daniel Schwartz (b. 1929). *When suffragists, calling themselves 'silent sentinels', picketed the White House in 1917, President Woodrow Wilson invited them inside to get out of the cold, but they refused. Woman's Suffrage by Leonard Slater, McCall's Magazine, September 1961.* Oil, 25″ x 35″. Lent by the artist.

Tom Lovell (b. 1909). *Rescue. True Magazine.* Oil, 24″ x 35″. Lent by the New Britain Museum of American Art.

Robert Shore (b.1924). *Benito Cereno. Benito Cereno by Herman Melville, Limited Editions Book Club, 1966.* Acrylic, 28½″ x 40″. Lent by the artist.

Saul Lambert (b. 1928). *Bernie the Faust. PLAYBOY Magazine, November 1963.* Print, 17½″ x 25″. Lent by Playboy Enterprises.

Austin Briggs (1909–1973). *Bocce Players. Illustrators '62, 1962.* Print, 14½″ x 38″. Lent by Lorna B. Harris.

André François (b. 1915). *The Most Beautiful Game of All.*
Sports Illustrated, February 20, 1961. Tempera, 17¼" x 12¼".
Lent by Sports Illustrated.

André François (b. 1915).
I particularly liked to keep my eyes on the goal. That way I caught the action like a wide-screen movie.
Sports Illustrated, February 20, 1961. Tempera, 12¼" x 20". Lent by Sports Illustrated.

Howard Rogers (b. 1932). *Imported Impact: The Canadian Sports Spectacular.*
Americana Magazine, November/December 1967. Acrylic, 14" x 17¾". Lent by Joseph T. Mendola.

315

Antonio Petruccelli (b. 1907). *Map of Australia.*
The Lamp, Spring 1966. Acrylic, 18″ x 14″. Lent by Exxon Corporation.

Peter Blake (b. 1932). *The London to Brighton Run.*
The Lamp, Winter 1968. Collage, 11½″ x 9½″. Lent by Exxon Corporation.

Blake Hampton (b. 1932). *Joe Levine Unchained.*
Esquire, January 1961. Gouache, 18″ x 12″. Lent by the artist.

1970's

Randall Enos (b. 1936). *The Lord will provide, my child.*
Print Magazine, July/August 1973. Linocut, 27" x 21". Lent by the artist.

Murray Tinkelman (b. 1933). *Indian God. At the Center of the World,*
Macmillan Publishing Co., 1973. Pen and ink, $13\frac{1}{2}$" x $10\frac{1}{2}$". Lent by the artist.

Randall Enos (b. 1936). *Black Magic in Scotland.*
Esquire, January 1975. Linocut and collage, 13" x 17". Lent by the artist.

Mort Künstler (b. 1931). *The First American Locomotives. Calendar series for American Cyanamid, 1972.* Oil, 30″ x 40″. Lent by the artist.

Cal Sacks (b. 1914). *Swindles.*
Signature Magazine, 1970. Acrylic on wood, 8½″ x 18″. Lent by the artist.

Dennis Pohl (b. 1941). *Vatican Library.* 1972. Collage, 19″ x 20″. Lent by Jane Lander Associates.

Howard Koslow (b. 1924). *Yosemite Falls.*
Unpublished, 1974. Acrylic, 36″ x 24″. Lent by the National Park Service.

Don Ivan Punchatz (b. 1936). *America the Raped by Gene Marine,*
Avon Books, 1970. Acrylic, 36″ x 24″. Lent by the artist.

Wilson McLean (b. 1937). *Rooster Fight.*
Sports Illustrated, 1973. Acrylic, 23¼″ x 33½″. Lent by the artist.

Wilson McLean (b. 1937). *Boy on Sofa.*
Acrylic, 27½″ x 27½″. Lent by the artist.

Jerry Pinkney (b. 1939). *Santeria.*
Bronk, Atheneum Books, 1975. Watercolor and pencil, 21¼″ x 27¼″. Lent by the artist.

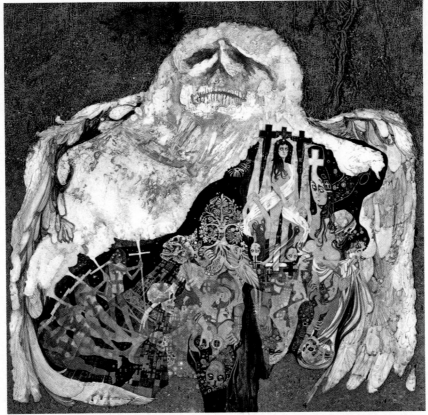

Ted CoConis (b. 1937). *Three Virgins of Death, Shostakovich Symphony #14.*
RCA Records, 1971. Mixed media, 29½″ x 30½″. Lent by the artist.

Bob Ziering (b. 1933). *Astaire. The Film Society of Lincoln Center, 1973*. Pen and ink, 18″ x 40″. Lent by the artist.

Daniel A. Long (b. 1946). *Old Man.*
Unpublished, 1973. Oil, 28″ x 21″. Lent by Jane Lander Associates.

John Martin (b. 1946). *Air Show. Boys' Life, 1972.* Oil, 15″ x 22″. Lent by Bob Crozier.

Gabriel Csakany (b. 1938). *Meeting.*
Chatelain Magazine, May 1971. Watercolor and pencil, 14″ x 19″. Lent by the artist.

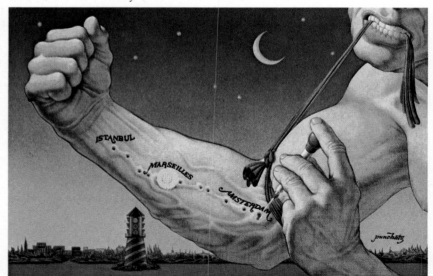

Don Ivan Punchatz (b. 1936). *How Heroin Missed its French Connection. OUI Magazine, 1975.* Acrylic, 11″ x 17″. Lent by the artist.

Howard Terpning (b. 1927). *Fishing the Père Marquette. Field and Stream Magazine, January 1973.* Mixed media, 11¾″ x 19¾″. Lent by CBS Publications.

Harvey Kidder (b. 1918). *Title unknown. 1971.*
Watercolor, 13¾″ x 21¾″. Lent by Joseph T. Mendola.

Robert M. Cunningham (b. 1924). *Lobster.*
Pastimes Magazine, December 1973. Acrylic, 13″ x 20½″. Lent by the artist.

Howard Terpning (b. 1927). *Over the Hill Together. Field and Stream Magazine, September 1972.* Mixed media, 14″ x 21¼″. Lent by CBS Publications.

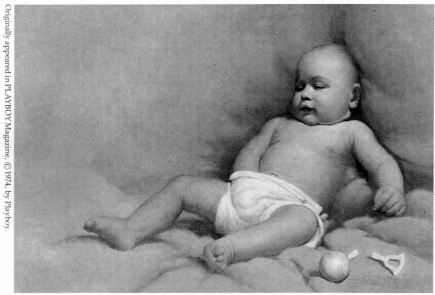

Jerry Podwil (b. 1938). *Getting Off.*
PLAYBOY Magazine, December 1974. Oil, 18″ x 25½″. Lent by Playboy Enterprises.

Charles Shields (b. 1944). *Clean Restrooms.*
Unpublished, 1975. Acrylic, 15¼″ x 22″. Lent by Daniele Deverin.

Walter Hortens (b. 1924). *Bridge Construction.*
Unpublished. Tempera, 19″ x 15″. Lent by the artist.

David A. Macaulay (b. 1946). *Untitled.*
Cathedral: The Story of its Construction, Houghton Mifflin Company, September 1973.
Pen and ink, 16″ x 12″. Lent by the artist.

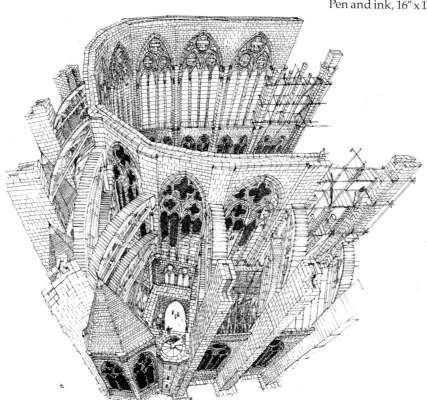

David A. Macaulay (b. 1946). *Untitled.*
Cathedral: The Story of its Construction, Houghton Mifflin Company, September 1973.
Pen and ink, 16″ x 16″. Lent by the artist.

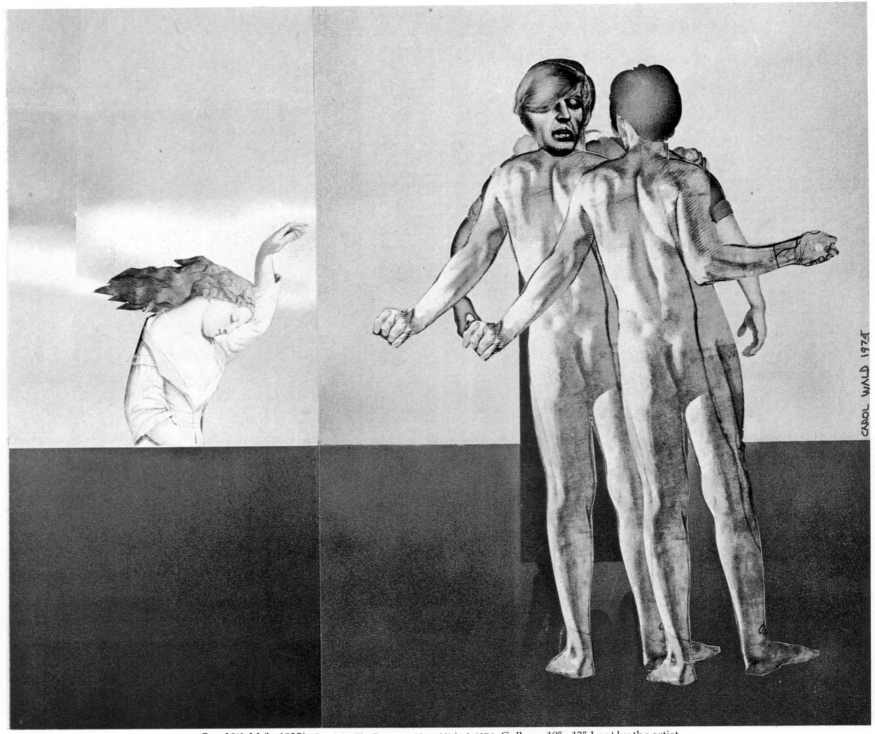

Carol Wald (b. 1935). *Gemini—The Dreamer. Unpublished, 1974.* Collage, 10″ x 13″. Lent by the artist.

Bob Pepper (b. 1938).
Puccini's Greatest Hits. RCA Records, May 1971.
Gouache, 14″ x 13″. Lent by the artist.

Ed Paschke (b. 1939).
The Great Girl Nut Contest.
PLAYBOY Magazine, December 1968.
Acrylic, 32″ x 34″.
Lent by Playboy Enterprises.
Originally appeared in PLAYBOY Magazine,

Harvey Dinnerstein (b. 1928). *Parade. Esquire, September 1972*. Oil, 74″ x 153″. Lent by the artist.

David K. Stone (b. 1922).
Man of La Mancha.
Record Cover for Pickwick Ltd., 1973. Oil,
48″ x 36″. Lent by the artist.

Doug Johnson (b. 1940).
The World of Ike and Tina Turner.
Record Cover for United Artists Records, 1973.
Gouache, 42″ x 20⅛″. Lent by the artist.

329

Lane Hamilton Yerkes (b. 1945). *Artist with Tophat. 1974.*
Pen and ink, 14″ x 11″. Lent by the artist.

Jim Spanfeller (b. 1930). *Self-portrait.*
Self-promotion piece, Winter 1974. Pen and ink, 23½″ x 19½″. Lent by the artist.

Gerry Gersten (b. 1927). *New York—1830.*
T.V. Commercial for New York Telephone Co., July 1972. Pencil, 32″ x 42″. Lent by the artist.

Bob Pepper (b. 1938). *Cranston: Today's Fabrics in the Tradition of Great Printmakers.*
Women's Wear Daily, November 1974. Gouache and dyes, 22″ x 13″. Lent by Essie Pinsker Associates.

Kim Whitesides (b. 1941). *My Affair with Fred Astaire.*
Rolling Stone, December 6, 1973. Watercolor and pencil and pastel, 17½″ x 12⅜″.
Lent by the artist.

Jim Sharpe (b. 1936). *Premier Chou En-Lai.*
Time, February 3, 1975. Acrylic and transparent inks, 28″ x 20″.
Lent by Time.

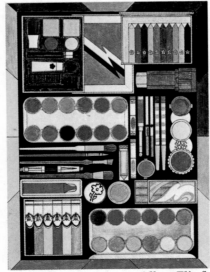

Albert Elia (b. 1941). *Untitled.*
Mademoiselle, February 1973. Pastel, 12″ x 17″. Lent by the artist.

Gerry Gersten (b. 1927). *Noah's Leopards.*
Art Directors Club of New York, 1974. Pen and ink and dyes, 20″ x 16″. Lent by the artist.

Jack Davis (b. 1924). *G.O.P. Elephant During Watergate.*
Unpublished for Time, 1974. Watercolor and pencil, 29½″ x 22″. Lent by the artist.

Shannon Stirnweiss (b. 1931). *Therapy for a Hunter.*
Field and Stream Magazine, February 1976. Oil, 16½″ x 24½″. Lent by CBS Publications.

Franz Altschuler (b. 1923). *Dashing Fellow.* PLAYBOY *Magazine,*
December 1971. Oil wash, 34″ x 52″. Lent by Playboy Enterprises.

Charles White III (b. 1940). *Ladies and Gentlemen—The Rolling Stones. April 1974.* Watercolor, 18″ x 60″. Lent by the artist.

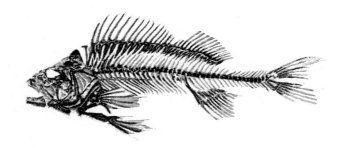

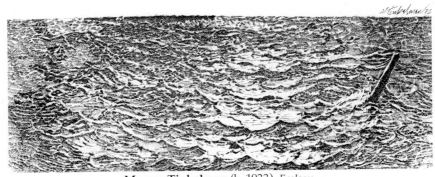

Murray Tinkelman (b. 1933). *Ecology.*
The New York Times, 1972. Pen and ink, $17\frac{3}{4}$″ x $22\frac{1}{2}$″. Lent by the artist.

Steven R. Kidd (b.1911). *Ichabod Crane pursued by Brom Bones, Tarrytown Bicentennial—1972, 1972.*
Print, 10½″ x 13¾″. Lent by the artist.

Stanley W. Galli (b. 1912). *Elk in Snowstorm.*
Echelon Publishing Brochure. December 1972. Acrylic, 28″ x 36″. Lent by the artist.

Roger Kastel (b. 1931). *Jaws.*
Jaws by Peter Benchley, Bantam Books, January 1975. Oil, 39″ x 30″. Lent by Bantam Books.

Charles Santore (b. 1935). *Alice Falling Down the Rabbit Hole. Pfizer Pharmaceuticals Poster, October 1974.* Acrylic, 34″ x 27″. Lent by Pfizer Pharmaceuticals.

Mort Künstler (b. 1931). *Stroud Farm.* 1976. Oil, 25" x 32½". Lent by the artist.

Jack Endewelt (b. 1935). *Father Ulivo and His Friends.*
Reader's Digest Children's Book, October 1974. Oil, 6¼" x 9¾". Lent by the artist.

David Kilmer (b. 1950). *Mercedes.* 1976.
Gouache, 13½" x 20½". Lent by the artist.

Allan Mardon (b. 1931). *The Shah of Iran.*
Time, November 1974. Watercolor, 16" x 12". Lent by the artist.

Sandy Huffaker (b. 1943). *Howard Cosell.*
Self-promotion piece, 1975. Pencil, 12" x 10". Lent by the artist.

Robert S. Lowery (b. 1950). *Fight Night—Madison Square Garden.*
Acrylic, 32" x 22". Lent by the artist.

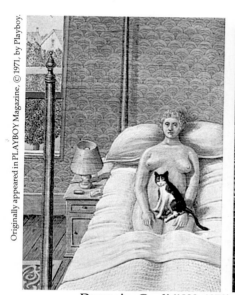   

Domenico Gnoli (1932–1970). *Spring, Summer, Autumn, Winter. PLAYBOY Magazine, January 1971.* Casein, 11″ x 30″. Lent by Playboy Enterprises.

Murray Tinkelman (b. 1933). *Fat Man on Rhino.*
Warlock Press, 1971. Pen and ink, 30″ x 23″ . Lent by the artist.

Robert T. Handville (b. 1924). *Muhammad Ali vs. Joe Frazier. Sports Illustrated, March 1, 1971.* Watercolor, 22″ x 28″. Lent by the artist.

Roy Carruthers (b. 1938). *All-Around Sportsman.*
WLS-TV Sports, January 1975. Acrylic, 31″ x 23¾″. Lent by Ong and Associates.

Edward Sorel (b. 1929). *First in War. First in Peace, First in the Hearts of his Country Club.*
The Atlantic Monthly, 1972. Watercolor and pencil, 17″ x 14″. Lent by the artist.

Bruce E. Barkley (b. 1950). *Ye Inside Story of Ye Boston Tea Party.*
Limited Edition Prints, June 1973. Mixed media, 24″ x 30″. Lent by the artist.

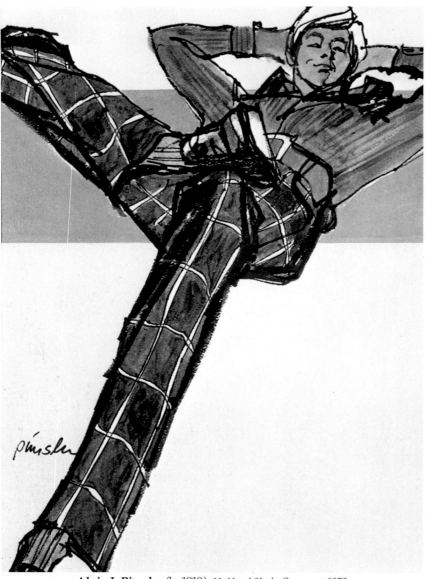

Alvin J. Pimsler (b. 1918). *Hubbard Slacks Company. 1972.*
Watercolor and magic marker, 12½" x 9". Lent by the artist.

Ken Riley (b. 1919). *Custer's Fall.*
Bantam Books, 1972. Oil, 23" x 14½". Lent by Bantam Books.

Nita Engle (b. 1925). *The Book of Christmas. 1974.*
Watercolor, 21½" x 29¼". Lent by the Reader's Digest.

Robert Van Nutt (b. 1947). *Lyric.*
American Heritage, 1974. Pencil, 11″ x 8½″.
Lent by the American Heritage Publishing Company.

Donald Moss (b. 1920). *The 15th at Oakmont.*
Sports Illustrated, June 11, 1973. Oil, 31″ x 25″. Lent by the artist.

Anthony Chen (b. 1929). *Crows and Great Horned Owl. About Owls,*
Scholastic Press, Fall 1975. Watercolor, 12½″ x 19″. Lent by the artist.

Gilbert Stone (b. 1940). *Jeremiah Johnson.*
Movie Poster, 1975. Acrylic, 48″ x 36″. Lent by the artist.

Robert E. McGinnis (b. 1926). *Run.*
Hearst Publications, 1975. Tempera, 16″ x 10″. Lent by the artist.

George S. Gaadt (b. 1941). *Last Stand at Fort Ligonier.*
Unpublished, 1975. Acrylic, 14½″ x 18″. Lent by the artist.

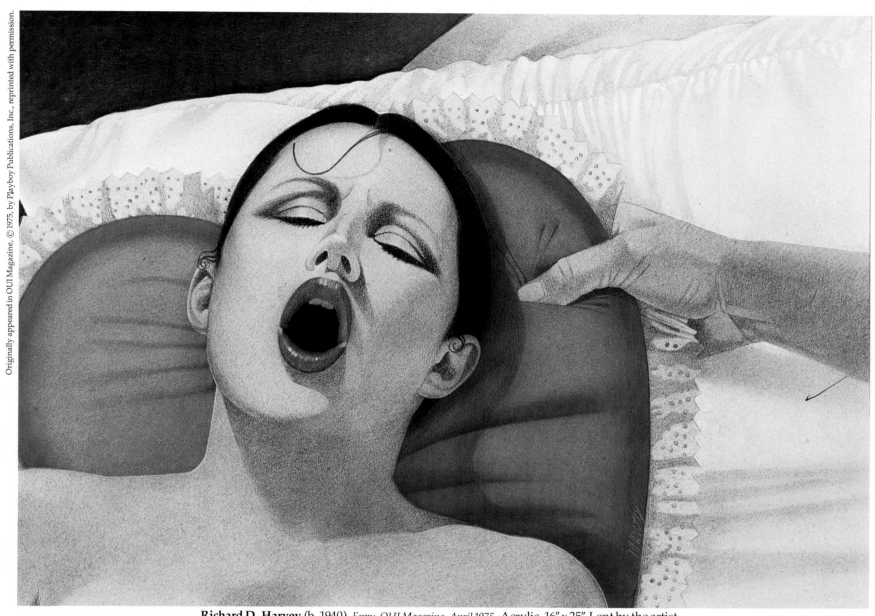

Richard D. Harvey (b. 1940). *Envy. OUI Magazine, April 1975.* Acrylic, 16″ x 25″. Lent by the artist.

Dennis Luzak (b. 1939). *The Turkey Vulture.*
Penthouse Magazine, November 1974.
Mixed media, 24″ x 19″. Lent by the artist.

Merrill Cason (b. 1929). *Zero and Zero, 1975.*
Acrylic and pastel, 15″ x 12″. Lent by the artist.

Jeffrey Schrier (b. 1943). *The Eternal Persistence of Laocoon the Turtle. 1975.*
Mixed media, 60″ x 40″. Lent by the artist.

Ivan Chermayeff (b. 1932). *War and Peace. 1974.*
Poster, 46½″ x 30¼″. Lent by the artist.

Burton Philip Silverman (b. 1928). *Patty Hearst.*
Newsweek, March 1, 1976. Watercolor, 10¼″ x 8″. Lent by the artist.

Mejo Okon (b. 1953). *Self-portrait, 1976.*
Fabric appliqué, 71″ x 48″. Lent by the artist.

Emanuel Schongut (b. 1936). *A Schoolyard Long Ago.*
Sesame Street, October 1974. Watercolor, 9⅜″ x 15½″. Lent by the artist.

Robert Giusti (b. 1937). *In a Bluebird's Eye. Holt, Rinehart & Winston, 1975.* Acrylic on canvas, 20″ x 14″. Lent by the artist.

Elizabeth Koda-Callan (b. 1944). *Framing Whistler's Mother. Self-promotion piece, May 1975.* Acrylic, 16¼" x 27½". Lent by the artist.

Charles Santore (b. 1935). *Tom Paine Writing 'Common Sense.'*
Unpublished. Acrylic, 16" x 16". Lent by the artist.

R. Crumb (b. 1945). *Cheap Thrills.*
Columbia Record Cover. Print, 12" x 12". Lent by CBS Records.

John C. Berkey (b. 1932). *Orr Station.*
Mixed a, 30" x 20". Lent by the artist.

John M. Thompson (b. 1940). *Larry Lampman.*
Self-promotional piece, 1976. Acrylic polymer, 36" x 36". Lent by the artist.

David Schleinkofer (b. 1951). *John Lenver.*
Stereo Review, September 1975. Gouache, $13\frac{1}{2}$" x $13\frac{1}{2}$".
Lent by Stereo Review.

350

Mark English (b. 1933). *Charles Dickens.*
Calendar Series for Borden & Co., 1971. Tempera, 24½″ x 25½″.
Lent by the New Britain Museum of American Art.

Robert Geissmann (1909–1976). *Title unknown.*
Reader's Digest. 1975. Acrylic, 14¾″ x 13″. Lent by the Reader's Digest.

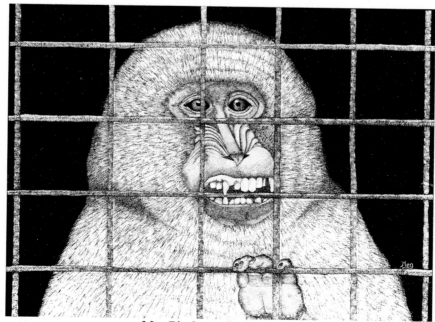

Meg Birnbaum (b. 1952). *Caged. 1976.*
Pen and ink, 20″ x 24″. Lent by the artist.

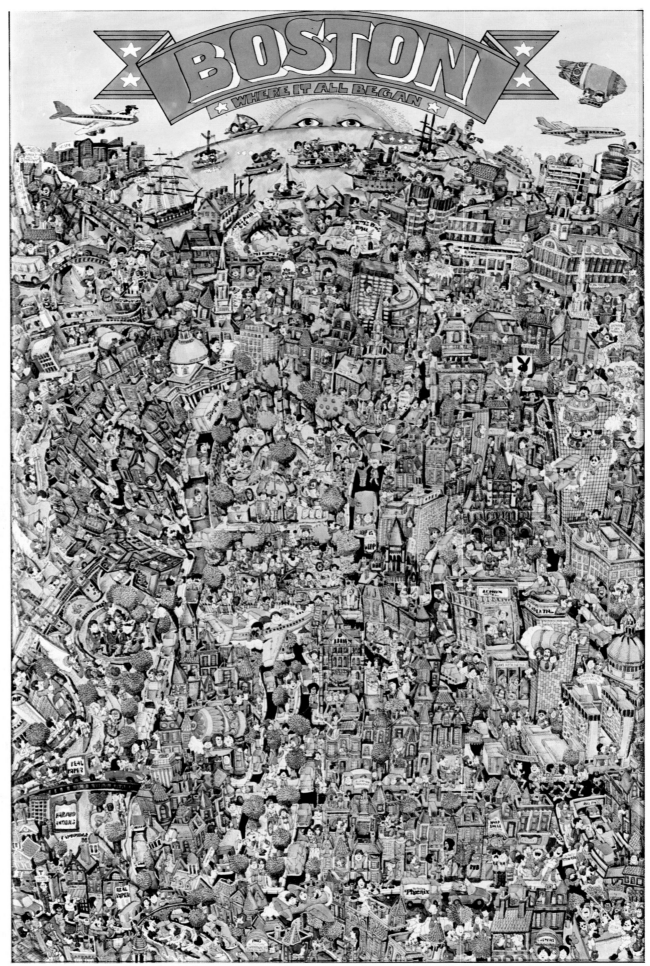

Joseph Veno (b. 1939). *Boston. July 1975.* Watercolor and pen and ink, 36″ x 24″. Lent by the artist.

Fred Otnes (b. 1926). *George Washington.* 1975.
Collage, 24″ x 20″. Lent by the Newspaper Advertising Bureau, Inc.

Mark English (b. 1933). *George Rogers Clarke.*
National Park Service, 1975. Lent by the artist.

Gordon Laite (b. 1925). *The General Store. Greeting Card.*
Watercolor, 12¼″ x 15″. Lent by Kirchoff/Wohlberg.

Ruth Brunner-Stroesser (b. 1944). *Sunday.*
Oil, 19¼″ x 21½″. Lent by the artist.

Gene Calogero (b. 1932). *Leaning Tower of Pizza.*
Self-promotion piece, December 1975. Pen and ink, 19″ x 15¼″. Lent by the artist.

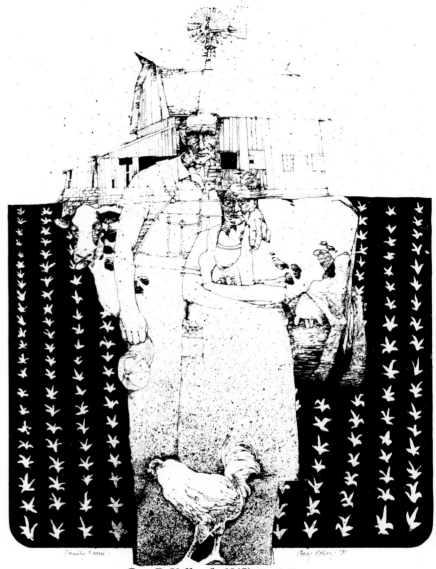

Gary R. Kelley (b. 1945). *Family Farm.*
Calendar Series for Northwestern Bell, December 1975.
Watercolor and pen and ink, 25″ x 20″. Lent by the artist.

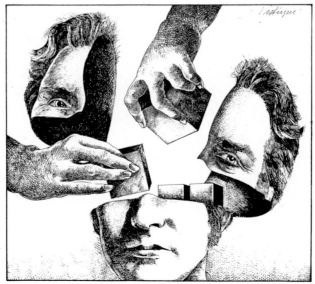

Gary Viskupic (b. 1944). *Brainwashing.*
Newsday, October 3, 1975. Pen and ink, 7¼″ x 8″. Lent by the artist.

Leo and Diane Dillon (both born 1933). *Whirlwind is a Ghost Dancing, E. P. Dutton Co., Inc., 1974.* Pastel and Acrylic, 15½″ x 8″. Lent by the artists.

Dennis Ziemienski (b. 1947). *Anteater.*
San Francisco Zoo Poster, 1976.
Watercolor and pen and ink, 8″ x 8″. Lent by the artist.

Harry Bennett (b. 1925). *Antigone and Sister.*
Limited Editions Club, Fall 1975. Dyes, 16″ x 13″. Lent by the artist.

355

Eraldo Carugati (b. 1921). *How Europe Stole Our Jazz. OUI Magazine, July 1975.* Gouache, 14″ x 22″. Lent by Playboy Enterprises.

Robert T. McCall (b. 1919). *Arizona Solar Farms—1990.*
Arizona Highways, August 1975. Acrylic, 29¾″ x 43½″. Lent by the artist.

Robert Benney (b. 1904). *Vietnam Episode, I Corps Area.* Oil, 30″ x 44″. Lent by the United States Marine Corps Museum.

Mort Rosenfeld (b. 1928). *Honor Coho.*
Field and Stream Magazine, May 1969. Acrylic and casein, 15½″ x 18″.
Lent by CBS Publications.

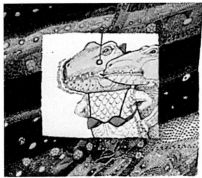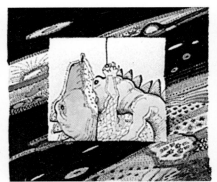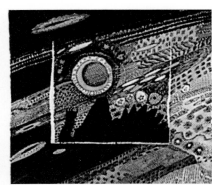

Jack Unruh (b. 1935). *How Dinosaurs Did It. Citadel Magazine, 1976.* Watercolor and pen and ink, 8″ x 22½″. Lent by the artist.

Roger Huyssen (b. 1946). *Furnace.*
Money Magazine, September 1975. Watercolor, 14¾″ x 16¾″. Lent by the artist.

Paul Giovanopoulos (b. 1939). *Magritte.*
Oil, 24″ x 30″. Lent by the artist.

Stan Watts (b. 1952). *Mother's Day—1956.*
Acrylic, 32½″ x 48″. Lent by the artist.

Leonard Baskin (b. 1922). *The Wild Owl.*
Catalogue for Towson State College Art Gallery, 1975. Pen and ink, 30½" x 22".
Lent by Kennedy Galleries, Inc.

Leonard Baskin (b. 1922). *Big Razor—Blackfeet Sioux.*
Catalogue for Towson State College Art Gallery, 1973. Pen and ink, 30¼" x 23¾".
Lent by Kennedy Galleries, Inc.

Eugene Karlin (b. 1918). *Colette: The Other Woman.*
December 1975. Pen and ink, 16" x 12".
Lent by the artist.

Leonard Everett Fisher (b. 1924). *Hardship at Valley Forge.*
Poster for Franklin Watts, Inc., 1975. Scratchboard, 36" x 24".
Lent by Franklin Watts, Inc.

Robert Andrew Parker (b. 1927). *The Blue Angel.*
The Lamp, Fall 1976. Watercolor and pen and ink, 8″ x 6″.
Lent by the Exxon Corporation.

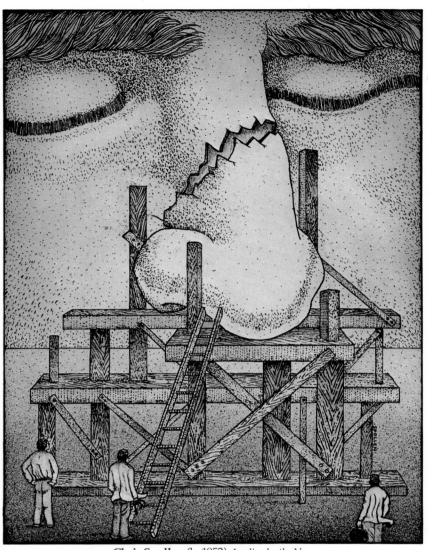

Chris Spollen (b. 1952). *Leading by the Nose.*
Emergency Medicine, November 1975. Hand-tinted etching, 12¼″ x 9½″.
Lent by the artist.

Anthony Chen (b. 1929). *Eagle and Other Birds of Prey.*
What is a Bird? Golden Books, Spring 1975. Watercolor, 12¼″ x 20½″. Lent by the artist.

Bill Utterback (b. 1931). *Ciné Duck.*
PLAYBOY Magazine, October 1970.
Tempera, 20¾″ x 16¼″.
Lent by Playboy Enterprises.

Gene Szafran (b. 1941). *Hand.*
Penthouse Magazine, December 1975. Plaster relief, 18″ x 18″. Lent by Artists Associates.

Jean Carlson (b. 1952). *Teddy. 1975.*
Fabric construction, 23″ x 23″. Lent by the artist.

Walter Einsel (b. 1926). *Reaching New Heights of Performance.*
Electronics Magazine, July 10, 1975. Wood and metal and fabric, 14¾″ x 14½″ x 5¾″.
Lent by the McGraw-Hill Publishing Company.

Philip Garris (b. 1951). *Fiddler, Blues for Allah.*
United Artists Record Cover, 1975. Acrylic, 19″ x 19″. Lent by the artist.

361

Miriam Wosk (b. 1947). *A Picture of Writing.*
Viva Magazine, August 1974. Acrylic, 13¾″ x 10¾″. Lent by the artist.

Guy Billout (b. 1941). *Untitled. Images,*
A Houghton Mifflin Reader for the Fifth Grade, 1971. Watercolor, 6⅞″ x 5½″.
Lent by Houghton Mifflin Company.

Di Fiori. *Growing up in Newport.*
American Heritage Magazine, August 1971. Pen and ink, 11¼″ x 8⅝″.
Lent by the American Heritage Publishing Company.

Stefan Martin (b. 1936). *Kenyon Review.*
Pen and ink, 9″ x 6¼″. Lent by Kirchoff/Wohlberg, Inc

Robert Andrew Parker (b. 1927). *War and Peace. Columbia Record Cover.* Watercolor, 14½" x 26". Lent by CBS Records.

Mark McMahon (b. 1950). *International Live Stock Show, Chicago Amphitheater, 1975.* Watercolor and pen and ink, 22" x 30". Lent by Handelan Pedersen, Inc.

Barron Storey (b. 1940). *The Miners. Swank, February 1975.* Pen and ink and acrylic, 18¾″ x 27¾″. Lent by Jane Lander Associates.

Kinuko Craft (b. 1940). *. . . and a Picture Tube Shall Lead Them.*
PLAYBOY Magazine, June 1976. Watercolor, 12½″ x 19″. Lent by Playboy Enterprises.

Anthony Chen (b. 1929). *Animals Reading.*
Xerox Corporation Poster, 1975. Watercolor, 11¼″ x 17″. Lent by the artist.

Jim Deigan (b. 1934). *Machine Design, June 1974.*
Acrylic, 17¼″ x 13″. Lent by the artist.

Stanley Meltzoff (b. 1917). *In the company of stingrays and a sand shark . . .*
Sports Illustrated, September 4, 1967. Oil, 31″ x 23″. Lent by the Garcia Corporation.

Leo and Diane Dillon (both born 1933). *Death Bird*
arper and Rowe Co., 1975. Acrylic 17½″ x 26½″. Lent by the artist.

Leo and Diane Dillon (both born 1933). *Kipling's Red Dog.*
Caedmon Record Cover, 1975. Watercolor and Acrylic, 12″ x 12″. Lent by the artists.

Robert T. Handville (b.1924). *Redfields. 1970.*
Watercolor, 25½″ x 25½″. Lent by the artist.

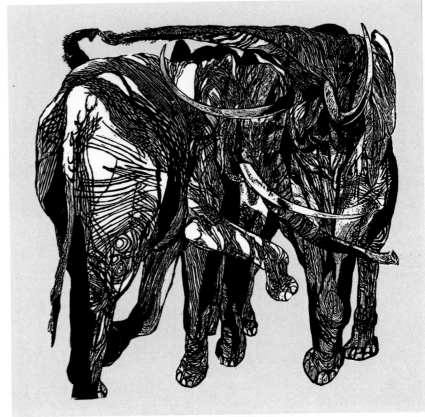

Jacob Landau (b. 1917). *Elephants.*
TV Guide, 1961. Signed print, 17½″ x 16½″. Lent by R. V. Hansmann.

Warren Linn (b. 1946). *The Numbers Aren't Everything.*
The New York Times, October 2, 1975. Scratchboard, 7¼″ x 9¾″. Lent by the artist.

Robert S. Lowery (b. 1950). *Carnegie Hall. 1974.*
Pen and ink, 20½" x 16½". Lent by the artist.

Daniel Maffia (b. 1937).
A Charming Field for an Encounter.
National Park Service Publication, 1976. Poster, 40½" x 26½".
Lent by the National Park Service.

Frederick Schneider (b. 1946). *His House.*
Unpublished, 1975. Pen and ink, 14" x 10".
Lent by the artist.

Sam Fink (b.1916).
Madison Avenue Magazine, October 1975. Watercolor, 15¾" x 22¼".
Lent by Pioneer-Moss, Inc.

Doug Johnson (b. 1940). *Illustrators 13.*
Society of Illustrators Annual Poster, 1971. Gouache, 38″ x 27″. Lent by the artist.

Don Weller (b. 1937). *Horses.*
Westways, May 1974. Watercolor and dyes, 16½″ x 14¼″. Lent by the artist.

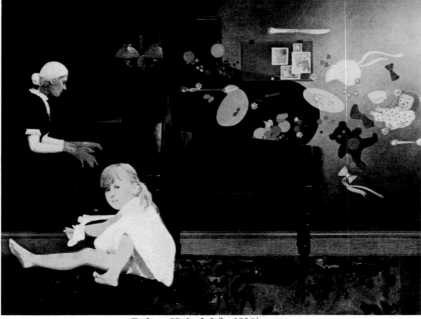

Robert Heindel (b. 1938). *Sybil.*
Reader's Digest Condensed Books, 1975. Acrylic, 18¼″ x 24″. Lent by Joseph T. Mendola.

Alan Magee (b. 1947). *Stones.*
Unpublished, 1976. Watercolor, 20″ x 28″. Lent by the artist.

Teresa Fasolino (b. 1946). *Happy's Cafe.*
Ms. Magazine, May 1975. Acrylic and collage, 19⅛″ x 14⅛″. Lent by the artist.

Bernard D'Andrea (b. 1923).
The Time Machine showed somebody built like a dumpling, busily making toys.
Santa Claus and the Time Machine by Donald Keith, Boys' Life, December 1973.
Watercolor and gouache, 21″ x 17″. Lent by the artist.

Edward Sorel (b. 1929). *Shopping for a Hat.*
Magical Storybook by Jay Williams, American Heritage Press, 1972.
Watercolor and pen and ink, 10¼″ x 21″. Lent by the artist.

Dickran Palulian (b. 1938). *Last Days of Earth.*
Penthouse Magazine, November 1974. Gouache, 12⅝″ x 23⅝″. Lent by the artist.

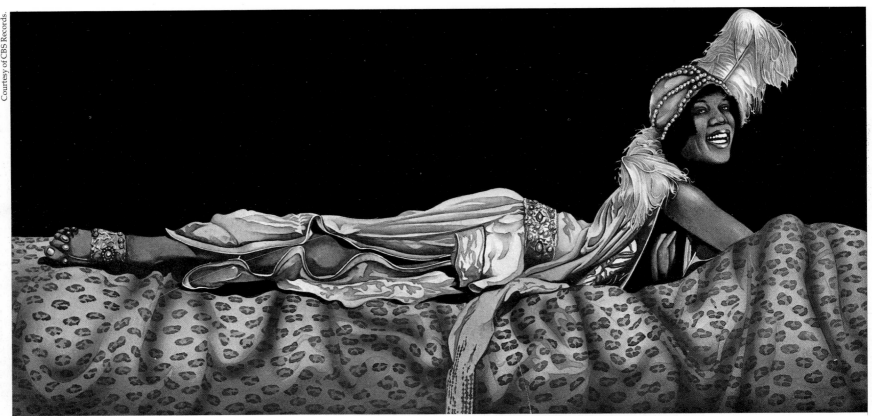

Philip Hays (b. 1932). *Bessie Smith. Columbia Records.* Watercolor and tempera, 12″ x 24″. Lent by CBS Records.

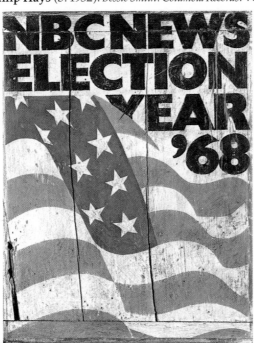

Cal Sacks (b. 1914). *NBC News Election Year '68.*
The New York Times Supplement, 1968.
Acrylic on wood, 12¾″ x 9¾″.
Lent by the artist.

Funs Von Woerkom. *Gandhi, Lenin and Mao.*
Horizon, Fall, 1971. Print, 12″ x 9″.
Lent by the American Heritage Publishing Company.

Albino Hinojosa (b. 1943). *Broken Shears. Uniquities, 1972.* Acrylic, 18″ x 36″. Lent by J & M Press Inc.

Austin Briggs (1909–1973). *Men at Desks.*
Crayon, 18″ x 15½″. Lent by the Society of Illustrators.

Kenneth Francis Dewey (b. 1940). *Watergate—So What?*
Senior Scholastic Magazine, October 1973.
Pen and ink, 15½″ x 10½″. Lent by Daniele Deverin.

Isadore Seltzer (b. 1930). *Rooster.*
Unpublished, 1976. Tempera, 29½" x 19½". Lent by the artist.

Boris W. Vallejo (b. 1941). *Of Man and Monsters.*
Of Man and Monsters, March, 1976. Oil, 22" x 16". Lent by the artist.

David Grove (b. 1940). *Shadows in the Showroom.*
Car & Driver Magazine, April 1975. Acrylic, 16½" x 27". Lent by the artist.

Reprinted from Car & Driver Magazine, © 1975, Ziff-Davis Publishing Company.

Gary Cooley (b. 1947). *Comes the Revolution.* 1975.
Gouache and egg tempera, 26″ x 20″. Lent by the artist.

Nancy Yarnall Martin (b. 1949). *You Turn Me On, I'm a Radio.*
Unpublished, 1976. Acrylic, 16″ x 13″. Lent by the artist.

Carol Inouye (b. 1940.) *Spring.*
Reader's Digest Condensed Books, 1976. Fabric sculpture, 30″ x 38″.
Lent by the Reader's Digest.

Erik Sundgaard (b. 1949).
The Art Annual. 1976. Watercolor and pen and ink, 11″ x 8″. Lent by the artist.

Steve Karchin (b. 1953). *How Many Miles to Babylon.*
Avon Books, 1976. Collage, 30″ x 24″. Lent by Miranda Hine.

John Groth (b. 1908). *Palio Start.*
John Groth's World of Sport, 1970. Pen and ink and brush, 25″ x 38″. Lent by the artist.

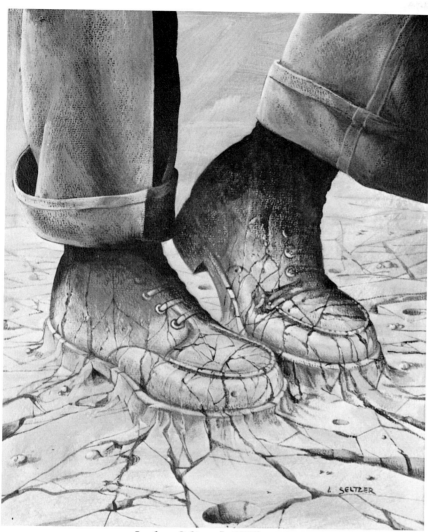

Isadore Seltzer (b. 1930). *Mud.*
Texaco Topics, 1976. Tempera, 13″ x 10½″. Lent by Harvey Kahn.

Milton Glaser (b. 1929). *No Man's Land.*
New York Magazine, November 1976. Ink wash, 15½″ x 12″. Lent by the artist.

Tien Ho (b. 1951). *Ballet Class. 1976.*
Watercolor, 8½″ x 11½″. Lent by Evelyne Johnson Associates.

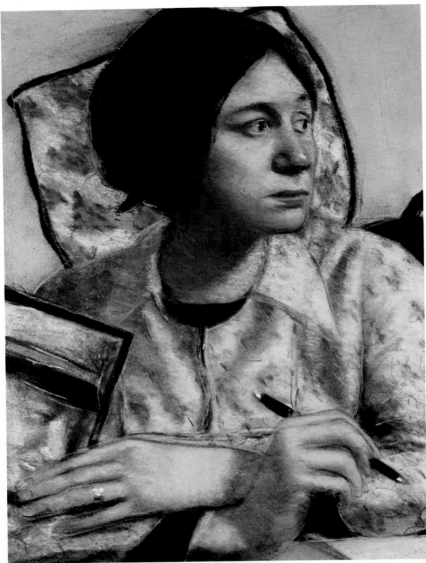

John Collier (b. 1948). *Girl With Pen.*
Redbook, 1975. Pastel, 15″ x 11½″. Lent by the artist.

William Edwards (b. 1953). *Magister Ludi.*
Magister Ludi by Herman Hesse, Bantam Books, 1970. Oil, 21″ x 17. Lent by Bantam Books.

Judith Jampel (b. 1944). *Bella Abzug.*
Unpublished for New Times, 1976. Fabric sculpture (photo by Vallini-Komar, Inc.),
24″ x 20″ x 12″. Lent by the artist.

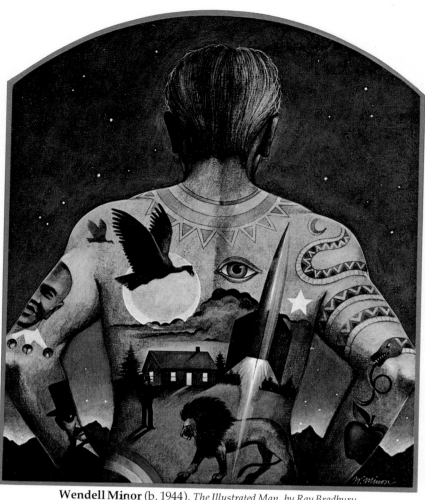

Wendell Minor (b. 1944). *The Illustrated Man, by Ray Bradbury,
Doubleday Inc., 1974.* Oil, 18" x 15". Lent by the artist.

Ray Cruz (b. 1933). *Samurai.*
Acrylic and pen and ink, 17" x 13¾". Lent by the artist.

Barbara Nessim (b. 1939). *Shoes. Audience,
March/April 1973.* Watercolor, 23¼" x 12". Lent by the artist.

Lou Myers (b. 1915). *Uncle Sam.*
The New Yorker, June 5, 1976. Pen and ink, 28" x 22". Lent by the artist.

Ben Wohlberg (b. 1927). *Fedora.*
Ladies' Home Journal, 1976. Oil, 12½" x 9½". Lent by Joseph T. Mendola.

John Clymer (b. 1907). *Horse Farm.*
Reader's Digest, April 1976. Oil, 27½" x 40". Lent by the New Britain Museum of American Art.

Siegbert Reinhard (b. 1941). *Rehearsal. Self-promotional piece, May 1976.* Paper sculpture, 46″ x 70″. Lent by the artist.

Zevi Blum (b. 1933). *Le Jardin de Pommes de Terre de Louis Quatorze.*
Horizon Magazine, Spring 1975.
Print, 11¾″ x 16″. Lent by the American Heritage Publishing Company.

Naiad Einsel (b. 1927). *The Westport Bicentennial Quilt. Americana Magazine, July, 1976.* Cotton appliqué, 108″ x 84″.
Hand sewn by 33 Westport women. Lent by the Westport Historical Society.

Diane Dawson (b. 1952). *Brother and Sister—*
A Grimm Fairy Tale. Unpublished. Summer 1975. Watercolor and pen and ink, 8⅜″ x 7⅜″.
Lent by the artist.

Denise Saldutti (b. 1953). *A Wolf in Sheep's Clothing. March 1975.*
Oil, 9″ x 7″. Lent by the artist.

Robert Andrew Parker (b. 1927). *The Great Sun Machine.*
The Lamp, Summer 1975. Watercolor, 5″ x 7″. Lent by the Exxon Corporation.

Dink Siegel (b. 1915). *Brandy and Ducks.*
Field and Stream Magazine, October 5, 1976. Watercolor, 14″ x 10″. Lent by the artist.

Robert Jones (b. 1926). *Rip Van Winkle. 1973.*
Watercolor and pen and ink, 18½″ x 13½″. Lent by Joseph T. Mendola.

Greg and Tim Hildebrandt (b. 1939). *Eowyn and the Nazgul. 1977*
J.R.R. Tolkien Calendar Ballantine Books, 1976. Acrylic, 32″ x 30″. Lent by the artists.

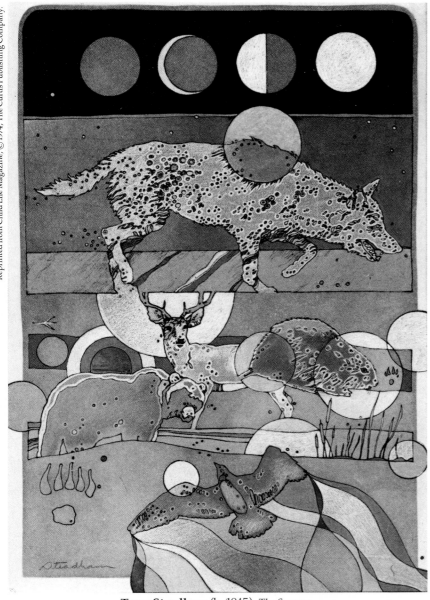

Terry Steadham (b. 1945). *The Seasons.*
Child Life Magazine, April 1974. Colored pencil and pen and ink, 13½" x 9½".
Lent by the artist.

Charles McVicker (b. 1930). *Mexico.*
Vista, 1973. Felt pen and acrylic, 19" x 14". Lent by the artist.

Jean-Claude Suares (b. 1942). *The War of the Mice.*
The New York Times. Pen and ink, 9¾" x 20¾". Lent by the Graham Gallery.

Fred Otnes (b. 1926). *Lincoln Center: American History Panorama.* Assemblage, 32″ x 74″. Lent by the artist.

Lou Brooks (b. 1944). *Philadelphia Bicentennial—1976.*
Unpublished, 1976. Collage and air brush, 28″ x 22″. Lent by the artist.

Roger Hane (1940–1975). *Information, Please.*
The Lamp, Summer 1972. Acrylic, 14″ x 10″. Lent by Exxon Corporation.

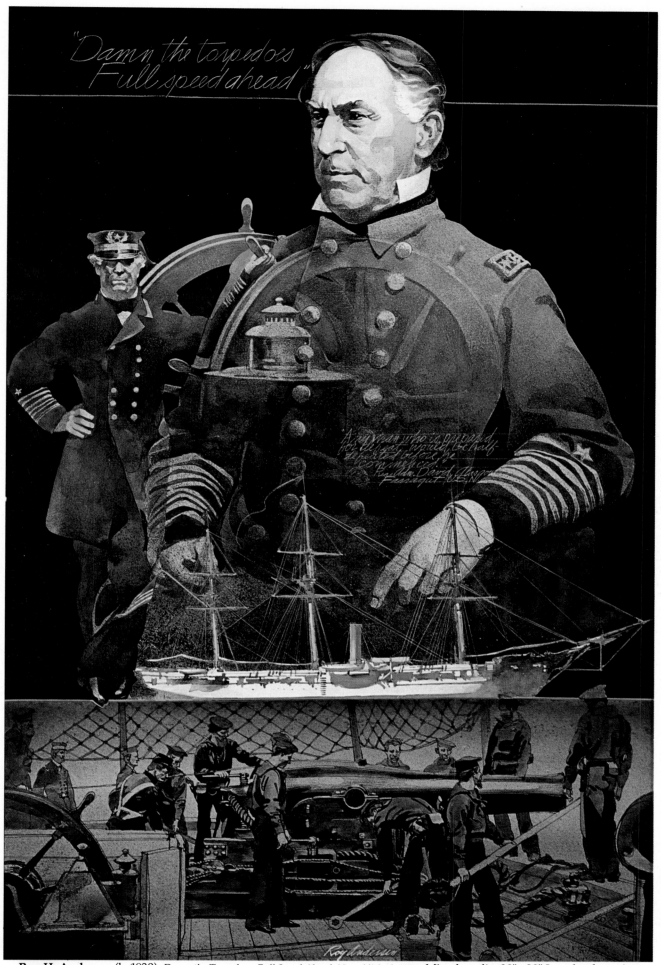

Roy H. Andersen (b. 1930). *Damn the Torpedoes, Full Speed Ahead. Unpublished, 1976.* Mixed media, 30″ x 20″. Lent by the artist.

Seymour Chwast (b. 1931). *In 1872 J. F. Blondel invented the first doughnut cutter . . .*
Pioneer-Moss Reproductions, 1975. Acrylic, 21$\frac{1}{8}$" x 13$\frac{7}{8}$". Lent by Pioneer-Moss, Inc.

Thomas Upshur (b. 1944). *Alice Cooper. Billion Dollar Baby,*
New American Library, 1975. Acrylic, 26½″ x 21½″.
Lent by the artist.

Robert E. Lapsley (b. 1942). *These are the times that try men's souls.*
Calendar Series for Coca-Cola Bottling Company, 1975. Watercolor, 15⅞″ x 15⅞″.
Lent by the Coca-Cola Bottling Company.

Alan E. Cober (b. 1935). *Sea Creatures.*
The Lamp, Spring 1973.
Watercolor and pen and ink, 11″ x 9″.
Lent by the Exxon Corporation.

David Palladini (b. 1946). *Still Life with Chinese Hen.*
Gentleman's Quarterly, 1975.
Pencil and acrylic, 20″ x 14¼″. Lent by the artist.

Reynold Ruffins (b. 1930). *The Monster Riddle Book, September 1975.* Acrylic polymer, 11½″ x 19½″. Lent by Charles Scribner's Sons, Inc.

Lorraine Fox (1922–1976). *Girl in the Tree.*
Unpublished. Oil, 22″ x 18″. Lent by Bob Crozier.

Milton Glaser (b. 1929). *Albert King.*
Utopia Records, 1976. Watercolor and colored pencil, 17″ x 11″. Lent by the artist.

William Chambers (b. 1940). *John Newcombe.*
Acrylic, 18″ x 14″. Lent by the artist.

Jözef Sumichrast (b. 1948). *Alphabet.*
VI Poster International Biennial—Warsaw, July 1976. Transparent dyes, 20″ x 30″.
Lent by the artist.

Thea Kliros (b. 1935). *Brooke Industry Creates in Trevira.*
Women's Wear Daily, May 20, 1975. Watercolor and pen and ink, 28″ x 22″.
Lent by Hoechst Fibers, Inc.

Ted CoConis (b. 1937). *Girl in the Orange Hat.*
Cosmopolitan, August 1975. Oil and pencil and gouache, 28″ x 22″.
Lent by Dr. and Mrs. Robert J. Ellingson.

Judy Dean Clifford (b. 1946). *Untitled.*
Simpson Lee Paper Brochure, September 1974. Watercolor, $15\frac{1}{2}$″ x $16\frac{1}{2}$″.
Lent by the artist.

Holly Hobbie (b. 1944). *Girl in Bonnet.*
Greeting Card for American Greeting Corp., 1976.
Pencil, $9\frac{1}{2}$″ x $6\frac{1}{4}$″.
Lent by American Greeting Corporation.

Shelley Freshman (b. 1950). *The Woods. Cricket, Bobbs-Merrill Publishers, October 1975.* Pen and ink, 7½″ x 10½″. Lent by the artist.

Frances Jetter (b. 1951). *Man Squeezing Rag.*
Institutional Investor, February 1976. Linocut, 8½″ x 18″. Lent by the artist.

Brad Holland (b. 1944). *Untitled.*
Galaxies, A Houghton Mifflin Reader for the Sixth Grade, 1971.
Watercolor and ink, 10″ x 7¾″.
Lent by Houghton Mifflin Company.

Elizabeth Malcynski (b. 1955). *Goose Girl.*
Unpublished. Watercolor, 9½″ x 12″. Lent by the artist.

Lorraine Fox (1922–1976). *Garden Fantasy.*
Unpublished. Watercolor and pen and ink, 22¼″ x 24¼″. Lent by Bernard D'Andrea.

Milton Glaser (b. 1929). *Jan Hammer—The First Seven Days.*
Atlantic Record Company,   1975. Watercolor and tempera wash, 12½″ x 25″.
Lent by the artist.

Jean Leon Huens (b. 1921). *Great People of the Bible.*
Reader's Digest, 1974. Watercolor, 10¾″ x 22″. Lent by the Reader's Digest.

Jean Leon Huens (b. 1921). *Sir Francis Drake's Golden Hind Rounding the Horn.*
National Geographic Magazine, February 1975.
Watercolor, 10″ x 8″. Lent by the National Geographic Society.

Shusei Nagaoka (b. 1936). *Japanese Rice Boat. 1975.*
Watercolor, 31″ x 25″. Lent by the artist.

Piero Ventura (b. 1937).
Venice. Piero Ventura's Book of Cities, Random House, Inc., October 1975.
Watercolor and pen and ink, 10¾″ x 19¼″. Lent by Random House, Inc.

Daniel Schwartz (b. 1929). *Centennial.*
As Levi and Elly Zendt began their dangerous journey West, they also began their marriage. If they lacked in knowledge, they had something better, youth and courage and a growing love that made them strong.
Ladies' Home Journal, 1975. Oil, 23" x 31". Lent by the artist.

Konrad F. Hack (b. 1945). *Oglala Sioux.*
Unpublished, 1975. Pencil, 15½" x 12". Lent by the artist.

Bernard Fuchs (b. 1932). *The Matador. Lithopinion, December 1974*. Oil, 22½″ x 32½″. Lent by the artist.

Harry J. Schaare (b. 1922). *U.S.C.G. Eagle.*
Decor Magazine. June 1976. Watercolor, 26″ x 36″. Lent by the artist.

Norman Adams (b. 1933). *Whitetail Deer.*
Sports Afield, October 1971. Gouache, 17¼″ x 12¼″. Lent by the Artists Associates.

Mercer Mayer (b. 1943). *Mickey Go Home.*
Penthouse Magazine. Watercolor and pen and ink, 10½″ x 7¾″. Lent by Joe Brooks.

Paul Williams (b. 1934). *Hold Up.*
Pen and ink, 14″ x 28½″. Lent by Joseph T. Mendola.

Walter Spitzmiller (b. 1944). *Indian Princess.*
Calendar series for Keeler Morris—1975, *1974.* Magic marker and spray, 24″ x 24″.
Lent by the artist.

Bart Forbes (b. 1939). *Chief Joseph.*
Calendar Series for Sun Graphics, Inc., 1975. Watercolor, 18″ x 18″. Lent by the artist.

Raymond Ameijide (b. 1924). *Illustrators 17.*
Society Illustrators Annual poster, 1975. Felt sculpture, 22″ x 20″. Lent by the artist.

Franklin McMahon (b.1921). *Plaza Mayor,
Madrid. U.S. Catholic, 1974.* Pencil and wash, 22" x 30".
Lent by the artist.

Franklin McMahon (b. 1921). *Chicago's Picasso.
Continental Bank Limited Edition Reproduction, 1973.* Watercolor and pencil, 22" x 30".
Lent by the artist.

James Lewicki (b. 1917). *Totem Dance.
The Golden Bough by Sir James Frazer, Limited Editions Club, 1970.*
Mixed media, 17" x 11". Lent by the artist.

Robert J. Lee (b. 1921). *A Personal Totem.*
Oil, 48" x 36". Lent by the Society of Illustrators.

Paul Giovanopoulos (b. 1939). *The Secret Life of Plants.*
Reader's Digest, 1975. Watercolor and pen and ink, 12½″ x 9″. Lent by the artist.

Bob Ziering (b. 1933). *Herself.*
Columbia Records Promotion, 1974. Pen and ink, 25″ x 18″. Lent by the artist.

Mark Barensfeld (b. 1947). *Warriors.*
Self-promotion piece. Wood and metal, 32″ x 32″. Lent by the artist.

Norman Laliberte (b. 1925). *Vibrations.*
The Lamp, Spring 1972. Crayon and pastel, 32″ x 21″.
Lent by Exxon Corporation.

Anna Marie Magagna (b. 1938). *Brown Satin Lady.*
The New York Times, February 1969. Paste and ink, 20¾″ x 16⅜″. Lent by the artist.

Thomas Sgouros (b. 1927). *The Loyalist.*
Yankee, April 1976. Acrylic, 21¼″ x 24″. Lent by the artist.

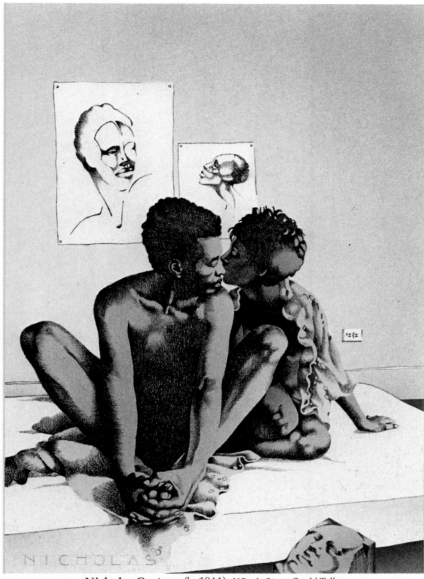

Carol Anthony (b. 1943). *Rollerskater, Sidewalk Champ.*
Mixed media, 60″ x 24″. Lent by Monique Knowlton Gallery.

Nicholas Gaetano (b. 1944). *If Beale Street Could Talk.*
Unpublished, 1975. Luina dyes, 11¼″ x 8⅜″. Lent by Daniele Deverin.

Gilbert Stone (b. 1940). *Privacy II.*
World Book Year Book, 1976. Acrylic, 18″ x 36″. Lent by the artist.

Miriam Schottland (b. 1935). *African Women.*
Unpublished, 1974. Tempera, 22″ x 16″. Lent by the artist.

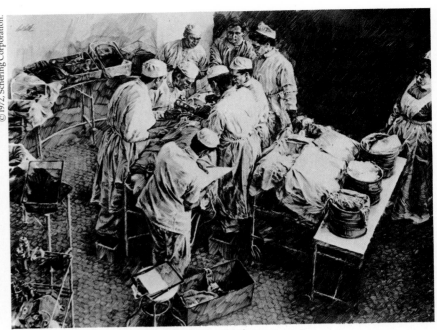

Paul Calle (b. 1928). *Dr. Halsted.*
Limited Edition Prints, 1972. Pencil, 40″ x 30″.
Lent by Johns Hopkins Medical Institution.

Roger Hane (1940–1975). *Indian Santanta.* 1972.
Oil, 19⅞″ x 14¾″. Lent by Cathy and Vin DiGerlando.

402

Sandy Huffaker (b. 1943). *President Ford and the Democratic Congress. The New York Times, November 10, 1974.* Pencil, 14″ x 7½″. Lent by the artist.

Stan Mack (b. 1936). *The Perfect Typewriter No. 2.*
The New York Times, Spring 1971. Pen and ink, 5⅜″ x 7″.
Lent by Ketchum, MacLeod and Grove, Inc.

Wally Neibart (b. 1925). *Skydiver.*
Time, 1975. Pencil, 23¾″ x 18″. Lent by the artist.

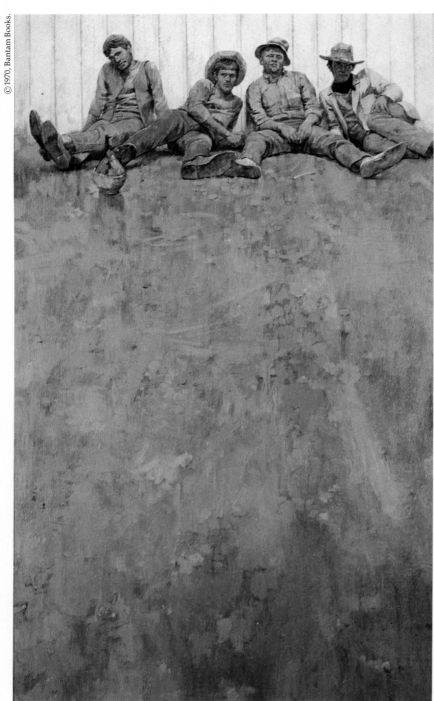

Ken Riley (b. 1919). *Tortilla Flat.*
Bantam Books, 1970. Oil, 34″ x 20″. Lent by Bantam Books.

Theodore Lodigensky (b. 1930). *Number 5.*
Scientific American, 1972. Tempera, 12″ x 12″. Lent by the artist.

David J. Blossom (b. 1927). *The Consultation.*
Medical Times, August 1972.
Acrylic, 31¼″ x 31¼″. Lent by Romaine Pierson Publishers, Inc.

Arno Sternglass (b. 1926). *On Guadalcanal with the Marines.*
America—An Illustrated Diary, November 1973. Gouache, 14″ x 11″. Lent by the artist.

Alan E. Cober (b. 1935). *Blue Whale.*
The Lamp, Spring 1973. Watercolor and pen and ink and tempera, 14″ x 10¾″.
Lent by the artist.

Garie Blackwell (b. 1939). *Woman with Mirror.*
Allied Chemical Promotion, 1975. Dyes, 18″ x 18½″. Lent by the artist.

Robert Weaver (b. 1924). *Construction Workers.*
Acrylic, 24″ x 19½″. Lent by Walt Reed.

Barron Storey (b. 1940). *Geronimo 1876*
—Man asks Indian: 'What was this land called before?' Indian answers in his own language.
Man says: 'What does that mean?' Indian says: 'Ours.' Flying Magazine, April 1974.
Acrylic and pen and ink, 14¼″ x 10¾″. Lent by Jane Lander Associates.

Ken Dallison (b. 1933). *1908 Grand Prix, Savannah.*
Car & Driver Magazine. Pen and ink and watercolor, 16¾″ x 25″. Lent by the artist.

Miriam Schottland (b. 1935). *Bien Hoa, 1970.*
Watercolor, 21″ x 28½″. Lent by the United States Air Force.

Ken Riley (b. 1919). *Wilderness Empire. Bantam Books, 1971.* Oil, 18½" × 23". Lent by Bantam Books.

Richard Ely (b. 1928). *Josephine Baker. Remembering Josephine by Stephen Papich, Bobbs-Merrill Co., November 1976.* Silkscreen, 30¼" × 26". Lent by the artist.

Bill Negron (b. 1925). *Jazzmobile Workshop. The Lamp, Winter 1971.* Crayon, 6½" × 8½". Lent by Exxon Corporation.

Jerry Pinkney (b. 1939). *Untitled.*
Fiesta, A Houghton Mifflin Reader for the Third Grade, 1971. Watercolor, 13⅜″ x 12¼″. Lent by Houghton Mifflin Company.

Joseph Ciardiello (b. 1953). *19th Century Images.*
Self-promotion poster, January 1976. Pen and ink, 38″ x 32″. Lent by the artist.

Albert Hirshfeld (b. 1903). *The Man Who Came to Dinner. 1972.*
Pen and ink, 19¾″ x 20″. Lent by Hallmark Cards, Inc.

Alan E. Cober (b. 1935). *Antonio, Janice, and Prince Paul.*
Lithopinion, Spring 1975. Watercolor and pen and ink, 16″ x 12″. Lent by the artist.

Tom Wilson (b. 1945). *Board Meeting.*
Washington Post, 1975. Pen and ink, 10″ x 16″. Lent by the artist.

Harvey Dinnerstein (b. 1928). *Terrorists. American Artist, May 1973.* Pastel, 21¼″ x 29¼″. Lent by the artist.

Noel Sickles (b. 1911). *A Time to Buy Horses.*
Reader's Digest, July 1976. Watercolor and gouache, 9″ x 9¼″.
Lent by the Reader's Digest.

Bob Peak (b. 1928). *Custer and Horse. Unpublished, 1972.* Oil, 47″ x 47″. Lent by the artist.

411

ABOUT THE ARTISTS

Abbreviations used in the biographies of the artists:

ACD	Art Center College of Design
ADC	Art Directors' Club
AEF	American Expeditionary Force
AG	Artists Guild
AIC	Art Institute of Chicago
AIGA	American Institute of Graphic Arts
AP	Associated Press
ASL	Art Students League
AWS	American Watercolor Society
CCAD	Columbus College of Art and Design
CCNY	City College of New York
CU	Cooper Union
FAS	Famous Art School
FIT	Fashion Institute of Technology
GAG	Graphic Artists Guild
GCSA	Grand Central School of Art
KCAI	Kansas City Art Institute
LC	Library of Congress
NAD	National Academy of Design
NYPL	New York Public Library
NYU	New York University
PAFA	Pennsylvania Academy of Fine Art
PI	Pratt Institute
PSD	Parsons School of Design
RISD	Rhode Island School of Design
S of I	Society of Illustrators
SVA	School of Visual Arts
TID	The Institute of Design
UCLA	University of California at Los Angeles
USA	United States Army
USAF	United States Air Force
USMC	United States Marine Corps
USN	United States Navy

Abbey, Edwin Austin (1852–1911). Born in Philadelphia, he studied art at the PAFA and joined the staff of *Harper's* in 1871. His authenticity of clothing was so noteworthy that it prompted a move to England where the costumes were more readily available. He did over 200 drawings for Shakespearean plays as well as numerous books including *She Stoops to Conquer, The Deserted Village* and *Old Songs*. Later in life, he was commissioned to paint murals such as the *Holy Grail* mural at the Boston Public Library and one at the Harrisburg State Capitol. There is a memorial of his works in the collection of the Yale University Art Gallery.

Abbot, Samuel Nelson (1874–1953). Born in Illinois, he studied in Paris under Laurens and Constant. His first illustration assignment was for *Hart Schaffner and Marx*, where he continued to design and illustrate their fashion catalogues for the next 25 years. During this period he also did illustration for *Ladies' Home Journal, The Saturday Evening Post* and *Collier's*.

Adams, John Wolcott (1874–1925). Born in Worcester, Massachusetts, he attended the ASL and also studied with Howard Pyle. He was best known for his illustrations of old songs, poetry and children's books including *Hoosier Romance* by Riley, which he illustrated for *the Century* in 1910. His works also appeared in *Scribner's* and *Harper's* magazines. He died in New York City.

Adams, Norman (b. 1933). Born in Walla Walla, Washington, he was trained at the ACD. In 1960 his first illustration, a watercolor, ran on the cover of *Today's Living* in the *Herald Tribune* magazine section. He has since done covers for *Sports Afield, Field and Stream, True* and *Reader's Digest*. His editorial work has been published in *Holiday* and *The Saturday Evening Post*, among others. A participant in the S of I Annual Exhibitions, he received the Mystery Writers' Raven Award.

Alajalov, Constantin (b. 1900). Born in Rostov-on-the-Don, he was brought up in pre-revolutionary Russia and by the age of 15 was illustrating a book of poetry by Baudelaire as well as the *Lives of Savanarola*. He attended the University of Petrograd, enjoyed a brief stay as a court painter and was a member of their new artists' guild. Having fled from Constantinople, Alajalov arrived in New York in 1923 and found work painting murals for Russian cabarets. Three years later he began a 20-year relationship with *The New Yorker* doing cover art and in 1945 he began working for *The Saturday Evening Post*, in addition to illustrating children's books.

Allen, Thomas B. (b. 1928). Born in Nashville, Tennessee, he studied at Vanderbilt University and received his BFA from the AIC. His work has appeared in *Esquire, Sports Illustrated, McCall's, Life, Redbook* and *Playboy*. He has also done illustrations for *CBS, Harper & Row* and *Signet Classics*. Gold medals have been awarded to him by the New York ADC and the S of I. From 1958 to 1964 he taught at the SVA in New York.

Altschuler, Franz (b. 1923). Born in Mannheim, Germany, he was educated in New York City at CU and TID. His professional career began in 1951 and he has since illustrated over 30 books. The recipient of awards in New York and Chicago, he has shown his work in galleries in Denver and Baltimore. His illustrations have been used as posters for the Chicago newspapers as well as for major magazines, including *Playboy* and *Skeptic*.

Ameijide, Raymond (b. 1924). Born in Newark, New Jersey, he attended PI. After a seven-year stint at Ross Advertising he went free-lance and later formed AKM Studio. His paper sculpture and felt constructions have appeared in *Art Direction* and *Graphis* as well as being shown at the ADC and the S of I of New York.

Amick, Robert Wesley (b. 1879). Born in Canon City, Colorado, he studied law at Yale University. After practicing law for two years in Ohio, he moved to New York to study at the ASL, then began illustrating for *Harper's, Scribner's, American* and *Harper's Bazaar*. Though he was also a proficient portrait artist, he was most fulfilled painting the Western scenes of his boyhood.

Andersen, Roy H. (b. 1930). Born in Chicago, he studied at the Academy of Fine Arts and the ACD. Associated with Jack O'Grady's Studio for a number of years, he came to New York in 1976. His illustrations have appeared in *National Geographic, Boys' Life, Sports Illustrated* and *Ladies' Home Journal*. He is a member of the S of I, and his work has been selected for its Annual Exhibitions; it has also been exhibited at the ADCs of Tucson and Washington and is part of the permanent collection of the LC.

Anderson, Alexander (1775–1870). Born in New York, he studied the work of the English artist Bewick and was later to be known as the father of American illustration. A physician and miniaturist, he was one of the first American artists to employ woodblocks for engraving. He used this method until the mid-1800's, although it was not widely accepted by his contemporaries. Among his many children's books was *The Only True Mother Goose Melodies*, 1833, published by *Munroe and Friends*. A founder of the NAD, he worked in New York until 1866, when he chose to retire in Jersey City where he died.

Anderson, Clarence William (b. 1891). Born in Wahoo, Nebraska, he trained at the AIC. In 1936 he illustrated his first book, entitled *Billy and Blaze*, which started his career. Though he was best known for his drawings of horses, his landscapes, always in vivid color, were another of his trademarks and prints of them were exhibited throughout the United States.

Anderson, Lyman Matthew (b. 1907). Born in Chicago, he

was educated at the AIC, GCSA and in private classes under Walter Biggs, Pruett Carter and Harvey Dunn. Acceptance in the 1939 *Art Directors Club Annual* started his career. He did a great many dry brush illustrations for the pulps until 1935 when he produced a syndicated strip for three years. Though his work appeared in major publications, he was most active in the field of advertising art until 1963 when he became an instructor for the FAS. He is a Life Member of both the S of I and Joint Ethics Committee.

Anthony, Carol (b. 1943). Born in New York, she was educated at Stephens College, Missouri, and graduated from RISD. An exhibition of her three-dimensional figures at the Museum of Contemporary Crafts was the beginning of a successful career leading to assignments for *Redbook, Vintage Books* and *The New York Times*. Her intriguing characters often develop from a prop as simple as a pair of old shoes. Her work is part of the Hirshhorn collection in Washington and the Museum of New Orleans. A member of the S of I, she works out of her home in Greenwich, Connecticut.

Armstrong, Rolf. An illustrator in the editorial and advertising fields, he executed many pastel drawings and oil paintings of beautiful women for clients such as *Shrine Magazine*, Oneida Silverware and Brown and Bigelow Calendars.

Arno, Peter (1904–1968). Born in New York City, he was a student at Yale University from 1922 to 1924, but had no formal art training at the time. 1925 marked the beginning of his long-standing relationship with *The New Yorker*, where his cartoons and covers appeared with great frequency. The consummate New Yorker, he brought his style and wit to his books of cartoons: *Dearie, Peter Arno's Parade* and *Peter Arno's Circus*.

Artzybasheff, Boris (1899–1965). Born in Kharkov, Russia, he received his art training at the Prince Tenisheff School in St. Petersburg. In 1919 he fled to the United States, where he worked as an engraver's apprentice while illustrating books by Balzac and Aesop. A long-standing relationship with *Time* magazine resulted in his production of over 200 covers. Among a number of citations awarded him was the prestigious Newberry Medal.

Atherton, John (1900–1952). Born in Brainerd, Minnesota, he studied art at the College of the Pacific and the School of Fine Arts in San Francisco. His advertising and editorial illustrations led to a One-Man Show in New York in 1936. He was an award winner in the 1943 *Artists for Victory* show for his piece, *Black Horse*, which is now owned by the Metropolitan Museum of Art. His first job was a cover for *The Saturday Evening Post* and later he produced three of their Franklin anniversary covers. A founding member of the FAS, he died in New Brunswick, Canada, while on a fishing trip.

Audubon, John James (1785–1851). Born in Les Cayes, Haiti, he fled with his family to France where, as a youth, he studied music, dance, painting and developed a keen interest in the wild creatures of the woods and fields. In 1803 he traveled to Philadelphia and continued his observation and accurate recording of wildlife. By the age of 35 he gave up his failing career in business to become a full-time naturalist and artist. He is best known for his great series, *Birds of America, Viviparous Quadrupeds of North America* and *Ornithological Record*. In 1833 he became an Honorary Member and Professional of the NAD. In 1864, 432 of Audubon's 435 drawings were purchased from his widow and now remain in the permanent collection of the New-York Historical Society Museum.

Bacon, Peggy (b. 1895). Born in Richfield, Connecticut, she studied under John Sloane and George Bellows at the

ASL. An author and illustrator, her work has been published by *Macmillan, Viking Press* and *Harcourt*. Her drawings of urban scenes have also appeared in *Vanity Fair, Town and Country* and *The New Yorker*. She produced a series of caricatures of famous artists which was published under the title "Off With Their Heads".

Bailey, Vernon Howe (1874–1953). After nine years of illustrating for local newspapers, he studied at the PAFA and subsequently went to London. Following his return to the United States with a book of sketches, he was commissioned by such periodicals as *Scribner's* and later *Harper's, the Century, Leslie's Weekly, Collier's* and *Everybody's*. While in Rome he received an unprecedented invitation to paint without restriction in the Vatican. He is best known for his technical drawings of cities and landscapes.

Balcom, Lowell Leroy (1887-1938). Born in Kansas City, Missouri, he began his career there at *The Star* after studying at the KCAI. After World War I duty painting officers' portraits, he visited the Virgin Islands and developed his lino-cut method. With a commission for several illustrations from the US Shipping Board, he travelled throughout the Orient and the Mediterranean, His editorial work appeared in *American Legion* and *Hearst's International*. He was a member of the Silver Mine Guild in Norwalk, Connecticut.

Bama, James Elliott (b. 1926). Born in the Bronx, New York, he attended the High School of Art and Design and the ASL as a pupil of Frank Reilly. His career began in 1949 and has included illustrations for hundreds of books and magazines such as *The Saturday Evening Post, Argosy* and *Reader's Digest*, as well as posters for a number of advertising firms. His artwork has been shown in galleries across the country and is part of the permanent collections in many museums. He retired from illustration in 1971 to live and work as a Western painter in Wyoming. The results of his efforts were recently recorded in a book, *Paintings by Jim Bama*, published by *Ballantine Books*.

Barclay, McClelland (1891–1943). Born in St. Louis, Missouri; his father was a surgeon of Scottish descent. He studied at Washington University and later attended the ASL and the AIC. He was a professional at 21, his work appearing in *The Saturday Evening Post, Ladies' Home Journal* and *Cosmopolitan*. His advertising art was well known, especially his Fisher Body Girl, a campaign on which he worked for ten years. As a government artist during World War I, he produced posters and camouflage, and as a pictorial artist on active duty with the Navy during World War II, he was reported missing in action in the Solomon Islands.

Barensfeld, Mark (b. 1947). Born in Cleveland, he attended Ohio University and Memphis State. His career began with an illustration for *St. Anthony's Messenger* in 1970 and his illustrations have since appeared in *Cincinnati Magazine* and *Writer's Digest*. He has produced posters for Ohio universities and his works have been shown at several Ohio museums and ADCs.

Barkley, Bruce E. (b. 1950). Born in New York City, he attended the ASL and received his BFA from SVA. A pupil of Steven Kidd, Jack Potter and Robert Weaver, he had his first illustration, *Boston Tea Party*, published in 1973. His work is owned by the United States Department of Interior, USAF, Walsh Galleries in Yonkers and the Pentagon.

Bartlett, William Henry (1809–1854). Born in London, he visited the United States four times between 1836 and 1852 and in 1840 a series of views from his early trips was published in *American Scenery* with text by N. P. Willis. He died aboard ship returning from the Orient in 1854. *History of the United States of North America* was published

posthumously with engravings taken from his interpretations of life in America. His drawings of the Near East were exhibited in Boston in 1856.

Barton, Ralph (1891–1931). Born in Kansas City, Missouri, he started working for the *Kansas City Star* while in his teens. After moving to New York in 1910, he did satirical drawings and caricatures for *Harper's Weekly, Puck, Judge* and later contributed to *Liberty, Vanity Fair* and *The New Yorker*, writing theater reviews as well. He illustrated a number of books in the 1920's, including Anita Loos' *Gentlemen Prefer Blondes*, his own *Science in Rhyme Without Reason* and *God's Country*.

Baskin, Leonard (b. 1922).Born in New Brunswick, New Jersey, he was apprentice to sculptor Maurice Glickman from 1937 to 1939. He attended Yale University and various schools in New York, Paris and Florence. In 1959 he illustrated *Auguries of Innocence* by William Blake, whom he admired greatly. Proficient in woodcut, wood engraving, pen and ink and lithography, he is also a noted wood sculptor.

Beard, Daniel Carter (1850–1941). Born in Cincinnati, son of artist James Henry Beard, he studied at the ASL under Beckwith, Sartain and Chase from 1880 to 1885. Animals, outdoor life and American history were the subjects of the artwork he producced for *Puck, Life* and *Judge*. His illustrations complemented Mark Twain's *A Connecticut Yankee in King Arthur's Court* (1889) and were the best known of the many pieces he did for Twain's books.

Beckhoff, Harry (b. 1901). Born in Perth Amboy, New Jersey, he studied art under Harvey Dunn and George Bridgman at the ASL and GCSA. In 1925 he began his career at *Country Gentleman* and has since worked for *Collier's, American, Woman's Home Companion, Reader's Digest* and others. His illustrations have been published in several books and exhibited at the Grand Central Art Galleries.

Bemelmans, Ludwig (1898–1962). Born in Austria, he studied in Germany until 1914; he then emigrated to the United States where he became a citizen four years later. Besides doing magazine illustrations for *The New Yorker, Vogue* and *Holiday*, he worked extensively in book illustration. As an author and artist he produced the *Madeline* series beginning in 1939. Very popular in the 1930's, he illustrated such books as *My War with the United States* and *Life Class*.

Benda, Wladyslaw Theodore (1873-1948). Born in Poznan, Poland, he attended Krakow College of Technology and Art. He also studied in Vienna before coming to New York in 1900 where he began illustrating for magazines and book publishers. He often received assignments to paint Eastern European scenes, including *A Russian Grandmother's Wonder Tales* for *Scribner's* in 1906. In his later years he began a second career as a designer, during which time he created the astonishing Benda Masks, laboriously constructed, highly decorative masks worn by stage and screen actors.

Bennett, Harry R. (b. 1925). Born in Lewisboro, New York, he studied at the AIC and American Academy of Art. His first illustration appeared in *Woman's Day* in 1950, but most of his work since then has been for book publishers, as demonstrated by the 982 paperback covers he has illustrated over the last 20 years. His works have been shown at the NYPL, The New-York Historical Society and several Annual Exhibitions of the S of I.

Bennett, William James (1787–1844). Born in London, he exhibited his watercolor landscapes, aquatint engravings and etchings from 1808 to 1825 in London. He moved to New York City in 1826, where he painted and engraved a

view of Bowling Green. In the early 1830's he sketched while traveling in Boston, West Point and Detroit. He died in New York City.

Benney, Robert (b. 1904). Born in New York City, he was educated at Cooper Union, ASL and NAD. In 1968 he was a combat artist with the Marines in Vietnam and has done extensive artwork for Naval Aviation and the USAF for Abbott Laboratories. His paintings are widely exhibited in museums such as the Corcoran Gallery, De Young Museum, Seattle Art Museum, Dallas Museum and the Pentagon.

Berkey, John Conrad (b. 1932). Born in Edgley, North Dakota, where he attended public school. His work has included advertising, editorial posters, calendars and book covers. He has been an illustrator for the past 20 years and is married with four children.

Betts, Anna Whelan. Born in Philadelphia, she studied under Howard Pyle and Robert Vonnoh. Her color illustrations appeared in *the Century, Harper's* and several other publications. A painter and teacher, she was also a member of the Philadelphia Watercolor Society.

Biggs, Walter (1886-1968). Born in Elliston, Virginia, he came to New York to study at the Chase School under Edward Penfield, Lucius Hitchcock and Robert Henri, along with classmates Edward Hopper, George Bellows and Rockwell Kent. His illustrations have appeared in many magazines such as *Harper's, Scribner's, the Century, Ladies' Home Journal, Good Housekeeping, McCall's* and *Cosmopolitan*. He taught at the ASL and GCSA and has exhibited in many prestigious galleries. The S of I elected him to the Hall of Fame in 1963.

Billout, Guy R. (b. 1941). Born in Decize, France, he studied art at the École des Arts Appliqués for four years. He has received two Gold Medals from the S of I since 1969, when his first illustration appeared in *New York Magazine*. *Esquire, Redbook, Ms., McCall's, Money, Town and Country* and *Vogue* have all published this man's charming illustrations.

Birch, Reginald Bathurst (1856-1943). Born in London, he came to New York in his teens but later returned to Europe to study in Paris, Antwerp and Munich. He is noted for his popular pen-and-ink drawings for children's books, including *Little Lord Fauntleroy* in 1886. He illustrated for many magazines as well, using pretty ladies and wide-eyed kids as subjects. He was active as an artist in his later years in Massachusetts, where he died.

Birnbaum, Meg (b. 1952). Born in Greenwich, Connecticut, she studied for two years in Massachusetts at the Montserrat School of Visual Art and Vesper George School of Visual Art. She began free-lance illustrating in 1972 with a piece in *Of Westchester Magazine* and presently works for *The Real Paper* in Cambridge, Massachusetts. Her artwork has been shown at the Beaux Arts Gallery, Mamaroneck Artists Guild Gallery and in the Annual Exhibition of the S of I.

Blackwell, Garie (b. 1939). Born in Los Angeles, she attended the Chouinard Art Institute for three years. Her first illustration was done for *Seventeen* in 1967 and she has since worked for *Cosmopolitan, Ladies' Home Journal, Mademoiselle* and Allied Chemical Corporation. She is now working in Cambridge, Massachusetts and researching the possible health hazards to artists resulting from the use of certain products used in the profession.

Blake, Peter (b. 1932). Presently living and illustrating in Somerset, England, he has worked for Standard Oil Company and Exxon Corporation. His work has been exhibited in The Tate and other major galleries.

Blashfield, Edwin Howland (1848–1936). Born in New York City, he moved to Paris in 1867 to study with Leon Bonnat. He returned to America in 1881 where, in collaboration with his wife, he published illustrated articles on ancient, medieval and Renaissance subjects in *Scribner's* and *the Century*. A successful muralist, he also wrote the book *Mural Painting in America* in 1914. He died on Cape Cod.

Blossom, David J. (b. 1927). Born in Chicago, the son of illustrator Earl Blossom, he studied at the Yale School of Fine Arts and ASL under Reginald Marsh. In 1947 he became an art director at the J. Walter Thompson advertising agency, but upon publication of his first illustration in 1961, he turned his talents to painting and drawing. Since that time he has illustrated several books and his work has appeared in *The Saturday Evening Post, McCall's, Good Housekeeping* and *Outdoor Life*. He received Awards of Excellence from the S of I Annual Exhibitions in 1962 and 1963 and the Hamilton King Award in 1972.

Blossom, Earl (1891–1970). Born in Siloam Springs, Missouri, he attended the AIC in 1920 and began his career drawing men's fashions, illustrating for the *Chicago American* newspaper and working on staff for Charles Daniel Frey Studio. He later worked for Pete Martin of *The Saturday Evening Post* where he began his inventive and often humorous style of fiction illustration. When Martin left the *Post*, Blossom moved to *Collier's* and subsequently appeared in *True, Bluebook, Liberty* and *American Legion Magazine*, among others. His work was seen in many ADC Annual Shows and is part of the collection of the New Britain Museum of American Art. His son, David, is presently a successful illustrator in New York.

Blum, Robert Frederick (1857–1903). Born in Cincinnati, he was a lithographer's apprentice at age 14, then studied at the McMicken Art School of Design at night and completed his training at the PAFA. Extensive travel resulted in his use of foreign subjects for most of his paintings. One such piece, *The Ameya or Itinerant Candy Vendor*, a product of his time spent living in Japan, is owned by the Metropolitan Museum of Art. His fine draftsmanship was evident in his illustrations done for magazines such as *Scribner's*.

Blum, Zevi (b. 1933). Born in Paris, he received a degree in architecture from Cornell University in 1957. After several years as a practicing architect, he began a career in illustration and is presently acting chairman of the Fine Arts Department at Cornell. A book illustrator with published works by *Doubleday* and *Pantheon Books*, he is a frequent contributor to the Op-Ed page of *The New York Times. Intellectual Digest, Rolling Stone* and *Atlantic Monthly* have also used his work.

Booth, Franklin (1874–1948). Born in Carmel, Indiana. His desire to be an artist was so great he would often take intricate wood or steel engravings from magazines and copy over them with pen and ink. In 1925 he published a book of 60 drawings in the decorative style which he often used to illuminate poetry and articles.

Bouché, René Robert (1906–1963). Born in Prague, Czechoslovakia, he studied briefly at the universities of Munich and Paris. He was a frequent contributor to *Vogue*, which assigned him to paint an editorial series on the 1948 Republican and Democratic conventions. Best known for the fluid elegance of his drawings, he greatly influenced future styles and modes of fashion illustration.

Bower, Maurice (b. 1889). Born in Ohio, he studied at the School of Industrial Art under Walter Everett and the Brandywine School in Delaware with Howard Pyle. While still at school, he began illustrating regularly for *St. Nicholas* magazine and later for the Hearst Publications. He signed a contract with *McCall's* to illustrate in Paris but

with the stock market crash in 1929, he turned to portrait work and teaching World War I veterans in Newark, New Jersey.

Bowler, Joseph, Jr. (b. 1928). Born in Forest Hills, New York, he started working at Cooper Union Studios in 1948. His first published illustration was for *Redbook* in 1949. He was acclaimed Artist of the Year in 1967 by the AG in New York, and his work appears at the Sanford Low Collection and the Hartford Museum. He has illustrated for all the major magazines and currently all his covers and illustrations are portraits. He is married and has two daughters.

Bozzo, Frank Edward (b. 1937). Born in Chicago, he was a pupil of Robert Shore and Eugene Karlin at SVA with classmates Paul Davis and Paul Giovanopoulos. In 1959 *Harper's* magazine gave him his first assignment, a pen and ink drawing which accompanied the article *How Much Poison Are You Breathing?* He has illustrated a number of children's books and worked for most major periodicals, including *Playboy, Esquire, Seventeen* and *New York Magazine*. Some of the organizations that have given him awards are the S of I, the ADCs of New York, Chicago and Detroit, AIGA and the Society of Publication Designers. His work hangs in many private collections.

Bracker, M. Leone (1885–1937). Born in Cleveland, Ohio, he was best known for his World War I posters, particularly *Keep 'em Smiling*. Accidental drowning caused his death in Rye, New Hampshire.

Bransom, Paul (b. 1885). Born in Washington, DC, he began working at the United States Patent Office at the age of 13 where he had on-the-job art training. His off hours were spent at the National Zoo where he developed a sketching style that continued throughout his career. In New York he worked on the comic strip *The News from Bugville* for the *Evening Journal* which led to assignments for *The Saturday Evening Post*. His unparalleled animal drawings were in demand for both editorial and book illustrations.

Brehm, George (1878–1966). Born in Indianapolis, he studied at the ASL under the guidance of Twachtman, DuMond and Bridgman. Both he and his brother Worth became well known for their depiction of children, especially boys, in everyday life. His first assignment was from *Reader's Magazine*, published by *Bobbs-Merrill Company*, and later he illustrated a series in *The Saturday Evening Post* and *Delineator*.

Brehm, Worth (1883–1928). Born in Indianapolis, he became fascinated with art, as did his brother George. His career was launched by *Outing Magazine*, which first bought his drawings. He is perhaps best known for his illustration of *Adventures of Tom Sawyer* and *Huckleberry Finn*, which were published by *Harper's*. He died at the early age of 44, having produced an abundance of artwork for *Cosmopolitan, Good Housekeeping* and *The Saturday Evening Post*.

Brett, Harold (b. 1882). Born in Middleboro, Massachusetts, he studied at the Museum of Fine Arts in Boston, ASL and as a pupil of Howard Pyle. He had a studio in Wilmington, Delaware where he worked for nine years until he moved to New York. His reputation was established as a book illustrator, his artwork often appearing in *Houghton and Company* publications. In later life, he devoted himself to the art of portraiture.

Briggs, Austin (1909–1973). Born in Humboldt, Minnesota, he studied at the Wicker Art School and briefly at Detroit City College. At age 16, he went to work in a studio doing Rickenbaker Auto advertisements, as well as local editorial work for the *Dearborn Independent*. Two years later he came to New York and soon after

appeared in *Collier's*. During the Depression he was able to do some movie posters for Fox Studios and attend the ASL. From the 1940's on, his work drew acclaim in *The Saturday Evening Post, Redbook* and *Cosmopolitan*. A Gold Medal winner in the S of I exhibitions, he is a member of their Hall of Fame. A constant innovator, he was always ahead of his imitators. Having lived most of his life in Connecticut, he moved to Paris, where he died.

Brodie, Howard (b. 1916). Born in Oakland, California, he studied at the California School of Fine Arts. He earned fame doing reportage during World War II in which, as an enlisted man, he worked for *Yank* magazine. His drawings of the Pacific battles were most striking, as were his later sketches in Korea and Vietnam. His work as a staff artist in San Francisco eventually led to a weekly feature in the Associated Press with assignments such as the Watergate hearings.

Brooks, Lou (b. 1944). Born in Abington, Pennsylvania, he has won awards from ADCs of New York and Philadelphia and the AIGA. He illustrates for *Oui, Viva, National Lampoon* and *Scholastic's Bananas*, for whom he illustrated the poster *The World's Gone Bananas* in 1977.

Brown, Arthur William (1881–1966). Born in Hamilton, Ontario, he studied at the ASL for three years with F. V. DuMond and Walter A. Clark. He received his start at the *Hamilton Spectator*, which published his first illustration, *The Maine*, as a front page spread, and by 1903 his works were appearing in major magazines. His New York success led to membership in the S of I and he later served as its president. His work for *Redbook* and *Ladies' Home Journal* was well received and his serial of *Mr. Tutt* was published in *The Saturday Evening Post* for many years. He illustrated for the top writers of his era including F. Scott Fitzgerald, O. Henry and Booth Tarkington and he was known to call on the most glamorous stars of the day to model for him. Elected a member of the Illustrators Hall of Fame, he spent most of his life in New York City where he died.

Brunner-Stroesser, Ruth (b. 1944). Born in Pittsburgh, she attended the Ivy School of Professional Art and has since had exhibitions and received awards in the Pittsburgh area, including the Pittsburgh ADC and the Humane Society. Her illustrations have appeared in *Fortune, Newsweek, Time, Sports Illustrated* and local Pittsburgh magazines, as well as in exhibitions at the Carnegie Museum and Three Rivers Art Festival.

Bull, Charles Livingston (1874–1932). Born in New York State, he studied at the Philadelphia Art School and later worked as a taxidermist for the National Museum in Washington, DC. He is well known for his animal illustrations, and his book, *Under the Roof of the Jungle*, is a collection of stories and drawings based on his trip to Guiana. He worked for the US Biological Survey banding birds and drawing preservation posters for publicity, concerning himself chiefly with the plight of the American eagle.

Bundy, Gilbert (1911–1955). Born in Centralia, Illinois, he spent his childhood in Oklahoma and Kansas. As a teenager he worked in an engraving house in Kansas City before coming to New York in 1929, where his first cartoons appeared in *Life* and *Judge*. Editorial illustrations for *Esquire* in the 1930's led to advertising work for such clients as Munsingwear and Cluett Peabody. During World War II, he reported on the Pacific theater for King Features Syndicate.

Calle, Paul (b. 1928). Born in New York City, he studied at PI for four years. Following his first illustration for *Liberty Magazine* in 1947, he produced many campaigns for major advertising agencies. He has recorded the NASA space program beginning with the Mercury program and in 1975 he covered the Apollo-Soyuz training team. Assignments for commemorative United States postal stamps followed and his works are in the collections of the Phoenix Art Museum, NASA and the Northwest Indian Center in Spokane. A Hamilton King Award winner, he has also exhibited illustrations and won awards in the S of I Annual Exhibitions.

Calogero, Eugene D. (b. 1932). Born in New York City, he attended the School of Industrial Arts in 1950 and had his first piece published in 1951. He has since illustrated several posters, most recently a poster for the Smithsonian Institution. His works have received many awards from the AIGA, the ADC, Type Designers Club and the Society of Magazine and Publication Designers.

Calyo, Nicolino (1799–1884). Born in Naples, Italy, he studied at the Naples Academy before coming to America in the 1830's. Known for his landscapes, historical paintings and portraits, he painted the Great Fire of 1835 in New York City. From 1847 to 1852 he painted scenes from the Mexican War, including his famous panorama of the Connecticut River which was exhibited in Boston, New York City, Philadelphia and New Orleans.

Carlson, Jean (b. 1952). Born in Burlington, Vermont, she attended the University of Vermont and RISD. In 1975 she won third place in the S of I Annual Student Scholarship Competition and has won various awards at New England Art Shows. She is presently teaching art at South Burlington High School in Vermont.

Carruthers, Roy (b. 1938). Born in South Africa, he studied art there for two years at Port Elizabeth Technical College. Beginning his career in London with an illustration for *Woman's Mirror* in 1966, he has since had illustrations published in *Redbook, Ladies' Home Journal, New York, Playboy* and *Oui.* His works are in the collections of the Ponce Museum and the Galeria de las Americas in Puerto Rico.

Carter, Pruett A. (1891–1955). Born in Lexington, Missouri, he was reared on an Indian reservation until his family moved to California where he attended the Los Angeles Art School. His first job was with the *New York American* and he later worked at the *Atlanta Georgian.* Moving closer to his chosen field, he became art editor for *Good Housekeeping* where he gave himself his first magazine illustration assignment. He moved to California in 1930, mailing his finished pieces to such New York publications as *Woman's Home Companion, Ladies' Home Journal* and *McCall's.* His tasteful illustrations showed his particular understanding of women, whom he portrayed as gentle and elegant without pretension. Greatly respected by his students, he taught at the GCSA in New York and the Chouinard Art Institute in Los Angeles.

Carugati, Eraldo (b. 1921). Born in Milan, he was educated at the Scuola Superiore D'arti Applicate for four years and began his career in Italy in 1948, producing many posters until 1970. He illustrated for the *Enciclopedia dei Ragazzi* in 1965 and in the United States has done work for *Playboy, Oui, Skeptic* and *Psychology Today.* His works are in the collection of the Oklahoma Historical Society.

Cary, William de la Montagne (1840–1922). Born in Rockland Lake, New York, he traveled West at age 20 to sketch the forts along the upper Missouri River. Back East he painted, from memory, Western subjects for *Frank Leslie's Illustrated Newspaper, Harper's Weekly* and *Scribner's* for over 30 years. Returning West in 1874, he accompanied the United States government's survey team and in 1894 he illustrated the account of his earlier Western trips, as written by one of his companions.

Cason, Merrill (b. 1929). Born in Marshall, Texas, he worked for 15 years doing display, television, graphic

design and illustration in Oklahoma City. Presently a free-lance illustrator in New York, he has taught in a number of schools and has had One-Man Shows in Texas, Oklahoma and Missouri. His artwork has been selected to hang in several S of I Annual Exhibitions.

Castaigne, J. André. Born in France, he studied art under Angoulême, a painter. In 1888 he became a member of the Artists of France and from 1885 until 1896 he painted portraits of famous people, an example of which is his piece entitled *Alexander le Grand à Memphis.* In 1899 he was decorated with the Légion d' honneur. A popular book illustrator, he collaborated with W. T. Smedley and Arson Lowell to illustrate the *Scribner* edition, *Love in Old Clothes.*

Catherwood, Frederick (1799–1854). Born in London, he worked as an apprentice architect from 1815 to 1820. He exhibited at the Royal Academy in London in 1820 and then began a life of travel throughout the world painting wonderful panoramas of the countryside. He toured Italy, Greece, Central America, Egypt, British Guiana, California and Mexico. He is well known for his illustrations of the Maya ruins of the Yucatan and Guatemala. He died in the sinking ship *Arctic* en route to America.

Catlin, George (1796–1872). Born in Wilkes-Barre, Pennsylvania, he studied law and set up shop as a miniaturist in Philadelphia in 1820. In 1830 he moved West and began his portrayal of the American Indians and their customs, for which he is best known. After eight years in the West, he left for Europe, where he spent 30 years, and then returned to the United States and died in Jersey City. The New-York Historical Society Museum owns an abundance of his Indian drawings.

Chambers, William (b. 1940). Born in Chicago, he graduated from the American Academy of Art in 1961 and later attended Northeastern Illinois University. His art career began in 1965 with an educational book illustration; he has since been a frequent contributor to *Ballantine Books* and *Playboy Press.* He has produced several posters and his illustrations have been accepted for the S of I Annual Exhibitions and the AG shows of Chicago.

Chapman, Charles Shepard (1879-1962). Born in Middletown, New York, he studied with Walter Appleton Clark at the ASL and later with William Merritt Chase. He earned a reputation as a superb watercolorist. He was a member of the Salmagundi Club and the NAD. His works are in the collection of the Metropolitan Museum.

Chapman, Frederick Trench (b. 1887). Born in Windsor, California, he attended the ASL, studied under George Bridgman and learned the linoleum cut process from Vojtech Preissig. He began his career working for New York department stores as well as for some newspapers. Later his line drawings appeared in *Collier's, Redbook* and *Everybody's.* He received several traveling assignments, including a London trip for *Condé Nast's Vogue* in the 1920's. His artwork is in the Smithsonian Institution and his dioramas were displayed at the West Point Museum. A member of the S of I, he lived much of his life in New Jersey.

Charmatz, William (b. 1925). Born in New York City, he attended the High School of Industrial Art with Henry Wolf and Helmut Krone. Beginning his career in 1946 with pen and ink illustrations for *Harper's Bazaar,* he has since worked for several magazines and illustrated many books, including *The Cat's Whiskers, The Little Duster, Endeerments* and *Horse Bus Stop.*

Chen, Anthony (b. 1929). Born in Kingston, Jamaica, he attended ACD and graduated cum laude from PI in 1955, having studied under Richard Lindner and Dong Kingman. In 1957 he first illustrated for *My Baby Magazine*

and began children's book illustration in 1966 with *Too Many Crackers* for Lothrop, Lee and Shepard. He has since illustrated books for *Reader's Digest* and *Better Homes and Gardens* as well as others. He has had numerous One-Man Shows in New York, Washington, Richmond and at the Delaware Museum. He was an instructor at Nassau Community College in 1974.

Chermayeff, Ivan (b. 1932). Born in London, England, he studied at Harvard University, the Institute of Design in Chicago and graduated with a BFA from Yale University, School of Art and Architecture. His many clients have included IBM, Philip Morris USA, Westinghouse Electric Corporation and others. Currently he serves as vice-president of Yale Art Association and is a member of the Yale Council Committee on Art and Architecture, Industrial Designers Society of America, Architectural League of New York and the Alliance Graphique Internationale. He is author of *Observations on American Architecture* published by *The Viking Press* in 1972.

Christy, Howard Chandler (1873–1952). Born in Ohio, he came to New York at age 16 where he studied at the ASL and for two years under William Merritt Chase. He accompanied Theodore Roosevelt's troops to Cuba and reported on the Spanish-American War for *Scribner's* and *Leslie's* which brought him early acclaim. His illustrations led to the famous Christy Girl which appeared in *McClure's* and other magazines. A varied career led him to paint portraits of such famous people as President and Mrs. Coolidge, Amelia Earhart, Will Rogers, Mrs. William Randolph Hearst and Crown Prince Humbert of Italy. He produced many large murals, including one at his beloved Hotel Des Artistes in New York where he lived for 30 years. His masterpiece remains the *Signing of the Constitution,* a 20½ x 30½ canvas, which now hangs in the Rotunda of the United States Capitol. He died in New York City, having completed his last mural some ten years earlier for the Ohio State Capitol.

Church, Frederick Stuart (1842–1924). Born in Grand Rapids, Michigan, he studied drawing and painting under Walter Shirlaw and L. M. Wilmarth in New York City. He began working for *Harper's Weekly* in the 1850's, making animal studies and endowing them with humorous characteristics. In 1875 he helped found the ASL and his works were exhibited at the Society of American Artists and the NAD. As an illustrator he was known for his whimsical humor, technical proficiency and his refined sense of tone. He is represented in the Metropolitan Museum of Art, City Art Museum in St. Louis and the National Gallery in Washington.

Chwast, Seymour (b. 1931). Born in New York City, he attended Cooper Union where he studied under Leon Friend with classmates Milton Glaser, Jay Maisel and Edward Sorel. His first published illustration was for *Seventeen* magazine in 1947 and he has received numerous awards from the ADC, AIGA and Cooper Union. His work has been shown at the Louvre in Paris, Lincoln Center, Brooklyn Museum, Art Museum of Amsterdam and throughout Italy. He has illustrated many children's books, magazines and posters and his work is owned by the Greengrass Gallery in New York and the Museum of Modern Art.

Ciardiello, Joseph G. (b. 1953). Born in Staten Island, he graduated from PSD in 1974, having illustrated for the Parsons Catalogue while still a student. He has illustrated books, including *The Great Houdini* and *Buffalo Bill,* as well as major magazines. He won a National Parks Purchase Prize in 1974 and his work is part of the collection of Mauro Graphics in Staten Island.

Clark, Matt (b. 1903). Born in Coshocton, Ohio, he was educated at the National Academy Art School in New York. *College Humor* published his first illustration in 1929 which led to a career with *The Saturday Evening Post* and other major magazines of the time. He was well known for his watercolor and pen and ink drawings of the early West, with particular attention to horses and cowboys.

Clarke, René (b.1886). Born in Eustes, Florida, he started as a staff artist for Calkins and Holden in 1912, later to become its President and Vice Chairman of the Board. He contributed to *Woman's Home Companion, McCall's* and *Collier's* in addition to several *Limited Editions* volumes. A member of the ADC, AWS and the Philadelphia Watercolor Club, he received a Book Gold Medal from Harvard and four ADC Gold Medals.

Clark, Walter Appleton (1876–1906). Born in Worcester, Massachusetts, he studied at Worcester Tech for two years and later left to train at the Massachusetts Nautical Training School. He came to New York in late 1894 to study at the ASL under William Merritt Chase. His brief career brought him medals at the Paris Fair of 1900 and the Pan American Fair. He is best known for his work at *Scribner's*, including Percy MacKaye's *Canterbury Tales*.

Clifford, Judy Dean (b. 1946). Born in Orange, California, she attended the University of Washington in Seattle and studied art at the Academy of Art in San Francisco for four years. Her career began with a series for the Simpson Lee Paper Co. and she has since won awards at the Western ADC Show and exhibited in the S of I Annual Exhibitions in New York and Los Angeles. She has worked for magazines and produced posters for Levi's and the San Francisco Ballet.

Clymer, John (b. 1907). Born in Ellensburg, Washington, he studied in Vancouver and Port Hope, Canada, as well as in Wilmington and New York. He illustrated several Chrysler advertisements before painting a cover for *The Saturday Evening Post* in 1947. In addition to illustrations in many major magazines, he has had special assignments for a number of Canadian publications and the Marine Corps.

Coale, Griffith B. (1890–1950). Born in Baltimore, he studied art in both Paris and Munich. His career as a muralist and portrait artist was interrupted by World War II, during which time he founded the Navy's Combat Artists Corps and served as a Lieutenant Commander. His murals can be seen in public buildings in New York City and his portraits of famous Americans are in the collections of Johns Hopkins University and the Maryland Historical Society.

Cober, Alan E. (b. 1935). Born in New York City, he began law studies at the University of Vermont until he returned to New York to attend SVA. His reputation as a top line and half-tone artist grew as his work appeared in books and magazines. The pen and ink drawings from his book *The Forgotten Society,* published by *Dover Press,* have been exhibited in galleries and museums nationwide. Named Artist of the Year in 1965 by the AG, he has received five Gold Medals, four Awards of Excellence and the Hamilton King Award from the S of I as well as two Gold Medals from the ADC. In addition, *The New York Times* has twice placed his children's books on their 10-Best list. President of the Illustrators Workshop, he collects folk art.

CoConis, Constantinos (Ted) (b. 1937). Born in Chicago, he spent a year at the American Academy of Art and three months at the AIC, before the appearance of his first illustration in *Sunset* in 1954. His distinctive style and intricate technique have earned him a reputation resulting in the publication of his work by almost every major magazine, including *Redbook, Cosmopolitan, Playboy* and *Time,* as well as for many publishers such as *Fawcett, The Viking Press* and *Random House.* Among his advertising assignments are movie campaigns and record covers. An award winner in the S of I Annual Exhibitions, he owns

and drives formula race cars.

Coll, Joseph Clement (1881–1921). Considered by many a master in the use of pen and ink, he started his career as a newspaper sketch-artist and later illustrated many mystery stories in which his skill to depict imaginative horror was realized. He worked for *Associated Sunday Magazine, Collier's* and *Everybody's,* having been greatly influenced by the artist Vierge. He died at the early age of 40, at a time when his talent was in great demand.

Collier, John (b. 1948). Born in Dallas, Texas, he attended Central College in Kansas for two years. He began illustrating Christmas cards in 1967. His career has blossomed in New York as illustrations for *Redbook* and *McCall's* have won him Gold Medals and an Award of Excellence at the Annual Exhibitions of the S of I. He has had exhibitions in Oklahoma City, Little Rock, Tulsa and New York.

Conacher, John C. (1876–1947). Though classically trained, he developed a style, full of comic detail, which appeared in his many pen and ink drawings for magazines in the early 1900's. *Everybody's* and *Judge* published his illustrations and his work for the Seaboard National Bank advertisements was selected for the ADC Annuals of Advertising Art.

Condak, Clifford Ara (b. 1930). Born in Haverhill, Massachusetts, he attended the Institute of Applied Arts and Sciences and the New School for Social Research in New York City. His first illustration, a tempera, appeared in *Therapeutic Notes,* a Parke, Davis and Company publication, in 1954. Since then his pieces have appeared in publications such as *Seventeen, Nugget, Playboy* and *Sports Illustrated.* His artwork and illustrations have been shown at the Museum of Modern Art in New York, Gallery of Modern Art in Washington, DC and San Francisco Museum of Modern Art.

Content, Dan (b. 1902). He received training at PI and the ASL. A pupil of Dean Cornwell, his illustrations for various adventure stories reflected Cornwell's teachings. His editorial work appeared in *Cosmopolitan, Good Housekeeping, Liberty, Ladies' Home Journal, Collier's* and *McCall's* as early as 1923. He taught at the Workshop School of Art in the 1940's.

Cooke, George (1793–1849). Born in St. Mary's County, Maryland, he started out in the grocery and china trade. In 1818, out of business, he went West and began painting portraits professionally, which was the start of his career as a historical and landscape artist. Daniel Pratt, a patron, built a gallery to display his work in Alabama. He was later represented at the Boston Athenaeum, the National Academy, Pennsylvania Academy and the Apollo Gallery.

Cooley, Gary (b. 1947). Born in Jackson, Michigan, he studied for four years at the Society of Arts and Crafts. Since 1969, when he entered the field of illustration doing black and white art for Detroit newspapers, his work has appeared in books, magazines and posters. The GAG of Detroit has awarded him three Gold Medals and he received a First Honor from the 1973 Ace Awards in Pittsburgh.

Cooper, Mario Ruben (b. 1905). Born in Mexico City, he was raised in Los Angeles and attended Otis Art Institute, Chouinard Art Institute and Columbia University in New York. His watercolors have earned him Gold Medals from the AWS of which he was at one time President. As an editorial artist his work has been seen in *Collier's* as well as *Woman's Home Companion, American* and *Cosmopolitan.* As an instructor, he has passed down the teachings of Harvey Dunn and Pruett Carter at both the ASL and GCSA. In addition to his extensive career in illustration, he is also a

renowned sculptor and a member of the National Sculpture Society.

Corcos, Lucille (1908-1973). Born in New York City, she attended the ASL. Her first assignments came in 1929 from *Condé Nast's Vanity Fair.* She became well known for her children's book illustrations, including *Grimm's Fairy Tales,* published by *Limited Editions Club,* and *Ungskah and Oyaylee.* Her work is owned by the Whitney Museum and Museum of Tel Aviv.

Cornwell, Dean (1892–1960). He began his training at the AIC before working for Chicago newspapers and later studying in Leonia, New Jersey under Harvey Dunn. *The Saturday Evening Post* published his first illustration in 1924, after he had been working at *Cosmopolitan* for six years. Every major magazine featured his very popular advertising and editorial work. Exquisite charcoal sketches were the preliminary base for his full-bodied paintings that were to inspire many later illustrators. As a result of his training in England under Frank Brangwyn, he also executed a number of murals, the most important of which are hanging in the Los Angeles Library and Lincoln Memorial in California. He devoted himself to his profession both as an instructor at the ASL and as President of the S of I from 1922 to 1926.

Cox, Kenyon (1856–1919). A student of Gerome and Carolus-Duran in Paris, he produced several drawings for the *Century* before returning to the US. His works were exhibited at the Chicago World's Fair of 1893. An author and critic as well as an artist, he often accompanied his works with poetry. Though mostly a pen artist, he also used photogravure for his book work, most notably Rossetti's *Blessed Damozel* in 1886.

Cox, Palmer (1840–1924). Born in Granby, Canada, he worked as a ship's carpenter and railroader in San Francisco in the early part of his life. He was given his first illustration job with a weekly comic paper called *Wild Oats,* but it was not until he was 40 that he began illustrating professionally for *St. Nicholas Magazine.* This led to his creation of the captivating little people known as *Brownies,* which were to be enjoyed throughout many generations. He wrote thirteen *Brownie* books of which over a million copies were sold during his lifetime.

Craft, Kinuko Yamabe (b. 1940). Born in Japan, she spent four years at the Kanazawa Municipal College of Fine Arts and one and a half years at the AIC. The winner of various awards and selected to show her work in S of I Annual Exhibitions, she has had assignments from *Psychology Today,* Science Research Associates and *Scott, Foresman and Company.* She currently lives and works in Chicago.

Craig, Frank (1874–1918). Having decided at an early age to pursue a career in art, he studied at Lambeth School of Art and the Royal Academy. He soon became a regular contributor to *The Graphic* and his black and white sketches were also seen in *Harper's* and *Nash's Magazine.* Having lived most of his life in London, he moved in 1916 to the warmer climate of Portugal where he died two years later. His portraits and paintings were quite popular in their day and are in the Tate and Durban Art Galleries and in galleries in France, Australia and New Zealand.

Crandell, Bradshaw (1896–1966). Born in Glens Falls, New York, he was educated at Wesleyan University and the AIC. In 1921 his first cover appeared on *Judge,* marking the beginning of his career which concentrated on cover design. His art graced the front of such magazines as *Collier's, Redbook, American, Ladies' Home Journal* and *The Saturday Evening Post.* For 12 years in the 1930's and 1940's he worked on *Cosmopolitan* covers doing a series of pastels of beautiful women, often using Hollywood stars for models. He was a member of the Dutch Treat Club, the Artists and Writers Association and the S of I.

Crawford, Will (1869–1944). Born in Washington, DC, he was a self-taught artist who worked on staff for the *Newark Daily Advertiser* and the *Sunday Call* while still in his teens. He illustrated for the *New York World* before establishing a studio with John Marquand and Albert Levering, later to be shared by Charles M. Russell. He was a successful free-lancer for *Life, Munseys, Puck* and *Cosmopolitan,* after which he worked in Hollywood as an expert on Indian costumes.

Crosby, Percy (1891–1964). He is best known for his comic strip *Skippy,* which he created, wrote and illustrated and which began in May, 1931. He also produced many sports drawings which led to his first exhibition in 1928 at the Anderson Galleries in New York. His work, executed almost exclusively in black and white line, hangs in galleries in Paris, Rome and Luxembourg. Married twice, he died in New York City.

Crumb, R. (b. 1945). Born in the eastern United States. His interest in comic art began at the age of eight when he wrote, drew and sold his own comic books. A self-taught artist, he has had his work published in many books and magazines. His book *Fritz the Cat* was the basis for the popular animated movie and his *Mr. Natural* appeared weekly in the *Village Voice.* Presently living in California, he works for such comic book publishers as *Print Mint* and *Last Gasp.*

Cruz, Raymond (b. 1933). Born in New York City, he studied art for five years at Cooper Union and PI. His first illustration was published in 1964 for the New York Graphic Society. Besides working for *Seventeen* and *McCall's,* he has illustrated several books for *Atheneum Press* and *Four Winds Press.* His works have been exhibited at the Museum of Contemporary Crafts in Houston and the S of I Annual Exhibitions.

Csakany, Gabriel S. (b. 1938). Born in Budapest, Hungary, he emigrated to Canada in 1956, attended the Toronto College of Art and studied under local professionals as an apprentice. He has had several magazine assignments in the United States and in Canada. As a designer and illustrator, he has won awards in Canada, the United States and Germany.

Cunningham, Robert Morris (b. 1924). Born in Herington, Kansas, he attended the University of Kansas, KCAI and ASL. His first illustration was done for American Cyanamid Company in the 1960's. The recipient of Gold Medals in 1966 and 1967 from the S of I, he has shown his paintings at the Brooklyn Museum and the Smithsonian Institution in Washington, DC.

Czermanski, Zolzislaw (1900–1970). Born in Krakow, Poland, he became a pupil of the famous Polish caricaturist Kazimierz Sichulski and later had his first exhibit, *Caricatures of Personalities of the Arts,* held in the Tatra mountains. He moved to Paris to study art with Fernand Léger and there began his career as a painter of everyday Parisian life. In 1931 he was invited to the United States to work for the newly founded magazine *Fortune.* His paintings have appeared in Warsaw, Paris, London, Geneva, Vienna, New York, Washington and Philadelphia.

Dallison, Ken (b. 1933). Born in Hounslow, Middlesex, England, he attended the Twickenham School of Art for two years. He began his career in 1956 with *Liberty* in Toronto, Canada. He lived in New York for many years and as a free-lance illustrator won several awards including a Gold Medal from the S of I. Presently he lives near Toronto with his wife and four children and is represented in the Ontario Gallery of Art.

D'Andrea, Bernard (b. 1923). Born in Buffalo, New York, he studied art at PI and the Brooklyn Art School. He worked in advertising firms before and after World War II and in the early 1950's he illustrated for *The Saturday Evening Post, Ladies' Home Journal, Boys' Life, Good Housekeeping* and *Seventeen.* A member of the S of I, he teaches art at PSD and PI. His wife, Lorraine Fox, was also an illustrator.

Darley, Felix Octavius Carr (1822–1888). Born in Philadelphia, the son of an English comic actor; his brother was also an artist. After the start of his career in 1842 in Philadelphia, he went on to illustrate many well known books for such authors as Tennyson, Poe, Hawthorne, Longfellow and Dickens. Best known as the illustrator of Washington Irving's *Rip Van Winkle* (1848), *The Legend of Sleepy Hollow* (1849) and *The Knickerbocker History of New York* (1850), he also designed booknote vignettes for *Toppan, Carpenter and Company.* He achieved acclaim and membership in the NAD in 1845.

Davidson, J. O. He worked for *the Century* and *Harper's Weekly* for many years while doing artwork for *St. Nicholas Magazine* and children's books. As an illustrator, he worked in tempera and was the artist most often chosen to paint ships and nautical scenes for *Battles and Leaders of the Civil War* published by *the Century.* A member of the Salmagundi Club, he was best known for his historical maritime scenes.

Davis, Floyd MacMillan (1896–1966). While still very young he began illustrating for small advertising firms. He is known for his depiction of southern people and he illustrated books by such famous authors as William Faulkner, Glenn Allan and Sigmar Byrd. During World War II, he was a correspondent-artist for the War Department and many of his paintings were reproduced in *Life* magazine. His war paintings are owned by the Pentagon and over the years he won several ADC Medals.

Davis, Jack (b. 1924). Born in Atlanta, he attended the University of Georgia and studied at the ASL. His first illustration was published in the Georgia Tech *Yellow Jacket,* a humor magazine. His distinctive caricatures have been seen in many TV film spots and movie posters for the major studios as well as in *Time, TV Guide, Audubon, Ladies' Home Journal* and *Life.*

Davis, Paul (b. 1938). Born in Cetrahoma, Oklahoma, son of a Methodist minister, he came to New York and studied with Robert Weaver, Tom Allen and George Tacherny at SVA. His first illustration was published in *Playboy* and he then joined Push Pin Studios with Milton Glaser and Seymour Chwast. In 1975 and 1976 the Paul Davis Exhibition was shown in Japan at a number of art museums. He has received more than 50 awards of distinctive merit for typography, design and illustration.

Davis, Theodore R. (1840–1894). Born in Boston, he moved to Brooklyn at age 15 and joined the staff of *Harper's Weekly* in 1861. As a special correspondent he traveled with the Union Army, during which time he was wounded twice. After the war he went on assignments for *Harper's* throughout the South and Far West. After 23 years with that magazine, he retired to Asbury Park in 1884. In his later years he became a historical consultant on the Civil War and free-lanced until his death.

Dawson, Diane (b. 1952). Born in Galveston, Texas, she attended Stephens College and RISD, studying under Tom Sgouros. She graduated from the SVA in 1975 and began her career that year with illustrations for *Ginn and Company.* She has illustrated several children's books and the cartoon strip *Burdseed* for *Scholastic's Bananas.*

Decker, Richard (b. 1907). A cartoonist and designer, he studied at the Philadelphia Museum School of Industrial Art. In 1939 he illustrated an *Evening Bulletin* series and was a regular contributor to *The New Yorker* and advertisers

in the Philadelphia area. He designed sets for seven major plays for Connecticut Playmakers, Inc.

Deigan, James Thomas (b. 1934). Born in Monongahela, Pennsylvania, he was educated at Temple University and Carnegie Institute of Technology. A resident of Pittsburgh for many years, he has been awarded prizes from the ADC there. He is married with two children.

DeMers, Joseph (b. 1910). Born in San Diego, California, he attended the Chouinard Art School and, as a fine artist, exhibited work at the Museum of Modern Art in 1933. After ten years as a production illustrator for Warner Brothers Studios, he became a successful book publisher in California. Ultimately, he moved to New York in the late 1940's to work at Cooper Studio. His free-lance work was seen in *The Saturday Evening Post, Ladies' Home Journal* and *McCall's.* Good business sense prompted him, Coby Whitmore and Joe Bowler to form a corporation through which they retained world rights for the many European reprints of their artwork. His paintings have been shown and are owned by many museums and galleries. A member of the S of I, he currently runs a gallery on Hilton Head Island in South Carolina.

Dewey, Kenneth Francis (b. 1940). Born in Brooklyn, New York, he studied under Robert Weaver and Phil Hays at the SVA. His first illustration was done for a magazine in Phoenix, Arizona in 1967. Three years later he wrote and illustrated a book entitled *Onyamarks.* His illustrations have been selected to appear in the S of I Annual Exhibitions of 1974, 1975 and 1976.

Diamond, Harry O. (b. 1913). Born in Los Angeles, he attended Los Angeles City College in 1932 and 1933 and Chouinard Art Institute in 1934 and 1935. He has received numerous awards as both illustrator and art director. His first published illustration was done for *Westways* magazine in Los Angeles in 1932 and he is presently the art director at Exxon Corporation. He is married and has three children.

Di Fiori, Lawrence. Based for some years in Philadelphia, he has illustrated for the *American Heritage* publications.

Dillon, Leo (b. 1933), **Dillon, Diane** (b. 1933). Born in the same year, Leo in New York and Diane in California, they studied together at PSD and SVA in New York under John Groth and Leo Leonni. As a team they have illustrated many children's books, including *The Hundred Penny Box,* 1974, *Why Mosquitoes Buzz in People's Ears,* 1975 and *Ashante to Zulu,* 1976. Their illustrations have appeared in *Ladies' Home Journal, The Saturday Evening Post* and others. Their work has been exhibited at Gallery 91 in Brooklyn, and they often travel to schools on the East Coast as guest speakers.

Dinnerstein, Harvey (b. 1928). Born in Brooklyn, New York, he attended Tyler Art School of Temple University for four years. His first illustration to be published was for a medical advertisement, followed by many assignments for advertising and editorial clients. He has illustrated several books, including *Tales of Sherlock Holmes, Remember the Day* and *At the North Wind.* Since 1946, when he won the Condé Nast Award, he has received numerous awards and his paintings are in the collections of major museums and universities throughout the United States.

Dohanos, Stevan (b. 1907). Born in Lorain, Ohio, he attended the Cleveland School of Art, after which he embarked on a long, successful career. His first assignment was a watercolor done for *McCall's* in 1934 and within four years he had won an Award for Distinctive Merit from the ADC of New York. From 1943 to 1959, his tightly rendered paintings, usually depicting everyday incidents in small town America, appeared on over 120 covers of *The Saturday Evening Post.* He has also designed

25 United States postage stamps and his artwork is owned by the Whitney Museum of Art in New York City. A founding faculty member of the FAS, he was elected to the S of I's Hall of Fame in 1971.

Doolittle, Amos (1754–1832). Born in Cheshire, Connecticut, he is known as one of the earliest American engravers of copper. Trained as a silversmith and jeweler, he taught himself the art of engraving. A series of four engravings of the Battles of Lexington and Concord, drawn by Ralph Earl and engraved and published· by Doolittle in 1775, are probably his best known works. His engravings included biblical stories, bookplates and portraits. His two sons, also engravers, carried on after his death in New Haven, Connecticut.

Dorne, Albert (1904–1965). Born in New York City, he learned his trade, after leaving school at an early age, by taking odd jobs in art studios and advertising agencies. He worked under Saul Tepper in New York while supporting himself as a clerk and a professional boxer. Starting inauspiciously with a sheet music cover illustration, he rose to the top of his profession, receiving the Horatio Alger Award for his achievement. His superb draftsmanship and strong compositions were seen in most major magazines in the 1930's and 1940's. He dedicated himself to the profession through his work as the President of the S of I, founding director of the FAS and co-founder of the *Code of Ethics and Fair Practices*. He received an honorary degree from Adelphi University and the First Gold Medal from the New York ADC for his distinguished career.

Doty, Roy (b. 1922). Born in Chicago, he received his art training at CCAD. After service with the US Army in World War II, during which time he worked with *Yank* and *Stars and Stripes,* he began his free-lance career. His illustrations have appeared in over 50 books and in advertising and editorial journals. Two of his long-standing clients are *Consumer Reports* and *Popular Science.* His work, ranging in style from decorative to cartoon, has also been seen in advertisements for Macy's, The Bowery Savings Bank and in the comic strip *Laugh-In* based on the TV series.

Dove, Leonard (d. 1964). A frequent contributor of cartoons and covers to *The New Yorker* in the 1940's and 1950's, he worked in pen and ink and watercolor.

Dunn, Harvey T. (1884–1952). Born in Manchester, South Dakota, he attended the AIC and was later invited to study with Howard Pyle. He adopted Pyle's teaching philosophy and in 1906 opened his own school with Charles Chapman in Leonia, New Jersey. His students included Dean Cornwell, Harold Von Schmidt, Amos Sewell and Mead Schaeffer. He later taught at the ASL and GCSA. His illustrations reflected his Midwestern cowboy background and he contributed a series of paintings about his heritage to the South Dakota Art Collection. A prolific illustrator, he worked for all the major magazines and was an official war artist during World War I. His works are in the collections of the Smithsonian Institution, International Art Gallery and the National Gallery in Washington.

Dupas, Jean-Théodore (1882–1964). Born in Bordeaux, he studied under Carolus-Duran and A. Besnard. A member of the Artists of France, he won the Prix de Rome in 1910 and, in 1941, received the Chevalier de la Légion d'honneur from the French Art Institution. Some of his best known works are *Les Pigeons Blanc, Le Jugement de Paris, La Paix* and *Les Antilopes.* When he came to the United States, he worked for Cheney Brothers Silk Company doing advertising and fashion illustration.

Eby, Kerr (1889–1946). Born in Japan, the son of Canadian Methodist missionaries, he came to America at age 18 to study at PI and the ASL. He produced a very popular volume entitled *War,* from his sketches of France in World War I, which was published by *Yale University Press* in 1936. He spent most of World War II in the Pacific where he produced many sketches. Other illustrations of his appeared in books and magazines such as *Life* and *the Century.* An extensive collection of his work is housed at the New York Public Library.

Edwards, William Alexander (b. 1924). Born in New York City, he studied at the Whitney Art School in Manor Haven under Alfred Freundeman. His first published illustration was a cover, entitled *Big Nickelodeon,* for *Bantam Books.* Since 1962, he has illustrated for magazines and books, the most notable being his covers for Herman Hesse's novels *Demian, Steppenwolf* and *Magister Ludi: The Glass Bead Game.* A prolific portrait artist, he has had work exhibited in galleries in Bridgeport and Waterbury, Connecticut.

Ehrhart, S. D. One of the top cartoonists for the dailies and weeklies in the later 1800's, his work was predominantly in pen and ink.

Einsel, Naiad (b. 1927). Born in Philadelphia, she graduated from PI in 1947, beginning her career the next year with an illustration for *Seventeen.* Since 1950, her work has appeared in many major magazines and in exhibitions at the S of I, ADC and Greengrass Gallery. Among her many poster assignments was the Westport Bicentennial Quilt in 1976 which she designed and which 33 Westport women hand-stitched, under the guidance of J. L. McCabe.

Einsel, Walter (b. 1926). Born in New York, he attended PSD and graduated from the ASL and the Brooklyn Museum School. In 1953, his first work was published in *The New York Times Magazine.* He has since illustrated many magazines and books. His pen and ink and three-dimensional artwork has been exhibited at the Museum of Contemporary Crafts, Montreal Expo and the Fairtree and Greengrass Galleries in New York.

Elia, Albert (b. 1941). Born in Beirut, Lebanon, he studied for five years at the Beaux Arts in Paris and PSD in New York. *Mademoiselle* published his first illustration in 1964 and he has since worked for *Harper's Bazaar, The New York Times* and *Seventeen.* Since 1970, he has been involved in film and photography.

Ely, Richard (b. 1928). Born in Rochester, New York, he attended the Kunst Akademie in Munich and studied under Jack Potter at SVA. He has worked for magazines and publishing companies since the 1950's and his works are in the collections of the New York Public Library, the private collection of Princess Grace of Monaco and the Museum of Afro-American Heritage in Philadelphia. His paintings of Elizabeth Rethberg and George Cehanovsky hang in the Founder's Hall of The Metropolitan Opera House in New York.

Endewelt, Jack (b. 1935). Born in New York City, he studied under Jack Potter and Daniel Schwartz at SVA where he has been an instructor of book illustration and drawing since 1968. He has illustrated educational books as well as many covers for *Dell* and *Avon,* and his work has often been included in the S of I Annual Exhibitions.

Engle, Nita (b. 1925). Born in Marquette, Michigan, she attended Northern Michigan University and the AIC. After nine years as an art director in a Chicago agency, she decided to start free-lancing. She began illustrating children's books at *Chicago Text* publishers and later for such magazines as *Reader's Digest* and *Playboy.* A member of the AWS, she has exhibited in Illinois, Michigan, California and England.

English, Mark F. (b. 1933). Born in Hubbard, Texas, he attended the University of Texas for one year before going to Los Angeles to study under John LaGatta at the ACD. His first job was in Detroit in an advertising studio and soon his editorial illustrations were appearing in *Redbook, Ladies' Home Journal* and *McCall's.* He has been awarded many medals from the S of I where he is currently a member. Named Artist of the Year in 1969 by the AG, he received awards from several ADCs in the United States He has been a contributor to the National Park Service Art Program and has exhibited at the Brandywine Gallery.

Enos, Randall (b. 1936). Born in New Bedford, Massachusetts, he studied at the Boston Museum for two years. He began illustrating for *Harper's* and has since worked for many other major magazines. He illustrated the children's book *It's Not Fair* in 1976 as well as other books for *Simon and Schuster* and *Harper & Row.* He has done a considerable amount of film animation for NBC as well as for other companies, winning an award at the Cannes Film Festival in France.

Erickson, Carl O. A. (1891–1958). Born in Joliet, Illinois, he studied for two years at the Chicago Academy of Arts and began his career working for department stores in Chicago (Marshall Field and Lord and Thomas) as well as for advertisers. Arriving in New York City in 1914, he continued doing advertising illustration until 1920 when he began a very successful career as a fashion artist. Shortly thereafter he moved to Paris where for 20 years he reigned supreme in the fashion field. His elegant illustrations, often the final draft of 20 or more preliminary sketches, first appeared in *Vogue* in 1923. He returned to America in 1940, after the Nazi takeover of France, to continue his work for *Condé Nast.*

Everett, Walter H. Born in New Jersey, he traveled by bicycle to Delaware to attend Howard Pyle's composition class. He worked his way through the School of Industrial Arts in Philadelphia‚ where he later taught for many years. His paintings were distinguished by their highly stylized, posterlike quality, composed of flat shapes that were delineated by color and value. Though his work was usually printed in black and white, the pieces that did appear in color, particularly in *Ladies' Home Journal,* showed the full brilliance of his illustration.

Falls, Charles Buckles (1874–1960). Born in Fort Wayne, Indiana, he worked at an early age on the *Chicago Tribune.* His career as a book illustrator and author began in 1923 with his *ABC Book.* He later worked extensively for *Viking, Grosset* and *World Books,* for whom he illustrated Robert Louis Stevenson's *Kidnapped* and *Treasure Island.* During his life he produced many different forms of art, including murals, posters, woodcuts and set designs. While on a trip to Haiti in 1945, he filled many notebooks with sketches, which later appeared as book illustrations.

Falter, John Philip (b. 1910). Born in Plattsmouth, Nebraska, he studied at the Kansas City Art Institute and in New York at the ASL. Beginning his career in 1929 at *Youth Magazine,* he has since illustrated for many major magazines and book publishers, including *Macmillan* and *Reader's Digest.* He served in the Navy in World War II as a special artist, producing some 180 posters. A member of the Player's Club, the Philadelphia Sketch Club and S of I, he was elected to the latter's Hall of Fame in 1976.

Fangel, Maud Tousey. Born in Boston, she attended the Massachusetts Normal Art School, Cooper Union and ASL. Her career was highlighted by her pastel drawings of babies, which appeared in magazines such as *Ladies' Home Journal, McCall's* and *Woman's Home Companion.* Her advertising clientele, which included Cream of Wheat, Swift and Co. and Squibb, all called on her for baby scenes. She worked for many years as a cover designer for magazines and produced many portraits.

Fasolino, Teresa (b. 1946). Born in Port Chester, New York, she attended the SVA where she studied under Robert Weaver. She also attended PI and the ASL. Her career began at *Ingenue* and she has worked for *Travel and Leisure, Playboy, Redbook* and *The New York Times*.

Fawcett, Robert (1903–1967). Born in London, he moved to Canada as a child and in 1924, after studying at the Slade School of Art, London, began his career in New York. He went on to produce illustrations for magazines and advertising clients, as well as to paint murals for the Commonwealth Institute and to write a book on the art of drawing, demonstrating his superb draftsmanship and mastery of composition. His intricate, atmospheric illustrations were published in *Look, · Collier's* and *The Saturday Evening Post,* appearing in the latter for the first time in 1945. A founding faculty member of the FAS, he was President of the Westport Artists and later elected to the S of I Hall of Fame.

Feind, Anna Nordstrom. Her paintings of pretty girls for *The Saturday Evening Post* are her best known works. She also produced several posters during World War I.

Fellows, Lawrence (1885–1964). Born in Ardmore, Pennsylvania, he attended the Philadelphia Academy of Fine Arts, followed by studies in England and France. Upon his return he did many humorous drawings for *Judge* and *Life*. His tasteful line drawings, utilizing large areas of white space, were suited to fashion illustration and appeared often in *Vanity Fair, Apparel Arts* and *Esquire*. He was best known for his Kelly-Springfield Tire advertisements in the 1920's.

Fink, Samuel (b. 1916). Born in New York City, he studied at the NAD and ASL in the mid-1930's. His first work appeared in *The New York Times* in 1938. He has spent most of his career at Young and Rubicam as an art director and is author and illustrator of the book *56 Who Signed* for E. P. Dutton. He is represented in the collection of the Brooklyn Museum.

Fischer, Anton Otto (1882–1962). Orphaned in Munich, Germany, he spent eight years sailing on different vessels as a seaman before going to study at the Académie Julien in Paris under Jean Paul Laurens. His first illustration was done for *Harper's Weekly* which led to over 40 years of illustrating for *The Saturday Evening Post, Everybody's, Life* and *Scribner's*. He was best known for his marine paintings and in 1947 he wrote and illustrated his own book on his early sailing years, entitled *Fo'cs'le Days,* published by *Scribner's*.

Fisher, Harrison (1875–1934). His formal art training began in San Francisco at the Mark Hopkins Institute of Art. At an early age he began to make sketches for *The San Francisco Call* and *The Examiner*. Upon his arrival in New York, he was hired by *Puck* as a staff artist and his talent for drawing women was established. His Fisher Body Girl was a trademark for years and led to an exclusive contract with *Cosmopolitan*. Later in life he concentrated solely on portraits.

Fisher, Leonard Everett (b. 1924). Born in New York, he attended Yale University and received a Pulitzer Prize for Painting in 1950. His illustrations for over 200 children's books have earned him many awards. The designer of 10 US postage stamps, he has produced a poster series of the bicentennial and of great composers in 1976. Many museums have exhibited his works, which are also in the collections of the LC, NAD, New Britain Museum of American Art and several universities. He has been on the faculty of the Paier School and Dean of the Whitney Art School.

Flagg, James Montgomery (1877–1960). Born in Pelham Manor, New York, he sold his first illustration to *Life* at age 14, beginning a 20-year association with the magazine. Trained at the ASL, he published his first book, *Yankee Girls Abroad,* in 1898. After extensive travel, he settled in 1904 in New York where his name became a household word, with his work regularly appearing in major periodicals and popular books. His great admiration for beautiful women led to the creation of the Flagg Girls, his ideal. A member of many prestigious clubs, he drew and painted famous entertainers, the most noted being his close friend, John Barrymore. His appointment as State Military Artist in 1917 resulted in the production of 46 posters, the best known being his *I Want You* illustration which was done for a cover of *Leslie's Weekly*. In addition to his illustration, he found time to write a weekly column, books and short films. A constant traveler, he documented his trips to Hollywood in the volume of drawings and comments entitled *Celebrities* in 1951. After a life of great productivity and zest, he died in virtual obscurity.

Flanagan, John Richard (1895–1964). Born in Sydney, Australia, he was an apprentice to a lithographer while studying art. He came to the United States and worked on *Everyweek* magazine, illustrating Chinese stories, soon establishing himself as an authority on the Orient. His illustrations also appeared in *Bluebook* and *Collier's*. Working almost exclusively in pen and ink, both in color and black and white, he later decided to design stained glass windows. He served as an instructor at New York Academy of Arts for many years.

Foeller, J., Jr. A pen and ink and watercolor artist with a whimsical approach to satire. His works are in the collection of Mrs. Thomas Wilcox.

Fogarty, Thomas (1873–1938). Born in New York City, he studied at ASL under Mowbray and Beckwith. His professional work, in pen and ink or wash and crayon, appeared in major magazines of the day and in several books which he illustrated, including *The Making of an American, On Fortune's Road* and the David Grayson books. His teaching career at the ASL lasted from 1903 to 1922 and among his students were Walter Biggs, McClelland Barclay and Norman Rockwell. His works are part of the collections at the Metropolitan Museum of Art and the Brooklyn Museum.

Forbes, Bart John (b. 1939). Born in Altus, Oklahoma, he studied under John LaGatta at the ACD and also attended the University of North Carolina. He has received 34 Certificates of Merit from the S of I Annual Exhibitions. His first illustration was done for Bell Helicopter in Dallas, Texas in 1965. Periodicals such as *McCall's, TV Guide, Saturday Review, Time, Redbook, Penthouse* and *Money* have published his illustrations.

Forbes, Edwin (1839–1895). Born in New York City, he studied under painter Arthur F. Tait in 1859. *Frank Leslie's Illustrated Newspaper* hired him from 1861 to 1865 as a staff artist and after leaving *Leslie's* he spent the rest of his life doing sketches for etchings and book illustrations on the Civil War. Best known for his historical paintings and etchings, he published *Life Studies in the Great Army* in 1876 and *Thirty Years After: An Artist's Story of the Great War* in 1890. He died in Brooklyn, New York.

Fox, Lorraine (1922–1976). Born in Brooklyn, New York, she published her first illustration, a gouache, in *Better Homes and Gardens* in 1951. She went to PI and the Brooklyn Museum Art School where she studied under Will Burtin and Reuben Tam. She was a lecturer and teacher at PSD in New York City and a faculty member at the FAS. She had numerous illustrations published in most of the well known magazines and won Gold Medals from the S of I and the Philadelphia ADC.

François, André (b. 1915). Born in Timisoara, Rumania, he studied at the Beaux Arts in Budapest and later at the school of A.M. Cassandre in France. Since 1945 his illustrations have appeared in *The New Yorker, Punch, Graphis, Holiday, Fortune* and *Vogue* as well as in numerous books. His artwork has hung in exhibitions in New York and throughout Europe.

Frasconi, Antonio (b. 1919). Born in Montevideo, Uruguay, he held his first exhibition of woodcuts and monotypes in Montevideo in 1944. He was awarded scholarships from the ASL, National Institute of Arts and Letters and Connecticut Commission of the Arts. In 1956 he received the top prize for book illustration from the *Limited Editions Club* in New York. A traveling exhibit of his woodcuts has been circulated by the Missouri State Council of the Arts. Since 1973 he has been an Adjunct Associate Professor of Visual Arts at the SUNY at Purchase.

Fraser, Malcolm (1869–1949). Born in Montreal, he studied at the ASL under Kenyon Cox and in Paris at the Beaux Arts and Académie Julien. He spent most of his career in New York illustrating for magazines such as *the Century, St. Nicholas* and *Ladies' Home Journal*. During World War I, he served with the artists in the AEF and several of his paintings are housed at the Ormond War Memorial Art Gallery in Florida. He was a member of the Salmagundi Club.

Freshman, Shelley A. (b. 1950). Born in New York City, she attended PI for four years, studying under David Byrd and Alvin Hollingsworth. She began her career with a poster for the off-Broadway production *Geese* and illustrated the book *Cricket* for *Bobbs-Merrill* in 1975. Her works have appeared in the S of I 1975 and 1976 Annual Exhibitions.

Friedman, Marvin (b. 1930). Born in Chester, Pennsylvania, he attended the School of Art at the Philadelphia Museum. He studied under Henry C. Pitz, Albert Gold and Benjamin Eisenstat and has illustrated books such as *Chewing Gum* published by *Prentice-Hall* in 1976, *Pinch* by the *Atlantic Monthly Press* in 1976 and *Can Do Missy* by *Follet* in 1975. He has worked for all the major magazines, and his illustrations have been shown at the Philadelphia Museum of Art, Academy of Fine Art in Philadelphia, Pittsburgh Museum and Brandywine Museum in Delaware.

Frost, Arthur Burdett (1851–1928). Born in Philadelphia, he was a wood engraver and lithographer as a teenager. He trained briefly at the PAFA under Thomas Eakins, and his earliest pictures were of sporting subjects, especially hunting and fishing. The anthologies of his later drawings, depicting rural America, were most favorably received. Joining the staff at *Harper's* in 1876, he later went to the *New York Daily Graphic* where he was a cartoonist for 20 years. Loved by many Americans for his warm and humorous portrayal of animals and people in colloquial settings, he produced an enormous amount of pen and ink drawings during his lifetime. Among his best known books are the *Uncle Remus* editions by Joel Chandler Harris, published by D. Appleton and *McClure, Philips*. He died in Pasadena, California.

Frueh, Alfred J. (1880–1968). Born in Lima, Ohio, he is best known for his cartoon caricatures. *Hem and Haw,* the newspaper comic strip about a vaudeville team, was one of his earlier works and for many years he contributed to *The New Yorker*. A member of the Society of Independent Artists, he lived most of his life in New York City.

Fuchs, Bernard (b. 1932). Born in O'Fallon, Illinois, he studied at the School of Fine Art at Washington University. His career started in Detroit, where he produced illustrations for automobile advertisements. This success brought him recognition and assignments from such magazines as *Redbook, Lithopinion* and *Sports Illustrated*. Elegance and craftsmanship are constants of the innovative style that have earned him many awards and prompted the AG to name him Artist of the Year in 1962. A Hamilton King Award winner, he is the youngest member of the S of I Hall of Fame. As a faculty member of the Illustrators Workshop, he is passing on the knowledge that has made him a continuing influence in American illustration.

Fuller, Arthur D. (b. 1889). Born in Exeter, New Hampshire, he attended the Fenway School of Illustration, Chicago Academy of Fine Arts and studied with Harvey Dunn. He began his career with *Greenbook* and was soon receiving assignments from most of the major magazines. He contributed frequently to *Field and Stream*, hunting and fishing being two of his hobbies. He was a member of the Salmagundi Club, Westport Artists and S of I.

Gaadt, George S. (b. 1941). Born in Erie, Pennsylvania, he studied at the Columbus College of Art and Design. Since his first illustration, a silk-screen, appeared in 1961, he has received over 60 awards in many cities in the United States. In addition to corporate advertising work and editorial illustration for many major magazines, he has also done children's books for *Macmillan*. His work has been shown in galleries in Columbus, Ohio, Pittsburgh, Pennsylvania and at the S of I.

Gaetano, Nicholas (b. 1944). Born in Colorado Springs, Colorado, he attended ACD. *Art Direction* magazine published his cover in 1965 and since 1970 his editorial work has appeared in many magazines including *New Times, Travel and Leisure, Contempo* and *Newsday*. With advertising and book illustration to his credit, he has received numerous awards from the AIGA, ADC and S of I. He has produced posters for the Open Gallery in Los Angeles which has exhibited his work.

Galli, Stanley W. (b. 1912). Born in San Francisco, he did a number of odd jobs in Nevada and California before enrolling in the California School of Fine Arts, and later studied at the ACD. He worked briefly in a San Francisco studio and later as a free-lance illustrator. He has had assignments for magazines including *Country Gentleman, Sports Afield, McCall's* and *True*. Among his clients are *Random House* and United Airlines, for which he illustrated a series of posters in the 1960's. His works are in the collections of the USAF and the Baseball Hall of Fame.

Gannam, John (1907–1965). Born in Lebanon, he spent his early years in Chicago and at age 14 he became the family breadwinner. One of his many odd jobs was in an engraving studio where he began his artistic training and in 1926 he moved to Detroit where for four years he worked in an art studio. Coming to New York in 1930, he quickly found assignments, at *Woman's Home Companion* and later *Good Housekeeping, Ladies' Home Journal* and *Cosmopolitan*. His advertising illustrations were in high demand and although he used all media, his most prolific work was done in watercolor. A member of the AWS, NAD and S of I, he worked most of his life from his studio on West 67th Street. He is a member of the Illustrators Hall of Fame.

Garris, Philip (b. 1951). Born in Maryland, he received no formal art training. In 1976, the S of I awarded him a Gold Medal for his Grateful Dead album cover. He also illustrated concert posters for Bill Graham and the 1976 album cover for Kingfish. He is presently living in Sausalito, California.

Geisel, Theodore (Dr. Seuss) (b. 1904). Born in Springfield, Massachusetts, he studied art at Dartmouth College, Oxford University and traveled extensively in Europe. He wrote several screenplays and won the Academy Award in 1951 for his animated cartoon *Gerald McBoing-Boing*. In 1954 he went to Japan as a foreign correspondent for *Life* and later received an Honorary Doctorate of Humane Letters. He has illustrated over 10 picture books and is currently working on elementary school readers. Some of his most famous illustrated books are *If I Ran the Circus, Scrambled Eggs Supper* and *On Beyond Zebra*, published by *Random House*. A number of his books have been translated into animated television programs.

Geissmann, Robert (1909–1976). Born in New Washington, Ohio, he studied art at Ohio State University before serving with the Air Force in World War II as an art director with a film unit. He continued his illustration and design career in New York after the war but maintained ties with the service as director of the USAF Art Program. An active member of the S of I, he was President from 1953 to 1955. In 1967, he helped found the New York GAG and served as its President for many years.

Georgi, Edwin (1896–1964). He began his art training in an advertising agency and later free-lanced for many companies, including Hartford Fire Insurance Co., Crane Paper and Yardley and Co. His editorial work appeared in most major magazines, *The Saturday Evening Post* being a frequent user of his paintings of beautiful women. He worked most of his life from his studio in Norwalk, Connecticut.

Gersten, Gerry N. (b. 1927). Born in New York City, he attended the High School of Music and Art and Cooper Union Art School. He studied under the painter Robert Gwathmey and fellow classmates included Milton Glaser, Seymour Chwast, Reynold Ruffins and Edward Sorel. His first illustration was done for Sudler and Hennessey, Inc. in 1951. He illustrates for *Playboy, Esquire, Harper's, Time, McCall's, True* magazine and others. In 1975 the New York State Lottery poster was executed by this illustrator. Noted for his humorous caricatures, he is profiled in *Idea Magazine, North Light* and in the book *The Art of Humorous Illustration*. He is an active member of the S of I and his work has appeared often in their Annual Exhibitions.

Gibson, Charles Dana (1867–1944). Born in Roxbury, Massachusetts; at the age of 11 he studied at St. Gaudens under architect George Post. His formal training included two years at the ASL and in a short time he was a published artist. His first job was sold to *Life* and his work was soon appearing in *Cosmopolitan* and *Collier's*. The latter signed him to a six-figure contract in 1904 to produce the Gibson Girl, made famous in the books *The Education of Mr. Pipp* and *A Widow and Her Friends* in the 1890's. While honeymooning in England, he began a long friendship with *Punch* artists Phil May and DuMaurier. During World War I, he headed a government agency producing war posters, and also served as President of the S of I. The financial success from his elegant pen and ink illustrations led to his acquisition of the original *Life* magazine. He served for many years as its editor, retiring in the 1930's to his drawing board. He died in New York City. He was elected to the S of I Hall of Fame in 1974.

Giovanopoulos, Paul A. (b. 1939). Born in Kastoria, Greece, he came to America on scholarship to attend NYU School of Fine Art, and later SVA, studying under Robert Weaver. His career began with magazine illustrations for *Seventeen* in 1960. His children's book illustrations have won several awards from *The New York Times* and his artwork has been shown at the S of I Annual Exhibitions. New York, Baltimore, Philadelphia and Washington have shown his work. He has been an instructor at Parsons School of Design and SVA.

Giuliani, Vin (1930–1976). Born in New York City, he attended PI. He started as an industrial designer, but he became best known for his assemblage technique using wood shapes. Both his editorial illustrations for *Seventeen, McCall's, Redbook* and *Time* and his advertising work for Scovill Manufacturing, Exxon and Corporate Annual Reports earned him a reputation as a fine craftsman. His illustrations were selected for several Annual Exhibitions at the S of I.

Giusti, Robert G. (b. 1937). Born in Zurich, Switzerland, he attended Tyler School of Fine Art and Cranbrook Academy of Art until 1961. His artwork was first published in 1956 in *American Girl* and more recently in *McCall's, Redbook, Fortune, Idea* and *Penthouse*. He also illustrated many book covers and promotional posters. Exhibits of his work were held at the Cranbrook Museum of Art and the Greengrass Gallery in New York.

Glackens, William J. (1870–1938). Born in Philadelphia, he studied at the Pennsylvania Academy of Fine Arts and began his career as an artist-reporter for the Philadelphia newspapers with co-workers Everett Shinn and John Sloan. *McClure's* sent him to Cuba to cover the war with Spain, concurrent with the start of his work in magazine illustration. His drawings were impressionistic in style, influenced by Renoir and Manet, but after turning entirely to painting he became one of The Eight, founders of the Ashcan School.

Glaser, Milton (b. 1929). Born in New York City, he attended Cooper Union Art School with classmates Edward Sorel, Seymour Chwast and Reynold Ruffins. He was awarded a Fulbright Scholarship to study etching with the late Giorgio Morandi in Italy in 1952. A co-founder of Push Pin Studios, former design director and Chairman of the Board at *New York Magazine* and designer of *Village Voice*, he co-authored *The Underground Gourmet* and is a faculty member of the SVA. He is also designer of the Childcraft store and the decorative programs for the World Trade Center. His distinctive work has earned him many awards, including a Gold Medal from the S of I and the honor of a One-Man Show at the Museum of Modern Art.

Gnoli, Domenico (1932–1970). Born in Rome, he lived for many years in Majorca, Spain. Self-taught, at age 18 he was designing sets for the Old Vic theater and began his career as a portrait and graphic artist with exhibits in Rome and Brussels. His works have appeared in many magazines including *Playboy, Sports Illustrated* and *Holiday* and he has written several children's books. Since his death in New York in 1970 at the age of 37, his works have been acquired by major European museums and the Museum of Modern Art and the National Gallery in the United States.

Godwin, Frank (b. 1889). Born in Washington, DC, he was a pupil of James Montgomery Flagg at the Corcoran School of Art. He illustrated for all magazines and was known for his *Winston* books and the murals he painted at Kings County Hospital in Brooklyn and Riverside Yacht Club in Greenwich. He was a member of the S of I, Dutch Treat Club and the Salmagundi Club.

Gold, Albert (b. 1916). Born in Philadelphia, he studied under Henry C. Pitz at the Philadelphia College of Art where he is now a professor. He joined the Army in 1943, the year his first illustration appeared in *Yank*. Examples of the artwork he did as an Army War Artist can be seen in the *James Jones New Anthology of World War II Art*, published by *Grosset and Dunlap*. His illustrations have appeared in *Holiday, The Lamp* and in many children's books. His work, which has received many awards, has been shown at the Metropolitan Museum of Art, the New Britain Museum of American Art and the Philadelphia Art Museum.

Goodwin, Philip R. (1882–1935). A native of Norwich, Connecticut, he was educated at RISD, ASL, and also studied under Howard Pyle. His editorial work appeared in many magazines and he had exhibitions in New York at the Hammer, Kennedy and Latendorf Galleries. His interest in hunting and fishing led him to use these themes in many illustrations for *Scribner's Publishing Co.*

Gorey, Edward (b. 1929). A graduate of Harvard in 1950, he worked briefly in a publishing house and began his free-lance career in 1953. Aside from many editorial assignments for *The New York Times, Esquire* and *Holiday,* he has illustrated several children's books, of which the first was entitled *Unstrung Harp.* In the early 1950's he illustrated the Henry James novels for *Anchor Books* and has since published many albums of drawings. Presently living in Barnstable, Massachusetts, he has had exhibitions in Minneapolis and New York.

Gould, J. J. A native of Philadelphia, he was a student at the Pennsylvania Academy of Fine Art in the 1890's and studied under Thomas Anshutz with Maxfield Parrish, William Glackens and Frederic Gruger. His covers for *Lippincott's Magazine* in the late 1890's and those he illustrated with Guernsey Moore under the pseudonym Peter Fountain for *The Saturday Evening Post* earned him a reputation as one of the top poster artists of the early 1900's. He was living in Philadelphia as late as 1932.

Grafstrom, Ruth Sigrid (b. 1905). Born in Rock Island, Illinois, she studied at the AIC and the Colarossi Academy in Paris. A fashion artist for *Vogue* from 1930 to 1940, she later worked for *Delineator, Cosmopolitan* and *Woman's Home Companion.* She won many awards and citations from the New York ADC and the S of I, of which she had been a member.

Gramatky, Hardie (b. 1907). Born in Dallas, Texas, he attended Stanford University and Chouinard Institute under Pruett Carter. He initiated his career with a 12-page spread for *Fortune* in 1938, and went on to illustrate for major periodicals such as *Collier's, Good Housekeeping, Redbook* and *True.* Author-illustrator of *Little Toot,* he is the creator of 12 additional children's books and recipient of 40 watercolor awards. His paintings have been in museums and galleries worldwide as well as part of many permanent collections.

Grant, Gordon Hope (1875–1962). Born in San Francisco. His Scottish parents sent him to England by boat to study art, and during the voyage he began to develop a great appreciation of the sea. He studied art in London at Heatherly and Lambeth, later returning to America to work on *The San Francisco Chronicle* and *The Examiner.* His reporting of the Boer War and of Mexican border conflicts with Pancho Villa appeared in many papers including *Harper's.* A foremost watercolorist, he often painted nautical subjects, many of which are in collections at the Metropolitan Museum of Art and the LC.

Granville-Smith, Walter (b. 1870). Born in South Granville, New York, he was a pupil of Walter Satterlee, Carrol Beckwith and Willard Metcalf. He studied at the ASL in New York and later in Europe. He won over 40 awards in his lifetime and his piece entitled *Grey Day* is in the permanent collection of the Smithsonian Institution. The Salmagundi Club, National Art Club, Lotus Club and Art Club of Philadelphia all own this artist's work.

Green, Elizabeth Shippen (1871–1954). Born in Philadelphia, she attended the PAFA under Robert Vonnoh and Thomas Eakins. While studying with Howard Pyle at the Drexel Institute she met Violet Oakley and Jessie Wilcox Smith. The three artists shared a studio for many years and occasionally collaborated on children's book illustration. Her early illustrations appeared in *Ladies' Home Journal, The Saturday Evening Post* and several children's books. The majority of her work, however, was for *Harper's,* which had her under exclusive contract. Noted for their decorative, almost stained glass quality, her illustrations were, for the most part, of children.

Groth, John (b. 1908). Born in Chicago, he went to the AIC and the ASL. His first piece, a cartoon, was published in 1930 in *Ballyhoo* magazine. His ink and wash illustrations appeared in *Holiday* and *Esquire* and in several books such as *The Grapes of Wrath* and *War and Peace.* Among his many honors are citations from the US Army and USAF as a result of his work as a War Correspondent during World War II, in Korea, Indochina, the Congo, Santo Domingo and Vietnam. His work has been shown and is owned by many prestigious museums including the Metropolitan Museum of Art and the Museum of Modern Art.

Grove, David (b. 1940). Born in Washington, DC, he went to Syracuse University and began a career as a photographer in the early 1960's. He settled in Paris in 1964 as a free-lance illustrator. Returning to the United States in 1969, he presently lives in San Francisco where he is President of the S of I of San Francisco. His artwork appears frequently in books for *Ballantine, Avon, Dell, Fawcett* and *Bantam,* earning him awards in Los Angeles and New York.

Gruger, Frederic Rodrigo (1871–1953). Born in Philadelphia, he attended the PAFA with William Glackens and Maxfield Parrish. His first work appeared in newspapers, including the *Philadelphia Ledger,* but his career is usually identified with magazines, especially *The Saturday Evening Post.* His charcoal pencil drawings were seen in *the Century* for many years.

Hack, Konrad F. (b. 1945). Born in Chicago, he attended the AIC and University of Chicago between 1964 and 1968. He produced movie promotion art and sports advertisements for WGN-TV in Chicago. Serving as a combat artist in Vietnam with the 19th Military History Detachment, he earned the Bronze Star and Army Commendation Medal. Recently he has illustrated books for the *Franklin Library* and the *Hamilton Mint* for whom he also designed a set of bicentennial pewter plates.

Hambidge, Jay (1867–1924). He received his art training at the ASL as a pupil of William Merritt Chase and spent most of his career as an illustrator in New York where he was a member of the S of I. An author and historian, he wrote *Dynamic Symmetry: The Greek Vase* for the *Yale University Press* in 1920.

Hampton, Blake (b. 1932). Born in Poteau, Oklahoma, he attended North Texas State College where he received his BA. Influenced by his study with Octavio Medellin, a sculptor, he has produced many fine dimensional pieces in addition to his other work. His first illustration was done in 1946 in California and it was entitled *How the Froggy Lost His Whoop.* The Eisenhower Museum and the John F. Kennedy Library own his artwork.

Handville, Robert T. (b. 1924). Born in Paterson, New Jersey, he graduated first in his class at PI. He studied under Reuben Tam at the Brooklyn Museum Art School and went to school with Ellsworth Kelly. His first published illustration was done for *Elks Magazine* in 1948. He has done extensive work for many well known magazines and publishing houses, and has also been an artist-reporter for *Sports Illustrated.*

Hane, Roger (1940–1975). Born in Bradford, Pennsylvania, he received his training in advertising design and illustration from the Philadelphia College of Art. Among his many clients were *Fortune, New York Magazine, The Times* of London, *Ladies' Home Journal, Time, McCall's,* Exxon Corporation, Columbia Records and others. The Swiss magazine *Graphis* in 1975 published an article on his great insight and imagination in depicting the everyday world. In 1975 he received an Award of Excellence from the S of I as well as being elected Artist of the Year by the AG. The loss of a great talent, he was brutally killed at the age of 35 while riding his bicycle in Central Park, New York.

Hanna, Thomas King (1872–1952). Born in Kansas City, Missouri, he studied at Yale University and the ASL under Kenyon Cox and C. S. Reinhart. He illustrated for *The Saturday Evening Post, Scribner's, Life, Woman's Home Companion, Harper's* and *Liberty.* He is represented in the collection of the National Art Gallery in Sydney, Australia.

Harding, George (1882–1959). He was the younger brother of the illustrator Charlotte Harding and attended Howard Pyle's school in Wilmington where he began illustrating for *The Saturday Evening Post.* During World War I, he was one of the eight artists sent overseas to paint panoramas of battlefields and the effect of war on man. His war art is part of the permanent collection at the Smithsonian Institution in Washington. He later taught illustration at the PAFA.

Harris, Robert G. (b. 1911). Born in Kansas City, Missouri, he studied under Harvey Dunn and George Bridgman. He attended the KCAI, ASL and GCSA in New York. From 1938 to 1960 his illustrations appeared in *The Saturday Evening Post, Ladies' Home Journal, Redbook, Woman's Home Companion, McCall's* and *Good Housekeeping.* In 1962 he had a One-Man Show entitled *Portraits,* which was held at the Phoenix Art Museum in Arizona. He is currently working exclusively on portraits.

Harvey, George (1801–1878). Born in Tottenham, England, he came to the United States in 1820, first traveling through the Midwest and Canada before settling in Brooklyn. He began his career there as a miniaturist and landscape artist and was elected to the NAD in 1928. His most ambitious project, a series of 40 scenes of American life, was begun in 1833 in his new studio in Hastings-on-Hudson, New York, but it remained unpublished. He spent his later years in England.

Harvey, Richard D. (b. 1940). Born in Meadville, Pennsylvania, he studied under John LaGatta at the ACD and Phoenix College. Beginning in 1967 with an illustration for *Good Housekeeping,* he has since illustrated for *McCall's, Business Week, Time, Oui, Cosmopolitan* and others. Many of his illustrations have been paperback covers for *Avon, Dell, Pyramid* and *Ballantine.*

Hatherell, William. A corresponding member of the S of I in the 1940's, his works are in their permanent collection. He was also a member of the Royal Academy.

Hays, Philip (b. 1940). Born in Shreveport, Louisiana, he studied with Jack Potter at ACD. Shortly thereafter his free-lance career began in New York with *Seventeen* magazine, one of his first clients. With many record covers and other advertising work to his credit, he has been awarded medals by the ADC of New York and the S of I. Predominantly executed in watercolor, his works have been used by *Sports Illustrated,* Seagram's Distillers and Columbia Records.

Hayward, George (1834–1872). Famous for his work as a lithographer and printer, he resided most of his life on Pearl Street in New York. He often drew scenes of the city and is best known for his *View of Broadway* and *View of High Bridge* which were later reproduced in *Munseys Magazine.* His works are in the Duyckinck Collection and the Eno Collection. He worked for *Henry McCloskey's Manual* and *D. T. Valentine's Manual* between 1857 and 1863.

Heindel, Robert Anthony (b. 1938). Born in Toledo, Ohio, he is a graduate of the FAS. Since moving to New York, he has done illustrations for *Redbook, Ladies' Home Journal, Time, Good Housekeeping* and *Sports Illustrated.* His work has appeared in several books including *Psycho, The Grapes of Wrath* for the *Franklin Library* and *Sybil,* for which he received an Award of Excellence from the S of I. In addition to a One-Man Show in New York, his illustrations have been exhibited in Cleveland and at the Smithsonian Institution. He is a founding faculty member of the Illustrators Workshop.

Heitland, Wilmot Emerton (b. 1893). Born in Superior, Wisconsin, he attended the Pennsylvania Academy of Fine Arts and ASL. He also studied at the Colarossi School in Paris and with Harvey Dunn and Walter Biggs. His career began at *Collier's Weekly* in 1922 and he was a frequent contributor to *Woman's Home Companion, McCall's* and *Cosmopolitan*. Noted for his watercolors, he is represented in many museums.

Helck, Peter (b. 1893). Born in New York City, he studied at the ASL and in England as a pupil of Frank Brangwyn. In 1911 he did advertising art for New York department stores and later editorial illustration for major magazines. His first love was the automobile, and he would often leave his studio in Benton Corners, New York to take motor trips across Europe. In 1961 he published *The Checkered Flag,* a collection of his race drawings. A member of the S of I Hall of Fame, he is also a founding faculty member of the FAS.

Held, John, Jr. (1889–1958). Born in Salt Lake City, Utah, he attended classes under Mahonri Young, the sculptor, and began his career as a sports cartoonist with the *Salt Lake City Tribune*. About 1910 he moved to New York, working as a newspaper artist and advertising illustrator, before beginning his very successful magazine career. His stylized flapper appeared in the 1920's and 1930's in most of the major magazines. His two cartoon strips, *Margie* and *Ra, Ra Roselie,* were very popular in the 1930's. During his later years he concentrated on sculpting and ceramics while acting as an artist-in-residence at Harvard University and the University of Georgia.

Henning, Albin (1886–1943). Born in Oberdorla, Germany, he was raised in St. Paul, Minnesota. A student of Harvey Dunn at the AIC, he also attended the GCSA in New York. Adventure illustration was his specialty, resulting in many assignments for boys' stories in publications such as *American Boy* and *Boys' Life*. He was most remembered, however, for his exciting paintings of World War I subjects, some of which appeared in *The Saturday Evening Post*.

Hildebrandt, Tim A. and **Hildebrandt, Greg J.** (b. 1939). Twin brothers born in Detroit, they attended Meinzinger's Art School in 1958 and began their career as an illustrating team in 1961 with *The Man Who Found Out Why.* Together they have produced several books, including *Mother Goose, Panda Book, Hippo Book* and *A Home for Tandy.* They also illustrated many book covers and the 1976–1977 *J. R. R. Tolkien Calendar* for *Ballantine.*

Hill, John (1770–1850). Born in London, he earned a reputation doing aquatints and engravings of landscapes before leaving for America in 1816. His first major work was for Joshua Shaw's *Picturesque Views of American Scenery* in Philadelphia. One of his most famous works was done for William Guy Wall's *Hudson River Portfolio.* He was the father of John William Hill, the landscape artist, and the grandfather of painter and etcher John Henry Hill.

Hill, John William (1812–1879). The son of the aquatint engraver John Hill, he was born in London. He served as an apprentice under his father in New York City and was employed by the New York State Geographical Survey where he began his career as a topographical artist. Later he drew views of American cities for Smith Brothers in New York City. Influenced by Ruskin's *Modern Painters,* he began to do flower and bird studies and naturalistic landscapes in watercolor. He died in West Nyack and in 1888 his son wrote and illustrated from his father's etchings *An Artist's Memorial.* His works are represented in the New-York Historical Society Museum Ayer

Collection and the Field Museum of Chicago.

Hinojosa, Albino R. (b. 1943). Born in Atlanta, he attended Texarkana and East Texas State University, studying under Jack Unruh and Otis Lumpkin. His first published illustration appeared in the *Greenville Texas Herald* in 1968 and he has since exhibited in Tennessee, Louisiana and New York. He is a member of the S of I of Los Angeles and New York. He is married and lives in Ruston, Louisiana.

Hirshfeld, Albert (b. 1903). Born in St. Louis, Missouri, he traveled and studied art in New York, Paris, London and Bali. He started his career at *The New Masses,* and in 1923 his first pen and ink caricatures appeared in *The New York World.* His drawings of political, television and, most notably, theater personalities have been published in magazines, books and in *The New York Times* for over 50 years. Examples of his unique drawings are owned by the Whitney Museum, Metropolitan Museum of Art and others.

Ho, Tien (b. 1951). Born in Shanghai, China, she attended the University of Dublin, Ireland and the ASL in New York, studying under Marshall Glasier. Her first illustration was an annual report cover, done for Topps Chewing Gum in February 1976. Her work has been shown at the S of I. In addition to being an illustrator, she is a fabric and fashion designer, known professionally as Tien.

Hobbie, Holly (b. 1944). The early influence of her farm upbringing in Connecticut infused her art with a homespun, fresh quality which captured the hearts of greeting card lovers all over America. Having attended PI and Boston University, she has been employed by the American Greeting Corporation for the past ten years. She has chosen to remain somewhat anonymous, maintaining a quiet life as a wife and mother of three.

Hoff, Guy (1889–1962). Born in Rochester, New York, he was a·pupil of Wilcox and DuMond. In 1916, he was awarded First Honorable Mention from the Albright Art Gallery in Buffalo. Best known for his paintings of women, he lived and worked in New York City for many years.

Holland, Brad (b. 1944). Born in Fremont, Ohio, he presently works in New York and his illustrations are seen frequently on the Op-Ed page of *The New York Times.* His magazine work for such publications as *Playboy, Redbook, Evergreen Review* and *National Lampoon* and his book illustrations for *Simon and Schuster* have won him two Gold Medals and an Award of Excellence from the S of I Annual Exhibitions. His drawings were part of an American Exhibition at the Louvre in Paris.

Holmgren, R. John (1897–1963). Born in St. Paul, Minnesota, he studied at the ASL and Columbia College where he was art editor for the literary magazine. From 1923 to 1960 he illustrated for all the notable magazines and advertising firms. Best known for his paintings depicting small town life, he spent most of his years in Freedom, New Hampshire, where he eventually died.

Holton, Leonard T. (b. 1906). Born in Philadelphia, he was an illustrator and co-author of books published by *Scribner's, Simon and Schuster* and others. He also illustrated for leading magazines and newspapers of the time. While living in Philadelphia in 1927, he joined the S of I and later became a Life Member.

Homer, Winslow (1836–1910). Born in Boston, he started sketching and illustrating in his school note-books before reaching his teens. At 19 he was apprenticed to a lithographer in Boston, for whom he designed sheet music and title pages. In 1858 he began his career

illustrating for *Ballou's Pictorial* and later *Harper's Weekly.* Moving to New York City in 1861, he studied painting under Frederic Rondel at the NAD. Interested in depicting war subjects, he painted *The Last Goose of Yorktown* and *Home, Sweet Home,* which were exhibited at the National Gallery in 1863. He continued working for *Harper's Weekly,* painting scenes from farm life, sea adventures and landscapes and in 1871 he did a series of illustrations for *Every Saturday,* a magazine published in Boston. Homer was considered at his best when painting his romantic views of sailing life, the majesty of turbulent seas and the lyrical beauty of the Bahamas, executed in sparkling watercolor. A prolific artist, he died at age 74, his great talent still much in demand.

Hooks, Mitchell Hillary (b. 1923). Born and educated in Detroit, he attended the Cass Technical High School. His first illustration was done in 1942 for an advertising firm. A leader in the field of paperback cover illustration for many years, he has illustrated a great number of books and magazines as well. An active member of the S of I, a contributor to the USAF art program, he lives and works in New York City.

Hornor, Thomas. Born in England, he was known for his etchings, engravings and topographical drawings. In 1828 he came to New York City where for the next ten years he portrayed city life and architecture. The New-York Historical Society Museum owns some of his drawings.

Hortens, Walter Hans (b. 1924). Born in Vienna, Austria, he studied in Egypt and Austria and is a graduate of Pratt Institute and the Académie Julien in Paris. His first assignment appeared in 1948 in *The New York Times* and since then his technical illustrations have frequently been seen in *National Geographic, Life* and *Time.* A veteran of World War II, he is a contributor to the USAF Art Program and a member of the S of I.

Hoskins, Gayle Porter (1887–1962). Born in Brazil, Indiana, he attended the AIC and also studied with Howard Pyle in Wilmington, Delaware. He established a reputation as an authority on military subjects and firearms. His illustrations of World Wars I and II and of the Battle of Little Big Horn have been reproduced as calendars and in books. His work is represented at the Custer Battlefield National Museum.

Howe, George (1896–1941). Born in Salzburg, Austria, he ran away to America at the age of 14. After studying in Paris for two years, he returned, making the United States his home. Before his career as a magazine illustrator began, he was forced to work at assorted odd jobs, from chauffeuring to scenery painting for movie companies. His illustrations, most of which were done in watercolor, executed in a flat, posterlike manner, were seen in *Collier's, American, Woman's Home Companion* and *Good Housekeeping.* One of his last assignments was a series of paintings that were seen as posters for the Barnum and Bailey Circus.

Huens, Jean Leon (b. 1921). Born in Melsbroeck, Belgium, he trained at La Cambre Academy prior to 1943, when his illustrations for a children's book by a Belgian publisher marked the start of his career. His illustrations have frequently been seen in America since 1962 when he began painting covers for *The Saturday Evening Post* and *Reader's Digest.* Most recently he has been a frequent contributor to *National Geographic.* The S of I has selected his works for several of their Annual Exhibits, and in 1973 The Sécurité Routieré Européenne awarded him First Prize for his poster *Against Drunkenness at the Steering Wheel.*

Huffaker, Sandy (b. 1943). Born in Chattanooga, Tennessee, he attended the University of Alabama and studied under Daniel Schwartz at the ASL. He was a political cartoonist for *The News and Observer* in Raleigh,

North Carolina before coming to New York as a free-lancer. His artwork has been seen in *Sports Illustrated, Business Week, Time* and *The New York Times,* which sponsored his nomination for a Pulitzer Prize in 1977. Exhibitions of his paintings and drawings have been held at the Greengrass Gallery, Puck Gallery and Hunter Gallery of Chattanooga. A member of the S of I, he presently lives and works in New York.

Hughes, George (b. 1907). Born in New York City, he studied at the NAD and ASL. For a short time he worked in Detroit as a special designer in the auto industry. He began his long-standing career with *The Saturday Evening Post* in the 1940's and did his first cover in 1948. Living in Arlington, Vermont for many years, he was a neighbor of Norman Rockwell, John Atherton and Mead Schaeffer. He now lives in Wainscott, New York.

Hurst, Earl Oliver (1895–1958). Born in Buffalo, New York, he studied at the Albright Art School, Cleveland School of Art and later at the University of Beaune in France. His work appeared on the cover of *Judge* as early as 1924 and very often in *Collier's* in the early 1930's. He was an active illustrator for magazines, working until 1956. He has had exhibits at the Silvermine Gallery, S of I and a One-Man Show at the Boothbay Harbor Gallery.

Huyssen, Roger (b. 1946). Born in Los Angeles, he attended the University of California at Santa Barbara and the ACD. After working briefly for a design firm in California, he moved to New York in 1974 as a free-lance illustrator for advertising and editorial clients. His airbrush and watercolor work has been seen on Columbia Records covers and several movie posters. He is a member of the S of I.

Inouye, Carol (b. 1940). Born in Los Angeles, she attended Chouinard Art Institute and UCLA. She began her career as a graphic designer and art director for several publishing houses. Her first published piece, entitled *Creative Living,* appeared in 1975. She wrote and illustrated the book *Naturecraft* and has done editorial illustrations for *Reader's Digest, Gallery* and *Guideposts.* Presently living in New York City, she is a member of the S of I.

Jamieson, Mitchell (b. 1915). Born in Kensington, Maryland, he attended the Abbott School of Fine Arts and studied at the Corcoran School of Art. During World War II, as an official combat artist, he began reporting on naval operations in the Pacific. These illustrations were reproduced in *Fortune* and *Life,* among others.

Jampel, Judith (b. 1944). Born in London, England, she attended Hunter College and SVA in New York. Her first published illustration was a self-promotional booklet entitled, *Sorry but we don't hire women because.* She works with nylon fabric, polyester fabric, real hair and props to create her three-dimensional figures. She received the Hamilton King Award and Award of Excellence from the S of I in 1975. Her artwork has been shown at the Greengrass Gallery in New York City.

Jetter, Frances (b. 1951). Born in New York, she attended PSD. In 1974 her career began with illustrations for a psychology book by *John Wiley and Sons.* She has designed bookjackets as well as editorial illustrations for *The New York Times, Institutional Investor, The Independent* (a United Nations publication) and others. Her illustrations have appeared in the Annual Exhibitions of the S of I and in *Graphis Annual.*

Johnson, Douglas (b. 1940). Born in Toronto, Canada, he studied at the Ontario College of Art for three years. The start of his career in Toronto in 1960 led to his success as an illustrator, his distinctive style being in great demand among magazine and book publishers. His work has been exhibited at the Art Gallery of Ontario, the Brooklyn

Museum and the S of I for which he produced the *Illustrators 13* exhibition poster. He was an instructor at SVA until 1974 and creative director of The Chelsea Theatre Center. He lives in New York and co-directs Performing Dogs, an advertising consultant group.

Jones, Robert (b. 1926). Born in Los Angeles, he attended the University of Southern California and ACD. He had practical training as an animator at Warner Brothers Studios before coming to New York in 1952 to join Charles E. Cooper Studio with whom he was associated for 12 years. Many magazines have published his work, most notably *The Saturday Evening Post,* and among his many advertising clients is Exxon Corporation, for whom he developed the Exxon Tiger as their symbol. A member of the S of I for 20 years, he was awarded a Gold Medal from their 1967 Annual Exhibition.

Jonson, James (b. 1928). Born in St. Louis, he attended Washington University and the Jepson Art School of Los Angeles. His first work appeared in *Westways* in 1948 and he has since won awards from the Los Angeles ADC, the S of I and First Prize at the National Art Museum of Sport Competition. He has illustrated several sports books and many magazines, including *Look, The Saturday Evening Post, Seventeen, Playboy, Boys' Life, Ski* and *Sports Illustrated.* His works are in the collections of Circle Galleries, Ltd. Currently he is producing lithographs at the American Atelier.

Justice, Martin (1892–1960). A resident of Hollywood, California for many years, he was a member of the S of I. During his career he illustrated for most major magazines.

Justis, Lyle (1892–1960). Born in Manchester, Virginia, he was considered a master of pen and ink despite his lack of formal art training. His first published works were sheet music illustrations which led to assignments from major magazines and several advertising clients. Among his best known illustrations were those done for the *Grosset and Dunlap* 1930 edition of Robert Louis Stevenson's *Treasure Island.* Noted for his historical drawings, he was a member of the Sketch Club and Pen and Pencil Club.

Karchin, Steve (b. 1953). Born in Brooklyn, New York, he attended PI from 1971 to 1974 where he studied under Jerry Contreras and David Byrd. His first work appeared in *Guideposts* in 1974. Selected for every Annual Exhibition of the S of I since 1973, his editorial illustrations have been published in *Redbook, American Way* and *Guideposts* and he has done several covers for *Avon.*

Karlin, Eugene (b. 1918). Born in Kenosha, Wisconsin, he received scholarships from The Chicago Professional School of Art, AIC and ASL. He is presently a teacher at the SVA and has won numerous awards from the ADC, AIC, S of I and AIGA. He has illustrated for all the major magazines and done extensive book illustration for such publishing houses as *Macmillan, Golden Press, Random House, Houghton Mifflin, Bantam* and many others.

Kastel, Roger K. (b. 1931). Born in White Plains, New York, he attended the ASL and Frank Reilly School of Art for six years. His first published work appeared in 1962 for *Pocket Books* at which time he was also free-lancing for advertising agencies. Included among the many paperback covers which he has illustrated is the much publicized *Jaws,* published by *Bantam.* His works have been exhibited at the Salmagundi Club and the Grand Central Gallery in New York.

Keats, Ezra Jack (b. 1916). Born in Brooklyn, New York, he had no formal art training, yet in 1948 his first illustration appeared in *Collier's.* A well known children's book illustrator, he received the Horn Book Award from the *Boston Globe* and two Caldecott Awards. The five UNICEF cards he contributed in 1965 raised $500,000 for medical

aid for needy children. All of his manuscripts and illustrations are owned by Harvard University.

Keller, Arthur Ignatius (1866–1925). Many years of study at the NAD and training under Loefftz in Munich resulted in the development of this man's brilliant technique in line and wash. His work was in demand at the turn of the century by such book publishers as *Bobbs-Merrill* and *Houghton Mifflin.* President of the S of I in 1903, he participated in the first Annual Exhibition of the Associated Illustrators of New York.

Kelley, Gary R. (b. 1945). Born in Algona, Iowa, he studied at the University of Northern Iowa and was a pupil of John Page, a print-maker. *Better Homes and Gardens* published his first illustration in 1970. His artwork is owned by the Artworks Gallery in Keokuk, Iowa and the Three-Rooms-Up Gallery in Minneapolis. Private collectors in Iowa, California, Florida, Arizona and Washington, DC own his paintings, drawings and prints.

Kemble, Edward Windsor (1861–1933). Born in Sacramento, California, he had no formal art training when he began his career in 1881 as a cartoonist and staff artist at the *New York Daily Graphic.* He contributed frequently to *Puck* and, after 1883, to *Life.* He is best known for his illustrations of rural southern life for such books as *Uncle Remus, Huckleberry Finn, Pudd'nhead Wilson* and *Uncle Tom's Cabin.*

Kent, Rockwell (1882–1971). Born in Tarrytown Heights, New York, he studied under artists Abbott Thayer, William Chase and Robert Henri. Not only a successful illustrator, he worked as a mural painter, writer, engraver and lithographer. He illustrated such famous works as *Candide, Moby Dick, Leaves of Grass* and *The Canterbury Tales.* In advertising he illustrated for Steinway and Sons, Rolls-Royce, American Car and others. Best known for his intricate woodcuts, he won the ADC Medal in 1931.

Keppler, Joseph (1838–1890). Born in Vienna, Austria, he studied at the Vienna Academy for several years. He came to America in 1868, settling in St. Louis, where he published, in German, the cartoon magazine *Puck,* which failed within six months. In 1873 he came to New York to join the staff of *Frank Leslie's Illustrated Newspaper.* Three years later he published *Puck,* this time successfully, and it soon became a very popular comic weekly. A contemporary of satirist Thomas Nast, his cartoon work and political caricatures appeared regularly.

Kidd, Steven R. (b. 1911). Born in Chicago, he studied at the AIC and later at the ASL, GCSA and PI in New York. His instructors, including Harvey Dunn, George Bridgman and Henry Varnum Poore, were some of the best known artists of their day. He started working in 1926 in Chicago and has since illustrated many books and magazines such as *Cosmopolitan, Redbook, Forbes* and *Argosy.* He is currently teaching at the ASL.

Kidder, Harvey W. (b. 1918). Born in Cambridge, Massachusetts, he graduated from the Child-Walker School of Design having studied with Lawrence Beal Smith and Arthur Lougée. His long career in editorial and book illustration began with *Houghton Mifflin* in 1939 and his artwork has since been used by *Reader's Digest, Ford Times, True, Argosy, Lithopinion, Golf Digest* and many others. A member of the S of I, he has participated in the USAF Art Program and the National Park Service Art Program.

Kilmer, David L. (b. 1950). Born in Waterloo, Iowa, he attended the Colorado Institute of Art in 1968 and 1969. His first published illustration was in 1970 for the Testor Corporation and he has since received awards from the Curtis Paper Company, *Art Direction* and the Chicago '75 exhibit. From 1973 through 1976 his work has been selected to hang in S of I Annual Exhibitions.

Kilvert, B. Cory (1881–1946). A graduate of the ASL, he was a prolific illustrator of children's books. His illustrations, often of golf scenes, appeared in *Life*. He devoted himself to watercolor and seascape painting in his later years, and died in New York City.

Kimmel, Lu (1908–1973). Born in Brooklyn, New York, he was a pupil of Will Taylor, Pruett Carter, George Luks, Max Hermann and Michel Jacobs at PI. In 1933, he won an award from the National Red Cross Poster Competition while illustrating regularly for *The Saturday Evening Post, Country Gentleman, Household Magazine, Field and Stream* and others. A member of the S of I, he lectured at the Queensboro Teachers' Association and was an art instructor at the Commercial Illustrations Studios in New York.

Kliros, Thea (b. 1935). Born in New York City, she attended Bennington College and Yale University before beginning her career in 1953 with a woodcut for *Seventeen*. Best known for her fashion illustrations, she has had her artwork exhibited in Washington, DC, and Spain.

Knight, Charles Robert (1874–1953). Born in Brooklyn, he attended the ASL and Brooklyn Polytechnic Institute. Known as both illustrator and scientist, he painted, lectured and wrote books on prehistoric man and animals for the American Museum of Natural History and the Field Museum in Chicago. *Life Through the Ages* published by *Knopf* in 1946 and *Prehistoric Man* published by *Appleton* in 1949 are two of his best known works.

Koda-Callan, Elizabeth (b. 1944). Born in Stamford, Connecticut, she attended Siena Heights College in Michigan, University of Dayton in Ohio and SVA in New York City. She studied under James McMullan and has done extensive work for *Scholastic Magazine* and *New York Magazine*. Her first published illustration was done for Arista Records in October, 1974.

Koslow, Howard (b. 1924). Born in Brooklyn, New York, he attended PI and the Cranbrook Academy of Art in Michigan. His career began in 1946 with a Hilton Hotel advertising series and went on to include book, poster and editorial illustration. Some of his clients are *Boys' Life, Popular Science, Reader's Digest* and the United States Postal Service. The Smithsonian Institution and the National Park Service own his work and his illustrations have been shown in galleries nationwide.

Kossin, Sanford (b. 1926). Born in Los Angeles, he studied at the Jepson Art Institute before coming to New York in 1952. Early in his career he was a frequent contributor to *Galaxy Magazine*, illustrating science fiction stories. He has recently been painting for paperback book publishers and has had exhibits in the S of I Annual Exhibitions several times. He illustrated a series on the Bay of Pigs for *Life* in 1963 and his work has appeared in *Argosy* and *The Saturday Evening Post*. His works are in the USAF Museum and the Douglas MacArthur Memorial.

Kuhn, Walt (1880–1949). Born in Brooklyn, he was the only one of eight brothers to survive childhood. At the age of 15, he sold his first illustration to *Truth* magazine. In 1899 he went West and began doing cartoons for the San Francisco *Wasp*, then left to study art at the Royal Academy in Munich. After 1905 he was making a living as a cartoonist, illustrating for *Puck, Judge* and *Life*. He later painted impressionistic landscapes, did over 3,000 studies of the nude, and worked on the creation of costumes and routines for theatre.

Künstler, Mort (b. 1931). Born in Brooklyn, he studied at Brooklyn College, UCLA and PI. In 1949 he published his first illustration, a black and white line drawing, for *Handy*

Football Library. He is best known for his intricate and realistic historical paintings. His works are owned by the Daytona Beach Museum of Arts and Sciences, Air Force Museum in Colorado, Favell Museum in Oregon and others.

LaGatta, John (1894–1977). Born in Naples, Italy, he attended the New York School of Fine and Applied Art, studying under Kenneth Miller and Frank Parsons. His early work in advertising earned him a reputation for depicting beautiful women. Soon in demand for editorial work, he illustrated covers for most major magazines during the 1920's and 1930's. After spending many years in New York he moved to Los Angeles and taught at the ACD. He died in Pasadena.

Laite, Gordon (b. 1925). Born in New York City, he attended Beloit College in Wisconsin and the AIC. Though he has used several media throughout his career, his work is predominantly in line. His children's book illustrations have been published by *Holt* and *Abingdon Press*, for whom he illustrated *Good King Wenceslas* and *The Story of Saint Nicholas*. He has lived most of his life in Gallup, New Mexico.

Laliberte, Norman (b. 1925). Born in Worcester, Massachusetts, he studied art at the Montreal Museum of Fine Art, Cranbrook Academy of Art and Institute of Design in Chicago. He received a Masters in Art Education from Illinois Tech. An author and illustrator, he has had over 50 One-Man Exhibitions and has designed many banners. Among the books he has illustrated is *The Rainbow Box*, a book of poems by Joseph Pentauro.

Lambdin, Robert (b. 1886). Born in Dighton, Kansas, he spent a year at the Read Art School in Denver, Colorado before taking a job as a staff artist with the *Rocky Mountain News*. He later worked for newspapers in Denver and Kansas City, graduating to feature article illustrations. In 1917, after his move to New York, *Greenbook* began to use his story illustrations and he later did advertising and book art. A highly respected portrait artist and a member of the National Society of Mural Painters, he is represented in the collection of The New-York Historical Society Museum.

Lambert, Saul (b. 1928). Born in New York City, he attended Brooklyn College and studied under Ad Reinhardt. His first published work appeared in *Esquire* in 1960 and his paintings have since appeared in most major publications. He has illustrated many books and produced posters for ABC and Columbia records. His works have been exhibited at the Bolles Gallery and the City Center Gallery in New York.

Landau, Jacob (b. 1917). Born in Philadelphia, he attended the Museum Art School and the New School for Social Research and later studied in Paris. His career in magazine illustration began with the editorship of *At Ease*. He has worked extensively in advertising design for IBM, Steuben Glass and others. An instructor at the Philadelphia Museum Art School, he has also served as chairman of the design department at PI.

Lapsley, Robert Ernest (b. 1942). Born in Memphis, he attended North Texas State University for three years before leaving for Los Angeles where he studied at the ACD until 1970. He has exhibited his work at the S of I Annual Exhibitions.

Lea, Tom (b. 1907). Born in El Paso, Texas, he studied at the AIC and under John Norton. His work for *Life* during World War II brought him considerable recognition and throughout his career he has illustrated over 50 books about the American West and the war, seven of which he also wrote. His works are in the collections of the University of Texas and the Dallas Museum of Fine Art.

He exhibited his artwork at the Whitney Museum in 1938.

Lee, Robert J. (b. 1921). Born in Oakland, California, he attended the Academy of Art College in San Francisco for four years. He served in the Air Force as a special service artist and later taught at the Academy Art College, PI and is presently Assistant Professor of Fine Arts at Marymount College. His first work appeared in *Western Advertising* in 1946 and he has since had several One-Man Shows and group exhibitions in New York, Chicago, St. Louis and San Francisco. His paintings have been exhibited in the Smithsonian Institution and several university museums.

Lewicki, James (b. 1917). Born in Buffalo, he attended PI and the Art School of the Detroit Society of Arts and Crafts. While attending PI he illustrated his first book, *New York: From Village to Metropolis* by Robert Swan. Winner of first prizes from Hallmark Cards and the Audubon Artists, in 1969 he illustrated *The Golden Bough* by Fraser for *Limited Editions*. He taught art for 15 years at CW Post College and later was department chairman and director of their graduate art program.

Leyendecker, Francis Xavier (1877–1924). Born in Germany, the younger brother of Joseph, who would later become famous in the illustration world, Frank gave up school at 13 to be apprenticed to Carl Brandt, a stained glass artisan from Vienna. In 1895 both brothers were sent to Paris where they studied art at the Académie Julien and Colarossi. After sailing to America in 1897, they opened their own studio in Chicago, which rapidly became a great success. Because of his desire to be a fine artist, Frank continued to design and make stained glass windows while illustrating covers for magazines, advertisements and posters. Always overshadowed by his brother, Frank left Joseph in 1923 and fell victim to drugs, dying at the early age of 47.

Leyendecker, Joseph Christian (1874–1951). Born in Montabour, Germany, he came to Chicago at age eight and later attended the AIC. In 1896 he and his brother, Francis (Frank), went to Paris to study at the Académie Julien. While still a student, he designed all 12 covers for *Inland Printer*, published in Chicago. Two years after the brothers opened their Chicago studio, he illustrated *The Saturday Evening Post* cover of May, 1899, the first of 321 paintings he executed for the *Post*. Six years later he began working for Cluett, Peabody and Co., originating the Arrow Shirt Collar Man which became the epitome of the elegant style sought after by the public. His exquisite paintings graced the pages of many magazines and advertised the apparel of B. Kuppenheimer, Hart Schaffner and Marx, as well as Interwoven Socks. Though his popularity had diminished by the mid-1930's, he continued working until his death in 1951.

Linn, Warren (b. 1946). Born in Chicago, he received his BFA from the AIC in 1968. His editorial illustrations have appeared often in *Playboy* since 1967. *Rolling Stone* and *The New York Times*, among others, have used his works. As a book illustrator he has painted covers for *St. Martin's Press* and *Scott, Foresman and Co.* The Chicago AG awarded him prizes in 1972 and 1973.

Llerena, Carlos Antonio (b. 1952). Born in Peru, he worked as an illustrator in South America before coming to the US in 1971. He studied at the Ringling School of Art and SVA, where he is presently an instructor. In addition to editorial art for magazines and children's books which he has illustrated, his works have also appeared on the Op-Ed page of *The New York Times*. While working in pen and ink for the most part, he has recently been doing woodcuts.

Lodigensky, Theodore (b. 1930). Born in Paris, France, he attended the Society of Arts and Crafts School in Detroit for four years, studying under Guy Palazzola. He began his career in Michigan in 1953 and has since illustrated for such magazines as *Automobile Quarterly, Car Classic, Playboy, Rod and Gun* and *Mechanics Illustrated*. An industrial designer as well as an artist, his works have been shown at the Detroit Museum of Art and the S of I Annual Exhibitions.

Loeb, Louis (1866–1909). Born in Cleveland, Ohio, he studied in Paris under Gerome and was elected to the NAD in 1906. He was a member of the Society of American Artists. His specialty was figure painting.

Long, Daniel A. (b. 1946). Born in Columbus, Ohio, he went to Southwestern College and the ACD. He now works for the United States Navy, Xerox, American Express, Panasonic, Merrill Lynch, the *New York Daily News* and London Records. His first illustration was done for Columbia Records in 1975. He illustrated the book *Human Sexuality,* published by *McGraw-Hill* in 1976.

Loomis, William Andrew (1892–1959). Born in Syracuse, New York, he attended ASL where he studied with George Bridgman and Frank DuMond. After returning from World War I, he worked in studios in Chicago and soon opened his own. During his long career he illustrated for magazines and also produced many advertising posters. He wrote books on figure drawing and pencil illustration and was an instructor at the American Academy of Art in Chicago for many years.

Lovell, Tom (b. 1909). Born in New York City, he received his BFA in 1931 from Syracuse University. In 1930 his first illustrations were published in a book entitled *Gangster Stories*. He has illustrated for all the major magazines and has won two Gold Medals from the S of I, two from the National Cowboy Hall of Fame and the Syracuse Centennial Gold Medal in 1970. His works are owned by the New Britain Museum of American Art, USMC Headquarters and the National Cowboy Hall of Fame in Oklahoma City.

Low, Will H. (1853–1932). Born in Albany, New York, he studied with the sculptor E. D. Palmer until he came to New York at age 17. After working on staff at *The Independent* and briefly with *Harper's,* he traveled to Paris to study with Gerome. In 1877 he returned to New York and contributed regularly to *Harper's*. It was not until 1885 that he began illustrating books, the best known being *Lamia* for *Lippincott* and *A Painter's Progress* for *Scribner's*.

Lowell, Orson Byron (1871–1956). Born in Wyoming, Iowa, he attended the AIC from 1887 to 1893; later, in New York, he illustrated for *Judge, Life, American Girl,* where he was on staff, and the Erickson Advertising Agency. He was President of the Member Guild Free-lance Artists from 1924 to 1925, and a life member of the S of I and New Rochelle Art Association. Best known for his social cartoons, drawings, paintings and posters, he also illustrated the books *The Court of Boyville* by William Allen White (*Doubleday*, 1899), and *Love in Old Clothes* by Henry C. Brunner (*Scribner's,* 1896).

Lowery, Robert S. (b. 1950). Born in Birmingham, Alabama, he received a scholarship to the ASL to study under Steven Kidd and Leslie Willett. He began his career as a sports artist with a pen and ink drawing of Muhammad Ali for *The New York Times*. Madison Square Garden has subsequently commissioned him to produce fight posters and his works have appeared in *Ring Magazine* as well as in NFL and NBA stories for *The New York Times*. His work is in the collections at the New York Jazz Museum, Madison Square Garden and ASL.

Ludekens, Fred (b. 1900). Born in Huoneme, California, he grew up in Canada and studied art briefly in California. He began as an artist for a San Francisco ad agency and

went on to become an art director for Lord and Thomas. In 1931 he came to New York and launched a second career as an editorial illustrator for the major magazines, among them *The Saturday Evening Post*. His illustrations of Western towns were particularly popular, as well as his more recent science fiction work. He headed the FAS in the 1960's while holding a creative position at Foote, Cone and Belding.

Luzak, Dennis (b. 1939). Born in Chicago, he received his BFA from the University of Notre Dame in 1961. He began his career as a designer for Chrysler and Ford Motor Company, but in 1969 joined the staff of Jack O'Grady Studios in Chicago. Later he moved to New York where his illustrations have appeared in major magazines and books as well as in the S of I Annual Exhibition.

Macaulay, David A. (b. 1946). Born in Burton-on-Trent, England, he studied at RISD, where he later taught. He has illustrated several children's books including *Underground* for *Houghton Mifflin* and *Pyramid* for *William Collins* in London, both of which were award winners in New York and Boston. He has had free-lance assignments for architectural journals and the *Washington Post*.

Mack, Stanley (b. 1936). Born in Brooklyn, New York, he attended RISD. His drawings have appeared on the Op-Ed page of *The New York Times* where he was Art Director of their Sunday *Magazine* section. His pen and ink work also appears in *Stan Mack's Real Life Funnies* in the *Village Voice*.

Maffia, Daniel J. (b. 1937). Born in Nevers, France, he attended the School of Industrial Arts where he was a pupil of Vogel. Among his clients are *Esquire, Limited Editions Club* and the National Park Service. His evocative paintings have been featured in *Idea* magazine's edition of New York illustrators and selected for inclusion in S of I Annual Exhibitions.

Magagna, Anna Marie (b. 1938). Born in Wilkes-Barre, Pennsylvania, she attended Marywood College in Scranton, ASL and SVA in New York. She has been on the faculty of PI since 1971. Her free-lance art career began in 1958 with the children's book *Christmas Miniature* by Pearl S. Buck which she illustrated for *John Day Co*. She has since worked for magazines such as *Vogue* and *Harper's Bazaar*. A member of the S of I since 1971, she lives in New York City.

Magee, Alan (b. 1947). Born in Newtown, Pennsylvania, he attended the Tyler School of Art and Philadelphia College of Art. His first published illustration was seen on the cover of *Scholastic Magazine* in 1969. Since then his work has appeared in *McCall's, Good Housekeeping, Penthouse, Viva, New York Magazine* and *The New York Times*. He has illustrated several book covers for *Ballantine, Fawcett, Bantam, Pocket Books* and *Random House,* and won a New York Book Publishers Award in 1976.

Malcynski, Elizabeth P. (b. 1955). Born in Brooklyn, she studied art for four years at the PSD. She illustrated the cover for *Day Care Magazine* in 1976 and has since illustrated for *Bantam* and Columbia Records. She is a descendant of George Luks of the Ashcan School.

Mardon, Allan (b. 1931). Born in Welland, Ontario, he graduated from the Ontario College of Art and studied at the Edinburgh School of Art and Slade School of Fine Art. His editorial illustrations are in great demand and are seen regularly in *Time* and *Sports Illustrated*. His *Time* covers have been exhibited overseas and he has shown work in the S of I Annual Exhibitions, the General Electric Gallery and Circle Gallery, which has issued his NBA lithographs as part of its 1977 Official Fine Art Sports Collection.

Marsh, Reginald (1898–1954). Born in Paris, he attended

Yale University where he began his career illustrating for the *Yale Record*. He came to New York in 1920 and served as a staff artist for the *Daily News* and as a cartoonist at *The New Yorker*. Best known for his paintings of New York scenes, he was in demand for his magazine work and, later in his career, for book illustration. He illustrated *Anatomy for Artists* in 1945.

Martin, Jerome (b. 1926). Born in New York City, he studied at Cooper Union and NYU. His first piece appeared in *Fortune* in 1959, which led to assignments for *Sports Illustrated, Playboy, Life* and *The Saturday Evening Post*. Numerous awards from the AIGA, ADC, and a Gold Medal from the S of I are the result of his efforts in the profession. His artwork has been shown at the Museum of Modern Art, Whitney Museum, Metropolitan Museum of Art and in the LC.

Martin, John (b. 1946). Born in Camden, New Jersey, he graduated in 1968 from the Philadelphia College of Art. Among his instructors were Albert Gold, Jack Freas and Ben Eisenstat. After military service as an art director for the psychological operations group in Vietnam, he returned to New Jersey, whereupon he began free-lancing. Among his clients are *Reader's Digest, Seventeen,* Nonesuch Records, Elektra Records and Bell Telephone Company as well as book publishers. His wife, Nancy, is also an illustrator.

Martin, Nancy Yarnall (b. 1949). Born in Camden, New Jersey, she studied at the Corcoran School of Art and Philadelphia College of Art under Ben Eisenstat and Albert Gold. Her work appeared in the Illustrators 18th Annual Exhibition at the S of I. She and her husband, illustrator John W. Martin, presently live in Pennsauken, New Jersey.

Martin, Stefan (b. 1936). Born in Elgin, Illinois, he studied for four years at the AIC under Ben Shahn. His work appeared in *Natural History* magazine in 1960 and he has had assignments from book companies including *E. P. Dutton, Coward-McCann, Scribner's* and *Grosset and Dunlap*. Best known for his paintings and woodcuts, he has twice won awards from the AIGA. He is represented in the collections of the Philadelphia Museum, LC, Metropolitan Museum of Art and AIC.

Mawicke, Tran J. (b. 1911). Born in Chicago, he studied at the American Academy and AIC. His career began in advertising in 1929 and later he had assignments from major magazines of the 1930's and 1940's. Among his clients were Pepsi-Cola, Phillips 66 and Camel Cigarettes. He began illustrating for book publishers in the late 1950's and has since worked for *W. W. Norton, Putnam's* and *Grosset and Dunlap*. A past President of the S of I (1960–1961), he has participated in the USAF Art Program and traveled overseas to record the Air Force Story. He has had many One-Man Shows and group exhibits across the United States.

Mayer, Mercer (b. 1943). Born in Little Rock, Arkansas, she attended the Honolulu Academy of Arts and ASL. She illustrated *A Boy, a Dog and a Frog* for *The Dial Press* in 1967 and has worked for magazines and book publishers.

McCall, Robert T. (b. 1919). Born in Columbus, Ohio, he studied at the Columbus Fine Art School. After serving as a bombardier in World War II, he returned to his career, in first Chicago then New York, frequently illustrating for *Reader's Digest, Popular Science, Life* and *Collier's*. His first love, science fiction, led him to many interesting projects, most notable of which was an assignment to paint a mural at the National Air and Space Museum. He has designed postage stamps for the space program and has been invited to record several space shots including the recent Apollo-Soyuz mission.

McCarter, Henry (1865–1943). Born in Norristown, Pennsylvania, he was a pupil of Thomas Eakins in Philadelphia; of Bonnat, Alexander Harrison, Toulouse Lautrec, M. Poll and M. Rixens in Paris. He illustrated for *Scribner's, the Century, Harper's* and *Collier's* and is best known for his beautiful paintings for Richard Watson Gilder's poems. In 1930, after winning many awards in illustration, he won the prestigious Joseph Pennell Memorial Prize from the Pennsylvania Academy of Fine Art. His works are owned by the Pennsylvania Museum of Art and the Pennsylvania Academy of Fine Art. He often lectured on modern painting.

McConnell, Gerald (b. 1931). Born in East Orange, New Jersey, he studied at the ASL under Frank Reilly, after which he apprenticed with Dean Cornwell. He began free-lancing in the mid-1950's, working for advertising agencies and publishers. He has served on the Board of Directors of the S of I since 1963 and its Executive Committee since 1967. A founding member of GAG in New York City, he has been on its Executive Committee since 1969. His works are in the collections of the S of I, USAF and National Park Service and have been shown in the galleries of Master Eagle, Fairtree, Greengrass and the S of I. He is best known for his three-dimensional art; his book on the subject, *Assemblage,* was published in 1976.

McGinnis, Robert E. (b. 1926). Born in Cincinnati, Ohio, he attended Ohio State University for four years and the Central Academy of Commercial Art. He began his career with *The Saturday Evening Post* in 1960 and has worked extensively for *Good Housekeeping* since then. As well as illustrating for paperback book publishers he has also produced over 50 movie posters, most notably those for the James Bond movies in the 1960's. A member of the S of I, he lives in Old Greenwich, Connecticut.

McKeown, Wesley Barclay (1927–1975). Born in Jersey City, he graduated in 1950 from the Newark School of Fine and Industrial Arts. Shortly thereafter, his illustrations appeared in advertisements, magazines and books as well as in technical and trade publications. A member of the S of I, he contributed to the USAF Art Program and was active on many committees before becoming President from 1968 to 1970. He was commissioned to produce a series of postage stamps on the metric system in 1974.

McLean, Wilson I. (b. 1937). Born in Glasgow, Scotland, he had no formal art training. In 1959 his first illustration was published by *Woman's Own* magazine and he has since worked for *Sports Illustrated, Esquire, Oui, Playboy, Penthouse, McCall's* and *Quest.* He has won a Gold Medal from the ADC Show, Awards of Excellence from the S of I, a Silver Medal from the One Show and a Clio for a TV commercial. The Greengrass Gallery has exhibited his work.

McMahon, Franklin (b. 1921). Born in Chicago, he attended the AIC, Institute of Design, American Academy of Art and the Chicago Academy of Art from 1939–1950. He studied under E. W. Ball, Francis Chapin and Paul Weighardt. In 1939 he published his first illustration for *Collier's.* Aside from being an illustrator who has worked for all major magazines, he has done eight 16mm documentaries on art, and in election years from 1964 to 1976 he made films for television on art and politics called *The Artist as a Reporter.* He has worked extensively for the American space program covering the launching of *Gemini III, Apollo X,* and *Apollo XI,* the first man on the moon.

McMahon, Mark Andrew (b. 1950). Born in Chicago, he attended the North Shore Art League, Deerpath Art League and Adam State College. He has worked for many magazines, including *Chicago, US Catholic, The Uptowner* and *Chicago Tribune.* His on-the-spot illustrations have led to assignments covering tennis, skiing and rodeo events

for TV and magazines. His work has been shown in many exhibits in Kentucky, Colorado and the Chicago area.

McVicker, Charles T. (b. 1930). Born in Canonsburg, Pennsylvania, he studied under John LaGatta at the ACD for four years. His career began in 1957 with an assignment for *Good Housekeeping* and he has since worked for *Popular Mechanics, Family Circle* and the *American Journal of Nursing.* His illustrations are part of the collections of the National Historical Society and the United States Capitol. A member of the AWS, he was elected President of the S of I in 1976.

Meltzoff, Stanley (b. 1917). Born in New York City, he studied at the Institute of Fine Arts of NYU, ASL and NAD. His first works appeared in *Stars and Stripes* prior to 1945 and in *Who* in 1946. In addition to his various poster and book illustrations, his pieces appeared in *Life, McCall's, The Saturday Evening Post, National Geographic* and *Sports Illustrated.* The ADC and the S of I in New York have awarded him many prizes for his paintings. His specialty as an art historian is Florentine Quattrocento painting.

Milbert, Jacques Gérard (1766–1840). Born in Paris, he came to the US in 1815 to study American flora and fauna. In 1825, a decade later, he returned to France and illustrated *Picturesque Views of North America.* He exhibited several landscapes and figure paintings at the American Academy during his stay and is best known for his landscapes, portraits, miniature paintings and draftsmanship. He died in Paris.

Miller, William Rickary (1818–1893). Born in Staindrop, England, he was trained by his father, Joseph Miller, a landscape painter. He moved to America in 1844 and settled in New York City where he did an enormous amount of American views and illustrations for books and periodicals. He worked in watercolor and oil, and from 1837 until his death he concerned himself with pen and ink drawings for a book entitled *1,000 Gems of American Landscape* which was never published.

Minor, Wendell Gordon (b. 1944). Born in Aurora, Illinois, he studied at the Ringling School of Art from 1963 to 1966. He worked as a designer for Hallmark Cards and his first works appeared in their *Cards Magazine.* He was an art director and designer, both in Chicago and New York, before beginning a free-lance illustration career in 1970. His clients include *Bantam, Random House, Avon, Dell* and other book publishers. He has had exhibitions in New York at the Greengrass and Chisholm Galleries and in New Mexico at the Brandywine Gallery. He is a member of the faculty at SVA.

Mitchell, Charles Davis (1887–1940). Born in Wilmington, Delaware, he maintained a studio in Philadelphia throughout his career. His charcoal and pencil drawings, often of beautiful women, appeared for many years in *Redbook, McCall's, Delineator, Cosmopolitan* and others. He was a member of the AG and Art Club of Philadelphia.

Mora, F. Luis (1874–1940). Born in Montevideo, Uruguay, he was an award winning student at both the Boston Museum School of Fine Arts and the ASL. His introduction to illustration followed in 1892 when he began working for major magazines and painting murals, the first of which was done in 1900 for the Lynn, Massachusetts Library. His portrait of President Harding still hangs in the White House. During his long career he utilized several media, but etchings and color washes predominated in his work. A member of the S of I, he died in New York City.

Moran, Edward Percy (1862–1935). Born in Philadelphia, he studied under his father, Edward Moran, marine painter. at the Pennsylvania Academy of Fine Art and also

at the NAD in London and Paris. His specialty was colonial scenes and other historical subjects. He worked under the name of Percy Moran, and was awarded the first Hallgarten Prize from the NAD in 1886 and the first Gold Medal from the American Art Association in 1888. He was a member of the AWS.

Morgan, Wallace (1873–1948). Born in New York City, he studied at the NAD for six years. This led to an early career with New York newspapers such as *The Telegram, The Herald* and *The Sun.* His works appeared in both books and magazines, earning him recognition as a member of the NAD in 1947 and as President of the S of I from 1929 to 1936. *Collier's* published *Abroad at Home,* his depiction of the Deep South, and he illustrated Richard Harding Davis's books as had Gibson and Christy. An instructor for many years at the ASL, he was later made an honorary member.

Moss, Donald (b. 1920). Born in Somerville, Massachusetts, he studied at PI and ASL with such eminent instructors as Paul Rand, Will Burton and Howard Trafton. His first illustration was done for *Collier's* in 1948. He has specialized in sports art for many years and has worked for *Sports Illustrated* for over 20 years. In 1976 he designed the United States Olympic stamps.

Mullins, Frank (b. 1924). Born in Springfield, Massachusetts, he received his BFA from PI in 1959 and his MA from Columbia University in 1966. His first illustration was a portrait of Murray Rose done as a cover for *Sports Illustrated* in 1961.

Myers, Louis (b. 1915). Born in Paris, he studied for many years at the New School for Social Research and the ASL. His first work, a children's book entitled *Clementina,* was published by *Western Publishing.* He has since illustrated many magazines and books in his unique cartoon style. He presently lives in Peekskill, New York.

Nagaoka, Shusei S. (b. 1936). Born in Nagasaki, he studied at Musashino Art University for three years. In the 1960's he had his first illustration published in *Boys Magazine* in Tokyo and has since received awards from the AIGA and the S of I in New York. His works are in the Yokohama Marine Museum in Japan.

Nast, Thomas (1840–1902). Born in Bavaria, he came with his family to America in 1846. His first illustrations appeared in *Frank Leslie's Illustrated Newspaper* when he was 15, and he was soon an accomplished reportorial and cartoon artist. He received assignments to London and Sicily in 1860 and during the Civil War he reported for *Harper's.* He was a regular contributor to *Harper's* until 1886, and his political cartoons were very influential. Boss Tweed and Tammany Hall in the 1870's and Horace Greeley during the 1872 Presidential campaign were among the many opponents that were the target of his biting drawings. He is also credited with initiating the donkey and elephant as political symbols. During his later years he free-lanced, but never regained his previous high standing. He died a few months after his appointment by President Roosevelt as American Consul to Ecuador.

Negron, William (b. 1925). Born in Bayonne, New Jersey, he studied at Cooper Union, SVA and the Pratt Graphics Workshop. For several years he held the position of art director for Clairol. His editorial illustrations have appeared in *The New York Times,* Exxon's magazine *The Lamp* and in several travel books. In addition to his editorial work, he is active in advertising design and book illustration for such clients as *Houghton Mifflin.*

Neibart, Wally (b. 1925). Born in Camden, New Jersey, he studied for four years under Henry Pitz at the Philadelphia College of Art, where he later returned to teach drawing. Since 1952, the year of his first illustration for the *Philadelphia Inquirer*, he has worked for many major magazines including *Esquire, Playboy, Good Housekeeping* and *The New Republic*. His works are in several private collections and have been shown in exhibitions at the Philadelphia Art Alliance, Widmeir and Cheltenham Art Center.

Nelson, G. Patrick. Residing in New York City, he contributed regularly to *Cosmopolitan* and the H. J. Heinz Company. A member of the S of I from 1911, he later joined the Salmagundi Club and the Authors' League of America in New York.

Nessim, Barbara (b. 1939). Born in New York City, she received a BFA from PI and taught at SVA from 1967 to 1975. Her works have been shown in the Louvre, Mead Gallery, Whitney Museum, AIGA and the Erotic Art Gallery and have received awards from the S of I, AIGA and ADC. Her poster works were commissioned by Lincoln Centre and WBAI.

Newell, Peter Sheaf (1862–1924). Born in Illinois, he first worked in a photographic studio before coming in 1882 to New York, where he studied briefly at the ASL. The creator of humorous cartoons for magazines such as *Harper's*, he later illustrated the children's books *Topsys and Turvys* and *Peter Newell's Pictures and Rhymes*.

Nurick, Irving (1894–1963). Born in Brooklyn, New York, he was trained at PI, the ASL and in Paris. His illustrations in *Ladies' Home Journal* for Elizabeth Woodward's *Sub Deb* articles were published for 15 years. The acclaim from this series and other magazine work led to assignments from such advertisers as Wesson Oil, Adams Hats, Sloane's Furniture and Kimberly Clark Products. A member of the AWS, Artists and Writers and a Life Member of the S of I, he had One-Man Exhibitions in the United States and in Paris, where he lived for many years. The NAD awarded him the Ranger Prize in 1957 and the Samuel Finley Breeze Award in 1960.

Oakley, Thornton (1881–1955). He attended the University of Pennsylvania, where he concentrated on architecture; however, his training in illustration resulted from his studies with Howard Pyle. His editorial work appeared in many major magazines including *the Century* and *National Geographic*, for which he painted a series entitled *American Industries Geared for War* in the 1940's. His works have been in several exhibitions and are in the collections of museums in the United States and abroad.

Oakley, Violet (1874–1961). Born in New York City, she attended the ASL, studying under Cecelia Beaux. She was a pupil of Howard Pyle at the PAFA. Among her most distinguished achievements are the murals for the Pennsylvania State Capitol Building.

Ogden, Henry A. (1856–1936). Born in Philadelphia, he became a staff artist at age 17 for *Frank Leslie's Illustrated Newspaper*. He left after eight years and worked for the Cincinnati-based Stobridge Lithograph Company as a New York staff artist. He is best known for his military art, and his plates can be seen in *Uniforms of the Army of the U.S., 1774–1907* and *Pageants of America, 1925—1929*.

Okon, Mejo (b. 1953). Born in Indianapolis, she studied at the Rochester Institute, Syracuse University and Herron School of Art until 1975. She began her career in Indianapolis with *Young World Magazine* in 1976. She has won a Gold Medal from the Indianapolis ADC and her work was accepted for the S of I Annual Exhibition in 1976.

O'Neill, Rose Cecil (1875–1944). Born in Nebraska. A self-taught artist, she wrote and illustrated the unpublished novel *Calesta* at age 19. Shortly thereafter she came to New York where she worked for *Truth, Life*,

Collier's and *Harper's* publications. She married in 1896 and became a staff artist for *Puck*. Five years later she was divorced, left *Puck*, and was soon married to its editor, Leon Wilson. In 1904 she wrote *The Loves of Edwy* for *Harper's* and illustrated her husband's novels. Early in 1908 she divorced Wilson and moved to Bonniebrook in Missouri, where she originated the Kewpies, the cherubic creatures that made her famous. The Kewpies first appeared in *Ladies' Home Journal* in 1909 and were later seen in *Woman's Home Companion, Good Housekeeping* and as a comic strip in *The New York Journal* in the 1930's. The ubiquitous use of her characters culminated in the creation of the Kewpie Doll in 1912.

Otnes, Fred (b. 1926). Born in Junction City, Kansas, he attended the AIC and the American Academy. Since 1946 his illustrations, exhibiting his fine draftsmanship, have appeared in many publications including *True, The Saturday Evening Post* and *Reader's Digest*. Recently he has concentrated on intricate and superbly crafted assemblages and elegant illustrations utilizing new photographic and printing techniques. He has received over 100 honors, including the Hamilton King Award from the S of I, and is a founding member of the Illustrators Workshop.

Palladini, David (b. 1946). Born in Roteglia, Italy, he studied art from 1964 to 1968 at PI under Jacob Landau and Gabriel Laderman. He produced a poster for Lincoln Center's Vivian Beaumont Theatre in 1965 and has worked for many major magazines and book companies. He has exhibited illustrations at the AIGA, S of I and Saks Fifth Avenue Galleries; his works are also in the collection of the Museum of Warsaw, Poland.

Palmer, Frances Flora Bond (1812–1876). Born in Leicester, England, she came to New York City in the early 1840's. By 1849 she was employed by *Currier & Ives* and became well known for her land and townscapes. Her most important work was a watercolor (which N. Currier lithographed) entitled *The High Bridge at Harlem, New York*. The only woman in her field, she was considered one of the best American lithographers, and her work for *Currier & Ives* extended for many years. She introduced the skill of printing a background tint and helped perfect the lithographic crayon. By 1857 she had done over 200 lithographs for *Currier & Ives*.

Palulian, Dickran P. (b. 1938). Born in Pontiac, Michigan, he studied for two years at the Society of Arts and Crafts in Detroit and began his career there in 1958. The recipient of awards from the Michigan Watercolor Show, Detroit ADC and GAG of Detroit, he has illustrated for many magazines and has often exhibited his work in the Detroit area.

Parker, Alfred Charles (b. 1906). Born in St. Louis, Missouri, he studied at the St. Louis School of Fine Arts of Washington University and came to New York in the mid-1930's. His illustrations depicting mothers and daughters for *Cosmopolitan* and *Ladies' Home Journal* were trendsetters of the era. Since his first assignment in 1933 for *Woman's Home Companion*, his illustrations have appeared in most women's magazines and have earned him a number of awards, including election to the S of I Hall of Fame in 1965. He has served as President of the Westport Artists and as a founding faculty member of the FAS. His artwork has been exhibited in the United States and Canada and is in many major collections. A long-time resident of New York and Westport, he now resides in Carmel Valley, California.

Parker, Robert Andrew (b. 1927). Born in Norfolk, Virginia, he attended the AIC and Atelier 17 in New York before beginning his career in 1954. His watercolors and etchings have since appeared in *Fortune, Sports Illustrated, Travel and Leisure* and *The Lamp*. In 1976 he produced a poster, entitled *Third Century*, for Mobil Oil. His paintings

have been part of exhibitions at the Whitney Museum, Museum of Modern Art and Los Angeles County Museum.

Parrish, Maxfield (1870–1966). Born in Philadelphia, he spent his early life in his father's studio in Massachusetts and later in New Hampshire. He studied architecture at Haverford College in 1888, but left to study art at the Pennsylvania Academy where he stayed until 1894. After further training at Drexel Institute under Howard Pyle, he opened a studio in Philadelphia which stayed in operation for many years. His first illustration for magazines brought him recognition and lucrative work in advertising. Edison Mazda Lamps was one of his long-standing accounts. He illustrated the desert life of Arizona for a series in *the Century*. His works sold as posters for many years through the House of Art in New York. In his last years he devoted himself to landscape work and murals. He painted the vast mural in the dining room atop the Curtis Publishing Company building in Philadelphia. With his wife, whom he met at Drexel, he raised his family at a personally designed home in Windsor, Vermont, called The Oaks. His work was often imitated, but no one could equal the incomparable use of light and brilliant color that made his paintings legendary.

Paschke, Edward (b. 1939). Born in Chicago, he studied at the AIC where he received both his BFA and MFA He has exhibited his work at the Whitney Museum, Museum of Contemporary Art in Chicago, Washington and Mexico City and the Darthea Speyer Gallery in Paris. The AIC, Brooklyn Museum, the Museum of Modern Art in Vienna, Austria and the Museum Boymans in Rotterdam own his work. He has taught painting, drawing and design at the School of the AIC, Barat College in Illinois and Columbia College in Chicago.

Patterson, Robert (b. 1898). Born in Chicago, he trained under Harvey Dunn, Walt Louderback and Carl Erickson. In 1922, after sharing a studio with his brother in Chicago, he moved to New York where he received fashion illustration assignments. Two years later he went to France on assignment for *Judge* and in 1927 began working in the Paris office of *Vogue*. He continued his art studies in Paris, returning to America in 1934 to pursue editorial work for *McCall's, Good Housekeeping, Ladies' Home Journal* and *American*. A member of the Westport Artists, he was an instructor at the FAS.

Patterson, Russell (1896–1977). Born in Omaha, Nebraska, he moved with his family to Canada and studied at McGill University. There he illustrated a French comic strip until he went to study at the AIC and the Academy of Fine Arts. His work for department stores gained him a reputation for interior design, a skill he utilized in the 1930's in Hollywood and on Broadway. With the advent of the Jazz Age the drawings he did for *College Humor* were highly popular. His flappers and style-setting collegians in raccoon coats and galoshes were eagerly imitated. Multi-talented, he designed costumes for Ziegfeld, and windows for Macy's, hotel lobbies and restaurants, in addition to illustrating for advertisements and magazines.

Paus, Herbert Andrew (1880–1946). Born in Minneapolis, he studied at the ASL under George Bridgman. After his first illustration, an editorial cartoon, appeared in 1896, he did many covers for *The Saturday Evening Post, Woman's Home Companion, Collier's, Popular Science* and *Redbook*. In World War I he did the poster *Over the Top* and later worked on many book illustrations such as *The Children's Blue Bird* by Madame Maurice Maeterlinck. In 1913 he designed the stage set for *The Betrothal* by Maeterlinck.

Peak, Robert (b. 1928). Born in Colorado, he received his art training at the ACD. After his arrival in New York, he was given assignments from advertising clients and periodicals such as *Cosmopolitan* and *Newsweek*. His deceptively simple style and innovative techniques have placed him in great demand among major magazines. A regular contributor to *TV Guide* and *Sports Illustrated*, he has also illustrated posters for movies such as *Rollerball*, *Mame* and *The Missouri Breaks*. Among his many citations are Artist of the Year in 1961 from the AG of New York and from the S of I, and the Hamilton King Award in 1968, in addition to several Awards of Excellence and Gold Medals from the Annual Exhibitions.

Peck, Clara Elsene (b. 1883). Born in Allegan, Michigan, she was educated at the Minneapolis School of Fine Arts and studied under William Merritt Chase. She illustrated for many women's magazines, using her particular talent for depicting women and children in a wide variety of roles and personalities. In her advertising work for Procter and Gamble, Metropolitan Life and Aeolian Company, she showed great sensitivity in her renderings of people, executed in a decorative style. She won many awards, exhibited her work widely and was a member of the AWS.

Pegram, Fred. During his career, he produced both illustrations and etchings for magazine and book publishers. While he lived in London, his work appeared in *Punch* and, for many years, in the books published by *James Connell and Sons* of Glasgow, Scotland. His technique of using detailed flower designs as decorations is best noted in his illustrations for *Marrayat* published by *Ready-MacMillan*.

Penfield, Edward (1866–1925). Born in Brooklyn, New York, he studied at the ASL and went on to become Art Editor for *Harper's* from 1890 to 1901. Although he did cover art for magazines such as *Collier's*, his outstanding contribution to the profession was his exquisite posters. Large, flat shapes, clean line and little detail were the hallmarks of his artwork. This style was often demonstrated in elegant illustrations of horse-drawn coaches, a favorite subject of his. In 1904, *Scribner's* published *Holland Sketches*, a series of illustrations inspired by his trips abroad. Through the example of his work, his art direction at *Harper's* and his instruction at the ASL, he had a profound impact on American illustration.

Pennell, Joseph (1860–1926). Born in Philadelphia, he studied art in Pennsylvania before leaving to spend many years in Europe. During his stay abroad he married Elizabeth Robins, with whom he wrote several travel books. *Harper's*, *McClure's* and *the Century* were among the publishers that sent him on working trips around the world. His great interest in engineering led to several reportage assignments of the Panama Canal and Niagara Falls. He returned to America and retired in Brooklyn Heights.

Pepper, Robert Ronald (b. 1938). Born in Portsmouth, New Hampshire, he attended Los Angeles City College and received a BA in advertising illustration from ACD. Since his first published work for *The Saturday Evening Post* in 1964, he has won awards from the Society of Publication Designers, Mead Library of Ideas and the S of I. His covers for *Ace*, *Ballantine*, *Avon*, *Dell* and the *New American Library* won him an award from Fantasy/Science Fiction Readers. He has also produced several posters and illustrated for major magazines.

Perard, Victor S. (1870–1957). Born in Paris, he studied art in France at the École des Beaux Arts and in New York at the ASL and the NAD. Later, he became an instructor at Cooper Union and the Traphagen School of Fashion. His works were often seen in *Scribner's*, *Harper's* and *the Century* magazines.

Peterson, Perry (1908–1958). Born in Minneapolis, Minnesota, he received his art training through the Federal Schools Course and later at the AIC. His career began with advertising assignments in Chicago and Detroit, but he soon moved to New York where he worked at the Byron Musser Studio. His free-lance career began in 1942, and he illustrated for *The Saturday Evening Post*, *Liberty*, *Good Housekeeping* and others.

Petruccelli, Antonio (b. 1907). Born in Fort Lee, New Jersey, he attended the Master School of United Arts in New York in the early 1920's. He began his career in 1929 with a *House Beautiful* cover and has since illustrated many books for *Time-Life*, as well as many magazines, over a 40-year period. His posters have won awards from *House Beautiful*, the American Society for Cancer Control and International Press Exhibition in Cologne, 1928. He designed the postage stamp for the Steel Centenary in 1957 and an award winning medal for the Franklin Mint in 1973.

Petty, Mary (1899–1976). Born in Hampton, New Jersey. Her works appeared in *The New Yorker* from 1927 until 1966, during which time she illustrated 38 covers, her last on Mother's Day in 1966. Her artwork was often satirical, preying on rich dowagers. In 1927 she married a New York cartoonist, Alan Dunn.

Pfeifer, Herman (b. 1879). Born in Milwaukee, Wisconsin, he studied art for a period of time with Howard Pyle. His illustrations appeared frequently in *Harper's*, *the Century*, *McClure's*, *Ladies' Home Journal*, *Good Housekeeping* and others. He was a member of the S of I and lived in New York.

Phillips, Coles (1880–1927). Born in Springfield, Ohio, he graduated from Kenyon College where he illustrated for the campus magazine. He soon came to New York where, after a brief stay in an advertising agency, he opened his own studio. He worked for *Life* and was especially known for his full color cover illustrations and his paintings of beautiful women. The Fadeaway Girl, his trademark, led to lucrative advertising assignments with Holeproof Hosiery and Community Plate Silverware.

Pimsler, Alvin J. (b. 1918). Born in New York City, he attended PI and the ASL, where he studied under Howard Trafton. His first published illustration in 1940, for L. Bamberger Company, led to his successful career as a fashion artist, his work appearing in ads for Saks Fifth Avenue for 25 years. Represented in the USAF Museum, Smithsonian Institution, Portraits, Inc., and Gallery of Sports, he has taught at SVA, PSD, FIT and served for two years as President of S of I.

Pinkney, Jerry (b. 1939). Born in Philadelphia, he studied at the Philadelphia Museum College of Art and went to school with Roger Hane. His first illustration was done in Boston for *Little, Brown* in 1963. He has since won many awards and illustrated for *Seventeen*, *Post*, *Boys' Life* and *Essence Magazine*. His work has been shown at the Brooklyn Museum, S of I, Brandeis University in Massachusetts and the Studio Museum in Harlem.

Pitz, Henry Clarence (1895–1976). Born in Philadelphia, he attended the Philadelphia College of Art and, after World War I, the Spring Garden Institute. Over 160 books were illustrated by him, as well as numerous periodicals including *Scribner's*, *Gourmet* and *The Saturday Evening Post*. Though he worked in all media, his specialty was pen and ink, the techniques of which he described in a number of instructional art books. His scholarship was reflected in his work of many years as Associate Editor of *American Artist* magazine. A recipient of many awards, he is represented in museums, corporations and private collections throughout the country.

Podwil, Jerome (b. 1938). Born in New York, he attended PI and the ASL from 1955 to 1960. He has illustrated for many major magazines, especially *Playboy*, and has received several awards, including a Gold Medal from the S of I Annual Exhibition, Awards of Excellence from Chicago 1974 and 1976, and a medal from the Communication Arts Annual.

Pogany, William Andrew (1882–1955). Born in Szeged, Hungary, he studied art in Budapest, Paris and Munich. London, in 1906, was where he began his productive career as a book illustrator. After coming to the US in 1915, he illustrated some of his best known works, including *Alice's Adventures in Wonderland*, *Gulliver's Travels* and *Willy Pogany's Mother Goose*. He also painted portraits and murals and served as art director for Hollywood Motion Picture Studios.

Pohl, Dennis (b. 1941). Born in Milwaukee, Wisconsin, he received his BA from the University of Wisconsin and his MFA from PI in Brooklyn. He studied under Dore Ashton and Arthur Okamura and his first published illustration, entitled *Vatican Library*, was done for *ESP Disk* in 1972. He has designed numerous album covers for RCA, Columbia, London, Arista and Savoy.

Potthast, Edward Henry (1857–1927). Born in Cincinnati, Ohio, he studied at the Cincinnati Art Academy and traveled throughout Europe, studying in Paris, Munich and Antwerp. Settling in New York in 1896, he began producing lithographs as well as pen and ink drawings for *Scribner's* and *the Century*. During his later years, he concentrated on oil painting.

Price, Garrett (b. 1896). Born in Bucyrus, Kansas, he attended the University of Wyoming and AIC. At age 16 he received his first training in Chicago at *The Tribune*. His career as a free-lance magazine illustrator at *Collier's*, *Scribner's*, *College* and *Humor* earned him a reputation for witty sketches, but he is best known for his covers for *The New Yorker*. A long-time resident of Connecticut, he was a member of the Westport Artists, Mystic Art Association and the S of I.

Price, Norman Mills (1877–1951). Born in Canada, he studied art in London and Paris, and is best known for the historical accuracy he brought to his assignments. His drawings, most often done in pen and ink, appeared in magazines and advertising campaigns. He was a charter member of the Guild of Free-lance Artists and a President of the S of I.

Prince, William Meade (1893–1951). Born in Roanoke, Virginia, he studied at the New York School of Fine and Applied Arts. After five years of doing advertising art in Chicago, he moved to Connecticut and began illustrating for major magazines in New York. He is particularly noted for his series of illustrations for Roark Bradford's Negro stories in *Collier's* magazine. He taught illustration and figure drawing and later became head of the art department at the University of North Carolina.

Prohaska, Ray (b. 1901). Born in Muo Dalmatia, Yugoslavia, he attended the California School of Fine Art in San Francisco for four years. His first published illustration was a watercolor done for the *Delineator* in 1930 and later he illustrated the books *Eddie No Name* (Pantheon, 1963) and *Who's Afraid* (Crowell Collier, 1963). He was an artist-in-residence at Washington and Lee University from 1964 to 1969 and at Wake Forest University from 1969 to 1975. His works are owned by the New Britain Museum of American Art and the Guild Hall in East Hampton, New York.

Punchatz, Don Ivan (b. 1936). Born in Hillside, New Jersey, he attended SVA and Cooper Union. He worked as an art director for several years before beginning free-lance illustration in 1966. His studio, The Sketch Pad, was organized in 1970. His work for magazines such as *Playboy*, *Oui*, *Penthouse*, *Esquire*, *True* and *Time* has earned him awards from the S of I and from many ADCs.

Pyle, Howard (1853–1911). Born in Wilmington, Delaware, he was sent by his Quaker parents to Philadelphia at age 16 to study art under Belgian Professor Van der Weilen. He studied at the ASL after coming to New York in 1876, and there his stories and illustrations began appearing in *Scribner's* and *St. Nicholas* magazine. He was an author as well as an artist and had a well earned reputation when he returned to Wilmington in 1879. Among his illustrated books were *The Merry Adventures of Robin Hood, Salt and Pepper* and *The Wonder Clock.* He was asked to try the new techniques in color reproduction at the turn of the century and this created a whole new era in illustration. His teaching career, by far his most important contribution, began at Drexel Institute in 1894 and he convinced them to sponsor summer training classes at Chadds Ford, Pennsylvania. These classes led Pyle to open his school in his Wilmington studio; it was here, from 1901 to 1910, that the top illustrators who were to emerge in the 1900's were schooled, and many, like Harvey Dunn, passed on the training to their students. Also an aspiring muralist, Pyle traveled to Europe in 1910 in search of larger studio space. He died in Florence, Italy.

Rabut, Paul L. (b. 1914). Born in New York City, he attended CCNY, ASL, and GCSA. In 1935 his first illustration was published for *Ainslee's Magazine.* His work has been shown at the Metropolitan Museum of Art, NAD in New York, International Watercolor Show in Chicago and Pennsylvania Academy of Fine Arts in Philadelphia. Not only an advertising illustrator for General Motors, Ford, Western Electric, General Electric, Shell Oil and US Steel, he is also an expert on primitive art and has lectured at PI, Newark School of Art and the S of I.

Rackow, Leo (b. 1901). Born in Spring Valley, New York, he attended PSD, then GCSA as a student of Harvey Dunn, and studied in Paris under Léger. Over the years he has received a number of New York ADC awards and several of his posters are in the LC collection. His illustrations have appeared in *The New Yorker, Liberty, Collier's* and *True.* The Museum of Modern Art, Dudensing Gallery and Harlow Gallery have all exhibited his work.

Raleigh, Henry Patrick (1880–1944). Born in Portland, Oregon, he studied art at Hopkins Academy in San Francisco, after which he became a reporter-artist for the *San Francisco Examiner* where William Randolph Hearst first noticed his enormous talent and sent him to New York to work on the *Journal.* He began extensive work for all the major magazines and was particularly gifted as an etcher, and also as an illustrator, using wash, line and colored inks to depict fashionable society. He won the Shaw Prize for Illustration from the Salmagundi Club in 1916 and the Gold Medal for Advertising Art in America in 1926.

Ramus, Michael (b. 1917). Born in Naples, Italy, he attended Exeter Academy at Yale University and the ASL, with additional training under Harry Sternberg, Howard Trafton and Elliot O'Hara. He has worked for *Life, Sports Illustrated, Smithsonian, American Heritage,* among others, and received the Award for Distinctive Merit in the 29th Annual Exhibition of the ADC.

Rea, Gardner (1892–1966). Born in Ironton, Ohio, he attended Ohio University in 1914, and later, the Columbus Art School. A free-lance cartoonist and writer, he worked for *Judge, Life* and *The New Yorker.* His cartoons were exhibited in museums all over the world and he was author and illustrator of the books *The Gentleman Says It's Pixies,* 1944, and *Gardner Rea's Sideshow,* 1945. He lived in Brookhaven, Long Island for many years.

Redwood, Allen Carter (1834–1922). A book and magazine illustrator, he worked for *the Century* in the 1880's, illustrating their *Battles and Leaders of the Civil War.*

His illustrations were usually done in pen and ink, capturing the intricate details of soldiers, war battles and the countryside. While serving in the Confederate Army he was captured in Virginia in 1862 but was later released.

Rehberger, Gustav (b. 1910). Born in Riedlingsdorf, Austria, he came to the US at age 13 and attended the AIC and Art Instruction School in Minneapolis, as a scholarship student. In 1949 he was awarded the Most Creative Painting from the Audubon Artists, and in 1966 he received the Stern Award. He has done a number of movie posters, such as *The Command, Moby Dick, Defiant Ones* and *Animal World.* He currently teaches and lectures at the ASL in figure drawing, composition and painting.

Reinhard, Siegbert (b. 1941). Born in Germany, he began his career in 1959 and two years later came to the United States. He has had his illustrations published in *Oui* magazine as well as accepted in several S of I Annual Exhibitions. Known for his incredibly intricate paper sculptures, he has utilized this skill in the design of many sets for television productions. He is presently working in Los Angeles, California.

Reinhart, Charles Stanley (1844–1896). Born in Pittsburgh, he studied in Europe at the Atelier Suisse and at the Munich Royal Academy. Upon returning to the United States in 1870, he began a seven-year relationship with *Harper's* where his character studies reflected a discerning eye for social types. His line and wash drawings appeared in publications until his death.

Reiss, Winold (1888–1953). Born in the Black Forest, Germany, he was trained as an artist by his father, Fritz Reiss, a well known painter and portrait artist. In 1913 he came to America for the sole purpose of studying the North American Indian in his native habitat. Through his sensitive, decorative depiction of the Indian, he helped restore and give substance to the legend of the red man. From 1933 he was an assistant professor at the College of Fine Arts at NYU. He designed mosaic murals of the history of American railroad for the Cincinnati Union Terminal Building.

Remington, Frederic Sackrider (1861–1909). Born in Canton, New York, he studied at the Yale University School of Fine Arts before heading West in 1880. Experiencing camp-life of the cowboy first-hand and witnessing Indian engagements, he brought excitement and realism to his drawings of Western scenes. After moving to New York in 1885, he produced many finished illustrations for books and magazines from his sketches of the West. In 1888 *the Century* published his illustrated edition of *Teddy Roosevelt's Ranch Life and The Hunting Trail,* and in 1898 he accompanied Roosevelt's Roughriders to Cuba as an artist-correspondent. Later in his career, his Indian and horse paintings were published in *Collier's Weekly* while he continued to illustrate for such authors as Henry Longfellow, Owen Wister, Charles King and Teddy Roosevelt. Collections of his works are in the Amon Carter Museum of Western Art in Texas, The Whitney Gallery of Western Art and the Remington Art Memorial in Ogdensburg, New York, near his birthplace.

Renaud, Phil (b. 1934). Born in Edmonton, Canada, he studied first at the Chicago Academy of Fine Arts and then, after a brief stint in a Chicago studio, attended ACD, studying under John LaGatta and Eugene Edwards. Returning to Chicago, he received many assignments from book publishers such as *Scott, Foresman & Co., Harper & Row* and *Rand McNally. Playboy, Atlanta* and *Chicago* have featured his editorial work. Recently he has been concentrating on fine art painting.

Revere, Paul (1735–1818). Born in Boston, he was trained as a silversmith by his father and in 1765 began engraving on copper. He worked as a political cartoonist, copper

worker, bell caster and watercolorist. During the Revolutionary War he was a courier for the Massachusetts Committee of Correspondence. His intense interest in the developing difficulties between the colonies and Great Britain became evident in his political cartoons which were effective propaganda for rebellion and were published in the *Royal American Magazine.* Historically, he is known as one of the earliest American engravers who captivated the interest of the people through his cartoon-like depictions of the Revolutionary War.

Rhead, Louis (1857–1926). Born in England, he studied there before coming to the US in 1883. His oil and watercolor work earned him a Gold Medal at the St. Louis Exposition of 1904. He is best known for his decorative color posters which appeared in *The Sun, The Herald* and *The Journal* in the 1890's. He illustrated classic works by such authors as Defoe, the Grimm brothers, Bunyan, Stevenson and Swift; he and his two brothers illustrated several of these books together.

Richards, Walter DuBois (b. 1907). Born in Penfield, Ohio, he studied at the Cleveland Institute of Art under Henry G. Keller, Frank Wilcox and Carl Gaertner. In 1930 his first published illustration was done in dry brush for *Child Life* magazine. He won the highest award in lithography from the Cleveland Museum, the Lily Saportas Award from the AWS in 1962 and a Special Award from the USAF in 1964. He has done extensive book, magazine and poster illustration since 1940 and his work appeared in the *200 Years of Watercolor Painting* exhibition in 1966 at the Metropolitan Museum of Art.

Riley, Kenneth (b. 1919). Born in Waverly, Missouri, he studied at KCAI and the ASL, where he was taught by Harvey Dunn, DuMond, Benton and George Bridgman. He illustrated *The Greatest Story Ever Told* by Anthony Trollope and he has done work for *The Saturday Evening Post, Life, National Geographic, Reader's Digest* and *McCall's.* His work is owned by the Custer Museum, West Point Museum and the White House Collection.

Riley, Nicholas F. (1900–1944). Born in Brooklyn, he attended PI and Mr. Scott School in Paris. His first illustration was a full color oil done for the *West Point Year Book* in 1928. *Good Housekeeping, The Saturday Evening Post, Woman's Home Companion* and *Field and Stream* are some of the magazines for which he illustrated. His portrait work was selected and hung at the Paris Grand Salon in 1925.

Roberts, Morton (1927–1964). Born in Worcester, Massachusetts, he graduated from Yale University School of Fine Arts. He illustrated for many major magazines, most notably *Life,* for which he painted a series on *The History of Russia* and *The Story of Jazz.* Among his many awards was the Edward Austin Abbey Fellowship from the NAD. He was an instructor of life drawing at PI.

Robinson, Boardman (1876–1952). Born in Nova Scotia, Canada, he studied at the Massachusetts Normal Art School and in Paris. He worked as an art editor and illustrator for several magazines and also painted murals for Rockefeller Center in New York and the Department of Justice building in Washington. He illustrated Dostoievsky's *The Brothers Karamazov* in 1933 and *The Idiot* in 1916, both published by *Random House.* Since 1930 he has been a teacher and art director at the Colorado Springs Fine Arts Center.

Rockwell, Norman (b. 1894). Norman Rockwell is one of America's best known and most loved illustrators, perhaps because his warm portrayal of human sympathies and emotions reflected the spirit of the country during the half century that his paintings graced the pages of all major magazines. He left high school to study art at the NAD and later at the ASL under the guidance of Thomas Fogarty and George Bridgman. The first of more than 300 covers he did for *The Saturday Evening Post* appeared in 1916, marking the onset of his long relationship with this magazine, which served as a forum for his superbly crafted, often humorous statements about the American people. In World War II the essence of Franklin D. Roosevelt's war aims was captured in Rockwell's powerful *Four Freedoms* posters, one of which, a version of *Freedom of Speech*, is part of the permanent collection of the Metropolitan Museum of Art. The list of awards and honors bestowed upon him is endless, ranging from his being cited as a Great Living American by the United States Chamber of Commerce in 1957 to his election to the S of I Hall of Fame in 1958 in recognition of the expert hand and keen sensibilities that have earned him a place in American history.

Rodewig, Doris (b. 1927). Born in Westfield, New Jersey, she attended PI and began her career as an illustrator in 1949. Since then she has shown her work in the National Arts Club, S of I, where she is a member, and the Salmagundi Club, which gave her the Best in Show Award in 1975. Her work hangs in the Pentagon and the Smithsonian Institution. Currently living in New York City, she is active in book illustration.

Rogers, Howard (b. 1932). Born in Medford, Oregon, he studied at the ACD, where he graduated with honors in Advertising Illustration. Before becoming a free-lance illustrator, he worked for McNamara Studio, Graphic House and New Center Studio in Detroit. He has won several awards including an Award of Excellence from the S of I.

Rogers, William Allen (1854–1931). Born in Springfield, Ohio, he began his career at the age of 14 as a political cartoonist for Midwestern newspapers. He later drew cartoons and served as an artist-reporter at *Harper's* and other Eastern newspapers. His autobiography, entitled *A World Worthwhile*, was published in 1922.

Rosenfeld, Mort (b. 1928). Born in Brooklyn, New York, he attended the School of Industrial Arts and the ASL. His first published illustration, an advertisement for US Rubber, appeared in *Life* magazine in 1948. Though primarily concentrating on editorial work, he has also illustrated books, including *Eight Bailed Out* (1952) and *Where Love Has Gone* (1960). The Silvermine Guild and New Haven Paint and Clay Gallery have exhibited his work.

Ross, Alex (b. 1908). Born in Dunfermline, Scotland, he came with his family to America and settled in the Pittsburgh area. He attended Carnegie Institute of Technology and later received an honorary degree from Boston College. His art career began in Pennsylvania, but he soon came to New York and worked in advertising. In 1942 he painted the first of 130 covers for *Good Housekeeping*. He has contributed to the USAF Art Program and his works are in the collections of the New Britain Museum of American Art, the Mormon Church (six murals exhibited at the New York World's Fair) and Fairfield University where he is on the board of trustees.

Ruffins, Reynold (b. 1930). Born in New York City, he graduated from Cooper Union in 1951, the year his first illustration was published. An early member of Push Pin Studios, he has worked in advertising agencies and been a partner in his own studio. A regular contributor to *Family Circle*, he designed and illustrated several children's books for *Charles Scribner's Sons*. The AIGA, ADC, S of I and *The New York Times Book Review* have all presented him with awards.

Russell, Charles Marion (1864–1926). Born in Oak Hill, Missouri, he became one of the best known Western artists, bringing an authenticity to his paintings that resulted from his travels and his work as a wrangler and cowhand. His knowledge of Indian lore and lifestyle was acquired during the several months he spent living with a tribe in Alberta, Canada. At age 16, with no formal training, he began sketching life in the cattle country of Montana. Some of his early works were published in *Harper's Weekly* and seen in his own showings in Montana's best known saloons. After the turn of the century he started to concentrate on book illustrating and received assignments from *Appleton*, *Putnam's* and *Macmillan*. He also wrote books on Western and Indian life, the best known of which is *Trails Plowed Under* published in 1927 by *Doubleday, Doran*. He lived most of his life in Montana, where his mural *Lewis and Clark Meeting the Flathead Indians at Ross's Hole* hangs in the State Capitol.

Saalburg, Leslie (1902–1975). Having studied briefly at the ASL, he continued his self education at various studios. His style, often color washes over line drawings, portrayed the old, genteel manners of the elegant and was much in demand for editorial and advertising clients. His work appeared in *Collier's, Vogue, Town and Country* and several portfolios for *Esquire*. Ford Motor Co., Cannon Mills and Hiram Walker Distillers were among his many advertising clients, earning him two awards from the New York ADC.

Sacks, Cal O. (b. 1914). Born in Brookline, Massachusetts, he studied with Kimon Nicolaides. Beginning his career in 1933, he has worked for the *American Heritage Publishing Co.*, illustrated many books and had shows with General Electric, the USAF and S of I, of which he is a member. He has two married children and resides with his wife, who is also an illustrator, in Westport, Connecticut.

Saint-Mémin, Charles Balthazar Julien Fevret de (1770–1852). Born in Dijon, France, he came to America in 1793 after the outbreak of the French Revolution. He started his career as a landscape artist and later became interested in portraiture, often reducing the profiles to miniature size and engraving them himself. From 1804 to 1809 he traveled around cities, painting portraits and landscapes. In 1814 he returned to Dijon, France where he served as director of a local museum until his death.

Saldutti, Denise (b. 1953). Born in Newark, New Jersey, she attended PSD, where she studied under Maurice Sendak. In 1974 she began illustrating and was selected to appear in the S of I Annual Show in 1975 and 1976.

Sample, Paul (1896–1974). Born in Kentucky, he received his art training from Jonas Lie. During his long career as an editorial and advertising illustrator he earned a reputation for painting country landscapes. Among his clients were Maxwell House Coffee and Ford Motor Company. His works were exhibited at the 1940 New York World's Fair and at the Golden Gate International Exposition. A long-time resident of New Hampshire, he was artist-in-residence at Dartmouth College and a member of the NAD.

Santore, Charles (b. 1935). Born in Philadelphia, he attended the Philadelphia College of Art. He began his career in 1959 with an illustration for *The Saturday Evening Post* after studying with Henry Pitz and Albert Gold. He has illustrated for most major magazines and was awarded Gold Medals from the Philadelphia ADC. In 1972, he received an Award of Excellence from the S of I and the Hamilton King Award.

Sarg, Tony (1882–1942). Born in Guatemala, he had no professional training when he began working for *Sketch Magazine* in London. He came to the United States in 1914 and organized a marionette workshop and animated cartoons before his first assignment appeared in *The Saturday Evening Post*. He was a frequent contributor to the periodicals of the 1920's and 1930's but also pursued the illustration of children's books and the designing of wallpaper, pottery and toys.

Sarka, Charles Nicolas (1879–1960). Rather than going to school, he traveled extensively in the South Seas, Africa, Tahiti and Morocco. He began illustrating for newspapers in Chicago, San Francisco and New York. By 1904, he was illustrating for *Judge, Cosmopolitan* and later most of the major magazines. He was a lifetime member of the AWS and was known for his mastery of watercolor and pen and ink.

Schaare, Harry J. (b. 1922). Born in New York City, he attended NYU School of Architecture and PI. His career began in 1949 with cover art for *Bantam Books* and he has since worked for most major book publishers and magazines, including *The Saturday Evening Post, True, Reader's Digest* and *Rolling Stone*. He has done many posters for movies and advertising and has exhibited in the Smithsonian Institution, the Pentagon, Grand Central Gallery, S of I, of which he is a member, and in numerous other galleries. The USAF has given him assignments in America, Europe and Asia.

Schaeffer, Mead (b. 1898). Born in Freedom Plains, New York, he studied at PI and privately with Harvey Dunn and Dean Cornwell. His career in magazine illustration began at a young age and before long his works appeared in most major magazines including *The Saturday Evening Post* and *American*. His World War II *Post* covers of the branches of the service, as well as his other *Post* artwork, formed an exhibit which toured the United States and Canada. He lived for some time in Arlington, Vermont, a lifelong friend and neighbor of Norman Rockwell. His works are in the collection of the S of I.

Schleinkofer, David J. (b. 1951). Born in Philadelphia, he attended Bucks County Community College and the Philadelphia College of Art. His first published illustration appeared in 1974 and he has since been illustrating paperback books and doing editorial work for *Cue* and *Cosmopolitan*. His artwork was selected for S of I Annual Shows in 1975 and 1976.

Schnackenberg, Roy (b. 1934). Born in Chicago, he received a BFA from Miami University in Ohio. After military service he joined the art staff at Foote, Cone and Belding in Chicago while pursuing his avocation for fine art. Galleries in Chicago have exhibited his paintings and sculptures in One-Man Shows. *Playboy* magazine, for which he works exclusively, has featured his editorial illustrations for the past 15 years.

Schneider, Frederick (b. 1946). Born in Los Angeles, he studied at PI, SVA and PSD in New York with Jacob Lawrence and Seymour Chwast. His first job appeared in *Crawdaddy* magazine in 1974 and he has since illustrated book covers, film strips, theater posters and editorial pieces for *Cue, Psychology Today* and *The New York Times*. He received an Award of Excellence from the S of I in 1976 and has had his artwork exhibited in Battle Creek, Michigan.

Schongut, Emanuel (b. 1936). Born in Monticello, New York, he received his BFA and MFA from PI where he was a classmate of James McMullan. His start in the illustration field was in 1963 with book covers for *Macmillan*. *Doubleday, Dodd, Mead, New York Magazine, Sesame Street* and *Electric Company Magazine* have all utilized his illustrating skills. He has several posters to his credit as well.

Schoonover, Frank Earle (1877–1922). Born in Oxford, New Jersey, he received his art training from Howard Pyle, first at Drexel Institute and later at Chadds Ford, Pennsylvania. His paintings reflect the accuracy of detail stressed by Pyle. He made two trips to Canada to sketch the Hudson Bay area and its Indians, later producing full color illustrations which appeared in magazines and books. Among his many illustrated editions are *LaFitte, The Pirate of the Gulf* and the *Hopalong Cassidy Stories*. He has been an instructor at the John Herron Art Institute in Indiana.

Schottland, Miriam (b. 1935). Born in Brooklyn, New York, she attended PI, the New School and ASL. Her free-lance work includes children's books, trade publications, corporate and editorial illustration, as well as the 1975 International Women's Year stamp and courtroom drawings for the ABC coverage of the Ellsberg hearings. The recipient of many awards, she was given the S of I Hamilton King Award in 1970.

Schrier, Jeffrey, A. (b. 1943). Born in Cleveland, Ohio, he was educated at the Cleveland Institute of Art, California Institute of the Arts and the New School for Social Research in New York. Although he began his career doing fashion illustrations in California in 1967, his range of work includes album covers for Warner Brothers, book covers for *Ballantine* and *Bantam*, editorial art for major magazines and several posters. Galleries in Los Angeles and New York, including the S of I Annual Exhibition in 1976, have exhibited his artwork.

Schwartz, Daniel (b. 1929). Born in New York City, he went to RISD and ASL under scholarship. He studied with Yasuo Kuniyoshi and John Frazier and in 1953 he published his first illustration for *Theatre Arts*. He has won seven Gold Medals from the S of I and the Purchase Prize from the Childe Hassam Fund of the American Academy of Arts and Letters. He has had numerous One-Man Shows and illustrates for all national magazines.

Seiden, Art (b. 1923). Born in Brooklyn, New York, he received his BA degree from Queens College. His first published illustration was for a children's book, *Three Mice and a Cat*, which was published in 1957 by Grosset and Dunlap. His work has been on display at the Lotus Club in NYC, University of Minnesota (Kerlan Collection) and the Watercolor Society at the NAD, where he is a member.

Seltzer, Isadore (b. 1930). Born in St. Louis, Missouri, he attended the ACD and Chouinard Art Institute. He illustrates for *McCall's, Playboy, Redbook, Cosmopolitan, Seventeen, Leisure*, and others. His works have been exhibited at the Louvre, the Whitney Museum and Benson Museum in Bridgehampton, New York.

Sewell, Amos (b. 1901). Born in San Francisco, he went to the California School of Fine Arts before moving East to attend the ASL and GCSA, where he studied under Harvey Dunn. His career began in 1936 with an illustration for *Country Gentleman*. He contributed for over 20 years to *The Saturday Evening Post*; his work was very popular in the 1940's and 1950's, earning him several awards from the S of I and ADCs. His painting entitled *What It Is Like to Die* won a Special Art Award in 1944.

Sgouros, Thomas (b. 1927). Born in Chicago, he went to the Massachusetts College of Art for a year and completed his studies at RISD under Joseph J. C. Santoro, John Frazier and Harve Stein. His first piece was published in 1949 while he was still a student. Since that time his artwork has earned him many awards and been shown in major museums nationwide. The Museum of Fine Arts in Jacksonville, Florida and the RISD Museum of Fine Arts have his work in their permanent collections. A participant in the Lecture Series at the S of I, he is currently the Chairman of the Design Division at RISD.

Shahn, Ben (1898–1969). Born in Kovno, Lithuania, he came to America in 1906. He worked as a lithographer's apprentice until 1930 when he completed his formal education at NYU, CCNY and the NAD. One of America's

most renowned artists, a traveler of Africa and Europe, his work is in private collections and museums around the world. He has earned innumerable prizes, including many Gold Medals from the ADC. His illustrations have appeared in *Fortune, Time, Seventeen, Esquire, Harper's*, on posters for the Office of War Information and at Syracuse University, where his famous interpretation of the Sacco-Vanzetti trial has been translated into a wall-sized mosaic.

Sharpe, James C. (b. 1936). Born in Vernon, Texas, he attended Texas Tech University and graduated from ACD where he was taught by John LaGatta. An illustration published in *Ford Times* in 1966 was his first, and he has since worked for *Bantam, Dell, Fawcett, Warner* and *Berkley* doing cover art. As well as illustrating books for the *Franklin Library* and numerous *Reader's Digest Condensed Books*, his work has appeared editorially in major magazines, including many *Time* and *TV Guide* covers. He is a member of the S of I, and his illustrations have been selected for their Annual Exhibitions.

Shields, Charles (b. 1944). Born in Kansas City, Kansas, he received his BFA from the University of Southern California, his MFA from ADC and later taught painting at Colorado Mountain College. His first illustration was done for the *Saturday Review of the Arts* in 1972 and he has since illustrated for *Rolling Stone, Sesame Street, Genesis, City of San Francisco, Human Behavior* and others. He has received awards from the S of I.

Shinn, Everett (1876–1953). Born in Woodstown, New Jersey, he studied at the Pennsylvania Academy of Fine Arts and began his career as a newspaper artist in Philadelphia. He moved to New York in 1900 to work for *The Herald* and *The World*. His editorial illustrations of city life, especially that of society figures, appeared in *Harper's, McClure's* and *Scribner's*. He was known as one of The Eight or Ashcan School and his work is represented in the collections of the Metropolitan Museum of Art, Whitney Museum and Phillips Memorial Gallery in Washington.

Shinn, Florence Scovel (1869–1940). Born in Camden, New Jersey, she studied at PAFA. She became well known for her book illustrations in line and watercolor such as those done for the series *Mrs. Wiggs of the Cabbage Patch* and *Lovey Mary* by Hegan Rice in 1903. She died in her home in New York City.

Shore, Robert (b. 1924). Born in New York City, he attended Cranbrook Academy in Michigan and PI. In 1952 he was awarded a Fulbright Fellowship in painting. His clients have included *Esquire, Collier's, Seventeen, Woman's Day*, CBS, NBC and *The New York Times* as well as many book publishers and advertisers. The Detroit Institute of Fine Arts, Smithsonian Institution and National Gallery in Washington, DC have all exhibited his artwork. In 1967 he was awarded a Gold Medal from the S of I for book illustration.

Sickles, Noel (b. 1911). His early career as a newspaper artist and cartoonist was the basis for his predisposition for clean, expressive line drawing. Having created his adventure strip, *Scorchy Smith*, he produced editorial and advertising illustrations. After instructional assignments from the Army and Navy Departments he produced a series of drawings of World War II for *Life*. American history illustration, his specialty, appeared in *The Saturday Evening Post, This Week, Life* and the *Reader's Digest*.

Siegel, Dink (b. 1915). Born in Birmingham, Alabama, he attended the NAD, ASL and American Academy of Art. His editorial work was first seen in *Good Housekeeping*, and this led to many years of assignments from other magazines and the subsequent appearance of his illustrations in *Playboy* and *Field and Stream*. Arrow Shirts, Ford Motor Company and film studios have used his

advertising art. He is a life member of the S of I and presently lives in New York.

Silverman, Burton Philip (b. 1928). Born in Brooklyn, New York, he trained at Columbia University and intermittently attended the ASL. Among his teachers were Reginald Marsh and Julian Levi. In 1955 he began working for *The New York Post* and since that time his illustrations have appeared in most national and international publications. A Gold Medal from the ADC One-Show was awarded to him in 1973; he also won six prizes from the NAD Annual Exhibitions. His work has been shown in many galleries as well as being presented in 14 One-Man Shows. The Philadelphia Museum, the Brooklyn Museum and the New Britain Museum of American Art all own his artwork.

Slackman, Charles B. (b. 1934). Born in New York City, he began his career in 1959 for *Esquire* and has worked for almost every national magazine, some of which are *New York Magazine, The New York Times, Playboy, Audience, Evergreen Review, National Lampoon* and *Time*. His work has appeared in numerous shows and galleries and was the subject of a feature article in *Communication Arts*. He has been an instructor with R. O. Blechman at SVA since 1963. He and his wife, a ballerina, live in New York City.

Smedley, William Thomas (1858–1920). Born in West Bradford, Pennsylvania, he studied at the Pennsylvania Academy of Fine Arts and later in Paris. He came to New York in 1878 with a practical background in engraving and worked as a draftsman for various periodicals. With the introduction of half-tone engraving, he began producing opaque water colors for *Harper and Brothers*. He often did portraits of fashionable people for magazines. A member of the National Watercolor Society, he received their Evans Prize in 1890.

Smith, Elmer Boyd (1860–1943). Born in St. John, New Brunswick, he studied art in France. His career as an author and illustrator spanned many decades. Among his best known books are *My Village* in 1896, *The Story of Pocahontas and Captain John Smith* in 1906 and *The Story of Our Country* in 1920. He also illustrated a series on life in the Southwest in 1903 for Mary Austin.

Smith, Jessie Wilcox (1863–1935). Born in Philadelphia, she attended the School of Design for Women in Philadelphia, and from 1885 to 1888 she studied under Thomas Eakins at the PAFA. Later, with illustrators Elizabeth Shippen Green and Violet Oakley, she attended Howard Pyle's school in Wilmington, Delaware. She illustrated for *Ladies' Home Journal, Collier's, Harper's, Scribner's, the Century* and *Good Housekeeping*, the last of which paid her $1,800 per cover. She was very successful in her lifetime, especially for her portrayal of children at work or play.

Smith, William A. (b. 1918). Born in Toledo, Ohio, he studied art in Toledo, Paris and New York. At the age of 13, he began his career as an illustrator working for the *San Francisco Chronicle*. His reputation as a print-maker, muralist and painter began with national advertising assignments in the early 1940's. In 1943 he began working for magazines, especially *Cosmopolitan*, and later illustrated books by Pearl Buck and Carl Sandburg as well as designing a number of United States postage stamps. His works are in the collections of the Metropolitan Museum of Art, LC and Los Angeles County Museum.

Snyder, Jerome (1916–1976). Born in New York. Though he had no formal art training, he became an active magazine and advertising illustrator. Known for his decorative and innovative style, he worked for magazines and book publishers such as *Crowell, Sports Illustrated* and *Scientific American*. Together with Milton Glaser, he wrote a weekly column entitled *The Underground Gourmet* in *New York*

Magazine. In addition to illustrating, he was an associate editor for *Sports Illustrated* from 1954 until 1961 and more recently art director at *Scientific American.*

Snyder, Wesley P. Born in Eldus Ridge, Pennsylvania, he attended Carnegie Tech before beginning his career in Pittsburgh. After seven years he moved to New York where he shared a studio with Alex Ross. His artwork appeared in several magazines before he illustrated *The Dimpled Saboteur,* his first assignment from *The Saturday Evening Post,* which appeared in 1947. During and after World War II he participated in the USO's hospital sketching program.

Sorel, Edward (b. 1929). Born in New York City, he attended Cooper Union and began his career as a founding member of Push Pin Studios in 1953. Five years later he started free-lancing as a political satirist and his work has appeared in *Ramparts, Esquire, Atlantic, Time* and *New York Magazine,* for the last of which he is a contributing editor. He has done several books and illustrates weekly in the *Village Voice.* In 1973 Cooper Union awarded him their Augustus St. Gaudens Medal for professional achievement.

Soulen, Henry J. (1888–1965). Born in Milwaukee, Wisconsin, he studied at the Chicago Academy of Fine Arts and later with Howard Pyle. He illustrated for most of the major magazines and received the Peabody Award for his magazine cover designs. During World War II he gave free art lessons to veterans at the Valley Forge Military Hospital. His illustrations were known for their strong patterns and rich colors.

Spanfeller, James John (b. 1930). Born in Philadelphia, he studied at the Philadelphia College of Art and Pennsylvania Academy of Fine Art. His first published illustration appeared in *Seventeen* in 1956. He has worked for most major magazines and illustrated over 40 books. He was voted Artist of the Year in 1964 and has received Gold Medals from the ADCs of New York and Washington and the S of I, where he is a member. He won the *New York Herald Tribune* Children's Book Award and was also nominated for the National Book Award. He currently teaches at PSD.

Spitzmiller, Walter (b. 1944). Born in St. Louis, Missouri, he attended Washington University. He began his career there and in 1974 was awarded a gold medal from St. Louis ADC. His editorial work has appeared in *McCall's, Redbook, Golf Digest* and *Sports Illustrated.* Exhibitions of his work have been held in colleges in Quebec City, Atlanta, St. Louis and in the S of I Annual Exhibition. He presently lives in Connecticut.

Spollen, Chris John (b. 1952). Born in New York City, he studied at PSD. His first job was an etching for *Crawdaddy* magazine in 1973. Awards for his work include the Society of Publication Designers Award of Merit, Second Place in the S of I Scholarship Competition and Second Place in the Staten Island Museum Spring Show. Illustrating for *Redbook, Viva, Emergency Medicine* as well as other major publications, he has shown his work in many galleries in the New York area.

Squires, C. Clyde (1883–1970). Born in Salt Lake City, Utah, he was apprenticed as an engraver there, and he later studied at the New York School of Art under Robert Henri and Kenneth Hayes Miller. In 1906 he published his first illustration for *Life* magazine which led to work with *Woman's Home Companion, Western Romances* and *Western Monthly.* One of his most famous paintings was entitled *Her Gift,* which appeared in *Success,* and was then reproduced in Australia and throughout Europe. He was best known for his romantic depiction of the West.

Stahl, Benjamin Albert (b. 1910). Born in Chicago, he

received his art training as an apprentice in a Chicago studio. He soon opened his own studio and was illustrating for such magazines as *Woman's Home Companion, Esquire* and *Cosmopolitan.* He began a long-standing relationship with the *The Saturday Evening Post* in 1937. A founding faculty member of the FAS, he instructed at the American Academy and the AIC. He lives in Mexico and has recently been concentrating on fine art painting and writing.

Stanlaws, Penrhyn. A native New Yorker, he specialized in paintings of glamorous women. A member of the S of I, his works appeared in the most fashionable magazines of the early part of this century.

Stansbury, Arthur J. (1781–1845). Born in New York, he became a licensed preacher in 1810. He produced most of his artwork in the 1820's, including several watercolors of New York City scenes. An illustrator of children's books and textbooks, he is best known for his *Plan of the Floor of the House of Representatives Showing the Seat of Each Member,* painted in 1823.

Steadham, Terry Evan (b. 1945). Born in Indianapolis, he there attended the John Herron School of Art and began his career in 1968. He received the Gold Award for Illustration from the Indiana ADC in 1970 and has been represented in the S of I Annual Shows of 1974, 1975 and 1976. Though he started working in advertising, he is currently free-lancing out of New York City, doing editorial work for children's magazines and other publications.

Sterner, Albert Edward (1863–1946). Born in London, he studied at the Birmingham Art Institute before coming to the United States at age 17. He worked in Chicago as a draftsman and lithographer and in 1885 moved to New York to open his own studio. His editorial illustrations in a variety of media appeared frequently in *Life, St. Nicholas, Harper's* and others. An instructor for many years in several New York schools, he was elected to the NAD in 1934 and was President of the S of I from 1907 to 1908.

Sternglass, Arno (b. 1926). Born in Berlin, Germany, he attended PI from 1944 to 1947. His illustrations have appeared in *Esquire, Look, Vogue, Redbook, Glamour, Seventeen, Horizon, The New York Times Magazine* and others. He has won awards in New York from the ADC, AIGA and the S of I.

Stilwell-Weber, Sarah S. (1878–1939). She studied art at Drexel Institute under Howard Pyle from 1894 to 1900 and later attended his summer classes at Chadds Ford, Pennsylvania. *The Saturday Evening Post* covers which she painted in the 1910's and 1920's earned her distinction in the magazine cover field. She is best known for her illustrations of children.

Stirnweiss, Shannon (b. 1931). Born in Portland, Oregon, he graduated from ACD in Los Angeles where he studied under John LaGatta, Reynold Brown and Pruett Carter and shared classes with Jack Potter, Phil Hays and Chuck McVicker. He received a Gold Medal from the New Jersey ADC and the Book Writers Award for the best illustrated dog book. He has illustrated 25 books, and many magazines, including *Field and Stream, Boys' Life, Reader's Digest, Argosy* and *Show,* have used his talents. His work has been shown in many galleries, including the S of I, where he was President from 1972 to 1974.

Stone, David K. (b. 1922). Born in Reedsport, Oregon, he attended the University of Oregon, graduating after serving in World War II. He studied art at the ACD in Los Angeles and also in Mexico. His career began in 1949 in New York with editorial work and he has won several awards since, from the S of I and the ADCs of St. Louis and Richmond. He served as President of the S of I and is a

contributor to the USAF Art Program.

Stone, Gilbert Leonard (b. 1940). Born in Brooklyn, New York, he graduated with honors from PSD after receiving scholarships there and at the Brooklyn Museum. Three years after his first illustration appeared in *Seventeen,* he was awarded the Prix de Rome. He has been the recipient of four Gold Medals from the S of I for his work in *Sports Illustrated, McCall's, Seventeen* and *Steelways.* His art is part of the permanent collection of the Brooklyn Museum and the Smithsonian Institution.

Stoops, Herbert Morton (1888–1948). Born in Idaho, he attended Utah State College before joining the staff of the *San Francisco Call.* He later worked at the *Chicago Tribune* while attending the AIC. His career as an illustrator of Western scenes began in New York with *Bluebook,* for which he was a frequent contributor. His illustrations also appeared in *Collier's* and *Cosmopolitan.* A member of several professional organizations and President of the AG, he was awarded the Isador Medal from the Salmagundi Club.

Storey, Ross Barron (b. 1940). Born in Dallas, Texas, he studied at the FAS, SVA under Robert Weaver and the ACD in Los Angeles where he is presently chairman in the illustration department. His career began in 1959 in Dallas and his artwork soon began appearing in *Sunday Magazine* of *The New York Journal American.* He has since illustrated for many magazines, including *Esquire, Life, This Week* and, recently, *Time.* He has won awards from the S of I and from several ACDs.

Street, Frank (1893–1944). Born in Kansas City, Missouri, he attended the ASL and studied with Charles Chapman and Harvey Dunn at their school in Leonia, New Jersey. His editorial illustrations appeared in *The Saturday Evening Post, Ladies' Home Journal* and *Cosmopolitan.* An active portrait and landscape artist, he taught a series of classes in his studio during his later years.

Suares, Jean Claude (b. 1942). Born in Alexandria, Egypt, he attended Sarola Suizzera di Genova and PI. His first published work appeared in *The Realist* in 1965 and the New York ADC awarded him a Special Gold Medal in 1971. A specialist in pen-and-ink editorial art, he has written several books on illustration and his works have been shown in the Musée des Beaux Arts in Bordeaux as well as the Musée des Arts Décoratifs in the Louvre.

Sullivant, Thomas S. (1854–1926). Born in Columbus, Ohio, he attended the PAFA. His witty drawings, predominately in pen and ink, were regularly seen in magazines at the turn of the century. A compilation of his humorous drawings, accompanied by his own anecdotes and poems, was published in 1946 by *The Old Wine Press* under the title *Sullivant's ABC Zoo.*

Sumichrast, Jözef (b. 1948). Born in Hobart, Indiana, he spent two years at the American Academy of Art. He has recently done a number of books, having written as well as illustrated *Onomatopoeia.* He has many posters to his credit, including those for *Graphis,* 1975 and 1977. *Communication Arts* and *Art Direction* have featured this artist and his work, examples of which are part of the permanent collections of the Library of Congress and the Chicago Historical Society.

Summers, Dudley Gloyne (1892–1975). Born in Birmingham, England, he studied in America at the New School of Design in Boston and at the ASL under Thomas Fogarty, Charles Chapman and F. R. Gruger. His first assignment was from *Maclean's,* a Canadian magazine, followed by publication in most American magazines. He taught at the American School of Design in New York and the Van Amburgh School of Art in Plainfield, New Jersey. A member of the S of I, he lives and works out of his studio in South Orange, New Jersey.

Sundgaard, Erik (b. 1949). Born in New Haven, Connecticut, he attended the Paier School of Art, where he studied with Rudolf Zallinger and Ken Davies. In 1970, his first published illustration appeared in *Yankee* magazine. His work has been hung in John Slade Ely House in New Haven and the S of I Annual Show in 1976.

Szafran, Gene (b. 1941). Born in Detroit, he was trained at the Art School of the Society of Arts and Crafts. Receiving his start in studios in Detroit, he produced many auto advertisements in addition to free-lance assignments. Among his many clients since his move to New York in 1967 are *Bantam Books, New American Library, Cosmopolitan, Fortune* and *Playboy*. He has exhibited his works in group shows at the General Electric and Master Eagle Galleries and has held a One-Man Exhibition at the S of I.

Taylor, Frank Walter (1874–1921). Born in Philadelphia, he attended the PAFA before studying abroad on scholarship. His illustrations for magazines, many accompanying his own stories, appeared frequently in major magazines. He was awarded a Medal of Honor for Illustration at the International Exposition of 1915.

Taylor, Horace Weston (b. 1881). Born in Chester, Pennsylvania, he was a pupil of Henry McCarter and Breckenridge at the Pennsylvania Academy of Fine Art. His editorial illustrations appeared regularly in *The Saturday Evening Post, Redbook, Ladies' Home Journal, Elks Magazine, American Boy* and *Maclean's*. Also an accomplished book illustrator, he often worked for *Harper's* and *Houghton Mifflin Company*.

Taylor, William Ladd (1854–1926). Educated in Boston, New York and Paris, he settled in New England where much of his subject matter reflected the life of the region. His paintings for *Ladies' Home Journal* were often reproduced in full color and many appeared as posters. *Our Home and Country*, published in 1908 by *Moffat-Yard and Company*, included many of his best known paintings of life in New England and the West.

Tepper, Saul (b. 1899). Born in New York City, he attended Cooper Union, ASL and the GCSA. Famous instructors included Harvey Dunn, George Bridgman and William DeLeftwich Dodge and fellow students were artists Jules Gottlieb and Dan Content. His first published illustration was an oil done for *Collier's* in 1925 called *Mid-Air*. His works are owned by the S of I, Joseph T. Mendola Galleries and Marbella Galleries. He has been a lecturer at PI, Cooper Union, New York ADC and the S of I. In addition to being a prolific painter, he is also a composer and lyricist.

Terpning, Howard Averill (b. 1927). Born in Oak Park, Illinois, he attended the Chicago Academy of Fine Art and American Academy of Art and was taught by Mosby and Haddon Sundblom. He has had many pieces accepted for the S of I Annual Exhibitions and his work is owned by the Pacific Northwest Museum in Spokane, Washington. Best known for his hunting and fishing pictures, he has illustrated extensively for *Field and Stream*.

Thompson, John M. (b. 1940). Born in Three Rivers, Michigan, he attended Miami (Ohio) University where he received a BFA in 1962. He has illustrated for numerous publishing companies including *Scholastic, Macmillan, Ace Books* and *St. Martin's Press*. RCA and Columbia Records presently utilize his skills and his artwork has appeared in the Aldrich and Berkshire Museums.

Thurber, James Grover (1894–1961). Born in Columbus, Ohio, he attended Ohio State University. While working as a reporter for *The Columbus Dispatch* and *The New York Evening Post*, he contributed free-lance stories to *The New Yorker*. In 1927 he became an editor for *The New Yorker*, the magazine that became the forum for his distinctive cartoons and sardonic writings portraying the plight of mankind. His first drawings were published in 1929 in *Is Sex Necessary?* and he quickly became a very popular cartoonist. His work appeared in *Forum, The New Republic* and *The Saturday Evening Post*. Despite failing eyesight, he wrote and illustrated many volumes, some of which were later the subject of television and film scripts.

Tinkelman, Murray (b. 1933). Born in Brooklyn, New York, he studied at Cooper Union and Brooklyn Museum Art School under Reuben Tam. His first published work was for *Seventeen* in 1951. He has received Gold Medals from the S of I, ADC and Society of Publication Designers and was named Artist of the Year by the AG. Associate Chairman at Parsons School of Design in New York, he is not only an illustrator but also a guest lecturer in various universities, and is engaged in writing and producing a video series on the *History of American Illustration*. He has illustrated for *American Heritage, McCall's, Audubon, Cosmopolitan, Boys' Life* and many others.

Ungerer, Tomi (b. 1931). Born in Strasbourg, France, he came to America in 1957 with a background in graphic arts. He settled in New York and produced advertising and editorial illustrations for *Esquire, Fortune* and *Harper's*. As a book illustrator and author, he published several volumes of his satirical cartoons. Most recently, his work has been seen on the Op-Ed page of *The New York Times*.

Unruh, Jack Neal (b. 1935). Born in Pretty Prairie, Kansas, he attended the University of Kansas and Washington University in St. Louis. In 1958 he began illustrating in Dallas, Texas, and has since received two Gold Medals, three Silver Medals, and an Art Director of the Year Award from the Dallas, Ft. Worth ADC. Though his work has appeared in *Seventeen* and *Redbook*, the bulk of his illustrations are done for advertising agencies in the Southwest.

Upshur, Thomas (b. 1944). Born in Detroit, he received his art training as an apprentice in a studio there. He began designing and illustrating before moving to New York, where he has since had editorial assignments from *Viva* and *Playboy*. His advertising clients include Eastern Airlines, Chicken of the Sea and Singer Sewing Machine Company, for whom he illustrated a TV spot with Albert Budin. He works predominantly in acrylics. His art has been selected for the S of I Annual Exhibitions.

Utterback, William Dean (b. 1931). Born in Arlington Heights, Illinois, he studied under John LaGatta and Morgan Henninger at the ACD in Los Angeles. *Moms Mabley at the White House* was his first illustration, done for Mercury Records in 1967. *Cine Duck* and other illustrations toured Europe and Tokyo in the *Beyond Illustration—The Art of Playboy* collection.

Vallejo, Boris W. (b. 1941). Born in Lima, Peru, he has specialized in book illustration since 1975. He attended Escuela Nacional de Bellas Artes and the SVA where he studied under Jack Potter. He has done over 75 book illustrations since 1975 and his work has appeared at the S of I, Greengrass Gallery and the Cornell Club in New York City.

Van Buren, Raeburn (b. 1891). Born in Pueblo, Colorado, he attended the ASL in 1913, before which he worked as a sketch artist for the *Kansas City Star*. He has illustrated over 350 stories for *The Saturday Evening Post*, was a regular contributor to *Redbook, The New Yorker, Esquire, McCall's, McClure's Syndicate* and *King Features Syndicate*, and created the comic strip *Abbie and Slats*. He was a member of the S of I, Artists and Writers and the Cartoonists Society. His home and studio are in Great Neck, New York.

Van Nutt, Robert (b. 1947). Born in New York City, he attended Cooper Union for four years and was a pupil of Peter Agostini and Stefano Cusomano. He has illustrated extensively for the *American Heritage Publishing Co.*

Veno, Joseph R. (b. 1939). Born in Stoneham, Massachusetts, he attended the Museum of Fine Arts in Massachusetts for five years. His first published illustration, executed in ink and watercolor, was for *Playboy* in 1968. He won a Gold Medal at the Boston Advertising Show and an Award of Excellence from the S of I. He is married and has one child.

Ventura, Piero (b. 1937). Born in Milan, Italy, he attended the Brera Academy there. His first published work was a children's book for *Random House* in 1975. He received an Award of Excellence in 1976 from the S of I, the Brooklyn Art Books Citation in 1977 and Fifty Books of the Year Award. He is married with three children.

Viskupic, Gary (b. 1944). Born in Brooklyn, New York, he attended Cooper Union where he illustrated for *At Cooper Union* magazine. He also attended the University of Illinois and has since illustrated several books for the university's *Depot Press*. His poster work, one of his main endeavours, has appeared in *Graphis Poster Annuals* and as a part of the Bicentennial Poster Show which toured the US and Europe. A contributing artist to *Car Driver*, he is currently chief illustrator for *Newsday*.

Von Schmidt, Harold (b. 1893). Born in Alameda, California, he studied at the California College of Arts and Crafts and San Francisco Art Institute and was instructed by Maynard Dixon and Harvey Dunn. His first illustration was published in 1915 for *Sunset Magazine*. A prolific artist known for his beautiful, realistic depiction of the West, he illustrated for over 30 major magazines, painted posters during World War I and World War II and illustrated many books including his own, *The Western Art of Harold Von Schmidt* and *Harold Von Schmidt Draws and Paints the Old West*. Married for 50 years, he was President of the S of I from 1938 to 1941, President of the Westport Artists in 1950 and a trustee of the AG in New York. His work is in private collections and museums across the United States and in 1968 he was the first artist to be awarded the Trustees' Gold Medal by the Cowboy Hall of Fame and Western Heritage Center.

Von Woerkom, Funs. Based for some years in New York, he has illustrated for *American Heritage's Horizon* and the Op-Ed page of *The New York Times*. Recently, he has concentrated on print-making.

Wald, Carol (b. 1935). Born in Detroit, she attended the Art School of the Society of Arts and Crafts, Skowhegan School of Painting and Sculpture and Cranbrook Academy of Art. She has had One-Woman Shows of collage at the Beilen and the Raven Gallery in Detroit. Her first published collage was for *The New York Times Sunday Magazine* in February, 1972. She wrote and illustrated the book *Myth America*, published by *Pantheon Books* in 1975.

Wall, William Guy (1792–1864). Born in Dublin, Ireland, he came to New York City in 1818 and won wide acclaim for his views of the Hudson River; 20 of these paintings were later published in the *Hudson River Portfolio*. He was a founder of the NAD and exhibited his works at the Pennsylvania Academy, Apollo Association and the NAD. Some of his paintings are owned by the New-York Historical Society Museum.

Ward, Edmund F. (b. 1892). Born in White Plains, New York, he attended the ASL, studying with George Bridgman, Thomas Fogarty and Edward Dufner. He was working for *The Saturday Evening Post* at age 20, illustrating for authors such as Zane Grey, Alexander Botts and Emerson Hough. While maintaining a studio in White

Plains, he painted murals for federal buildings in the area. He designed a United States postage stamp commemorating a Revolutionary War battle in upstate New York.

Watts, Stan (b. 1952). Born in Ponca City, Oklahoma, he studied under Don Ivan Punchatz at the University of Oklahoma. His first illustration was for the *National Lampoon* in February, 1975. He currently illustrates for *Avon Books, Texas Monthly, Oklahoma Monthly* and others, and his work has appeared at the Fred Jones Museum in Norman, Oklahoma.

Waud, Alfred R. (1828-1891). Born in London, he studied art at the Royal Academy. After emigrating to the US in 1850 he started his career as a newspaper artist, first in Boston and later in New York. During the Civil War his battlefield illustrations were published by the *New York Illustrated News* and *Harper's Weekly*. Harper's serialized his report on the post-war South and West. These later appeared in a book, Picturesque America. He contributed to *the Century's Battles and Leaders of the Civil War*. He died in Marietta, Georgia.

Weaver, Robert (b. 1924). Born in Pittsburgh, he attended the Carnegie Institute, ASL and later the Accademia Delle Belle Arti in Venice. His editorial work has brought him acclaim and several awards including a Gold Medal from the S of I in 1964. *Fortune, Life, Look, Seventeen, Town and Country* as well as other magazines have published his paintings and he presently contributes frequently to *Sports Illustrated*. He has had several exhibits in the United States including a One-Man Show in 1977 at SVA, where he has been an instructor for many years.

Weldon, Charles Dater. Born in Ohio, he was the pupil of Walter Shirlaw in New York and Munkacsy in Paris. He was awarded the Bronze Medal from the Charleston Exposition in 1902, and he was an active member of the Century Association, American National Academy (1889) and the NAD (1897). His watercolors, often of domestic scenes, showed the influence of the Japanese painters whom he admired.

Weller, Don M. (b. 1937). Born in Colfax, Washington, he attended Washington State University for four years. His first illustration was done for *Western Horseman Magazine* in 1957. The ADC and The One-Show in New York, as well as the Los Angeles ADC, have awarded him Gold Medals. *Boys' Life, Redbook, Esquire, Penthouse* and many other magazines have published his work.

Whitcomb, Jon (b. 1906). Born in Weatherford, Oklahoma, he attended Ohio Wesleyan University and Ohio State University where he studied with Milton Caniff, the cartoonist. In 1929 his illustration for *Collier's* was the first of a multiple of covers he executed for publications such as *Ladies' Home Journal, Woman's Home Companion, Good Housekeeping* and *The Saturday Evening Post*. He achieved popularity for his illustrations of young love and glamorous, elegant women, such as the series of articles about movie stars done for *Cosmopolitan*, entitled *On Location with Jon Whitcomb*. A member of the S of I, he resides in New York City.

White, Charles Edward, III (b. 1940). Born in San Diego, California, he studied under John LaGatta at the ACD. His first illustration, an advertisement for Hoffman Electronics in 1962, led to assignments from many magazines including *McCall's, Redbook, Esquire, Playboy* and *Viva*. The recipient of awards from the ADCs of Los Angeles, New York and Chicago, his poster of the Rolling Stones won a Gold Medal from the S of I. He presently operates a design, art direction and illustration studio in Los Angeles.

Whitesides, Kim (b. 1941). Born in Logan, Utah, he studied at the University of Utah and ACD, with classmates David Wilcox, Dave Willardson, Peter Lloyd and Charles White III. After studying under Lorser Flelteison and Alvin Gittens, he had his first illustration published for *Ladies' Home Journal* in 1967. *Playboy, McCall's, Redbook, Oui, Viva, Psychology Today, Look, Ladies' Home Journal, Rolling Stone* and *Penthouse* are some of the magazines for which he illustrates.

Whittingham, William Henry (b. 1932). Born in Detroit, he attended the University of Michigan for four years and worked at the Charles E. Cooper Studios. Beginning in 1958, with an illustration for *Guideposts,* he worked for many magazines until 1970, but is now doing portraits exclusively. His artwork has appeared at Portraits Incorporated in New York City.

Wiles, Irving R. (1862–1948). Born in Utica, New York, he studied at the ASL, then for two years in Paris under Lefebvre. In 1879 he had his first New York showing after which he produced many portraits and out-of-doors scenes, usually executed in transparent wash. He was elected to the NAD in 1897 and was also a member of the AWS.

Williams, John Scott (1877–1976). Born in England, he studied at the AIC under Fred Richardson, before beginning his career in 1905 with *The Saturday Evening Post*. His pen and ink drawings appeared in the major magazines and for many years he painted covers for *The New York Herald Tribune*. Later in life, he turned to mural painting, producing a very large mural for the Union Terminal in Cleveland, Ohio.

Williams, Paul (b. 1934). Born in Detroit, he attended the ACD in Los Angeles. Returning to Detroit, he joined the staff at New Center Studio before beginning a free-lance career in advertising and editorial illustration. His recent work has been used by *Good Housekeeping, Woman's Day* and the Girl Scouts of America.

Williamson, James W. (b. 1899). Born in Omaha, Nebraska, he graduated from Yale University in 1923. He is best known for his whimsical editorial illustrations which appeared first in the old *Life*. His work later appeared in *Vanity Fair* and *Judge,* and for over 30 years he illustrated for *The Saturday Evening Post*. Among his many advertising clients were Arrow Shirts, Ford Motor Company and Yardley. He was a member of the S of I. In the 1950's he left the United States to settle in Puerto Rico.

Wilson, Edward Arthur (1886–1970). Born in Glasgow, Scotland, he studied at the AIC and with Howard Pyle. He began his career in New York City in the early 1920's and soon was illustrating advertising campaigns for LaSalle-Cadillac and Victrola. From an early age he was enamored by sea life and his first illustrated book, for which he used wood blocks, was *Iron Men and Wooden Ships* in 1924. This book led to more than 70 others in his long career and his election to the Illustrators Hall of Fame in 1962. His book work was his first love and among his illustrated editions were *Robinson Crusoe, The Last of the Mohicans, Treasure Island, Around the World in 80 Days* and *A Journey to the Center of the Earth*. His works are in the collections of the Metropolitan Museum of Art, the Library of Congress and the NYPL. He was a long-time resident of New York City, moving later to Cape Cod.

Wilson, Thomas William (b. 1945). Born in Shreveport, Louisiana, he attended Georgia Tech and Georgia State University. A pen-and-ink drawing for *Georgia* magazine in 1973 was his first published piece and he has since illustrated for many major magazines. His work for American Greeting Corporation and the *Washington Post* has been selected for the S of I Annual Exhibitions. Represented by Middendorf Gallery in Washington, DC, he presently lives in Sausalito, California.

Winslow, Earle Bartrum (1884–1969). Born in Northville, Michigan, he attended the Detroit School of Fine Arts and the AIC. He went to school with Peggy Bacon and Lucille Blanche while a student of George Bellows, Andrew Dashburg and John Sloan. His first published illustration was for *Judge* magazine in 1919. He illustrated the *Gospel of St. Mark* for *Condé Nast* in 1932 and originated the newspaper cartoon *Bingville Bugle*, which is referred to in the book *Call Me Lucky* by Bing Crosby. He is a Life Member of the S of I, AG and the ADC, and his works are owned by the New Britain Museum of American Art and the Library of Congress in Washington, DC.

Wohlberg, Ben (b. 1927). He attended Kansas State College prior to his art training at the Chicago Academy of Fine Art and ACD. He began his career at *Redbook* in 1960 and has been a frequent contributor to *Ladies' Home Journal* and *Good Housekeeping,* and to several book publishers. He received an Award of Excellence from the S of I Annual Exhibition in 1962 and has exhibited his work at the AWS.

Woolf, Michaelangelo (d. 1899). He studied for several years in the best known art academies of Paris and Munich. His pen-and-ink illustrations, most often revealing the life of poor city children, were the trademark of his humorous style. The Graham Gallery in New York owns several of his drawings.

Worth, Thomas (1834–1917). Born in New York City. His first published illustration was a comic sketch done for *Currier & Ives* in 1855. He later became very popular for his racing scenes and was one of the most important artists whose work was lithographed by *Currier & Ives*. He was considered a comic and genre artist and lived most of his life in Islip, Long Island.

Wosk, Miriam (b. 1947). Born in Vancouver, British Columbia, she attended the Fashion Institute of Technology and the SVA where she was taught by Milton Glaser and Henry Wolf. Her first published illustration was for *Esquire* in 1971. She illustrates for *New York Magazine, Ms., Viva, Sesame Street, Vogue, The New York Times, Oui* and others. She was guest editor of *Mademoiselle* in 1968.

Wright, George Hand (1873–1951). He trained at the Spring Garden Institute and PAFA. His illustrations, generally of rural life, were often seen in *Scribner's, Harper's* and *the Century*. He devoted much of his free time to his profession as a member of the Westport Artists, the Salmagundi Club and as President of the S of I.

Wyeth, Newell Convers (1882–1945). Born in Needham, Massachusetts, he studied art at the Mechanic Art High School in Boston, Normal Art High School and the Eric Pape School of Art under Charles W. Reed. In 1902, at the age of 20, he went to study at Howard Pyle's school in Wilmington, Delaware. Returning from a trip out West with many drawings of cowboys, cattle and landscapes, he was immediately commissioned for his artwork by all the major magazines and book publishers. For the next four decades he continued illustrating such famous works as Robert Louis Stevenson's *Treasure Island* (1911) and *Kidnapped* (1913), Jules Verne's *Mysterious Island* (1918) and James Fenimore Cooper's *The Last of the Mohicans*. Wyeth painted in oil and worked on large canvases; this preference resulted in his five large murals representing maritime commerce for the First National Bank of Boston in 1924. Wyeth was a member of the NAD and the S of I.

Yerkes, Lane Hamilton (b. 1945). Born in Philadelphia, he attended the Philadelphia College of Art for five years. His first published illustration was for *Today Magazine* in Pennsylvania in 1962. His work has been shown at the Commercial Museum and he has illustrated for *Macmillan, Penthouse, Smithsonian Magazine* and *The Philadelphia Inquirer*.

Yohn, Frederick Coffay (1875–1933). Born in Indianapolis, he studied under H. Siddons Mowbray at the ASL. He began his career in 1894 working for *Harper's* and subsequently illustrated for many book publishers. For *Scribner's* he did historical and battle scenes, including illustrations for Henry Cabot Lodge's *The Story of the Revolution*. He was a member of the S of I and AG and a permanent collection of his work is in the LC. He died in Norwalk, Connecticut.

Zallinger, Rudolph Franz (b. 1919). Born in Irkutsk, Siberia, he attended Yale University School of Art where he received his MFA in 1950. He went to school with Morton Roberts, Ken Davies, Leonard Everett Fisher and Robert Vickrey and studied under Eugene Francis Savage. He received the Pulitzer Prize in painting in 1949. His work is owned by the Seattle Art Museum, Yale University and the New Britain Museum of American Art. He is presently a professor of drawing and painting at the Hartford Art School in Connecticut.

Ziemienski, Dennis Theodore (b. 1947). Born in San Francisco, he studied under Joe Cleary at the California College of Arts and Crafts, received a BFA in 1972 and began his career with an illustration for Payless Drug Stores in Oakland, California. He won awards in 1974 and 1976 from the S of I in Los Angeles and New York City. His illustrations appeared in *Crafts for Children,* published by *Sunset Press* in 1976.

Ziering, Robert M. (b. 1933). Born in Brooklyn, New York, he studied at NYU School of Education and began his art career with *Coronet* magazine. His works have been shown in galleries in New York and Boston including the Museum of Modern Art and New York Gallery of Sports. Among his clients are the New York Racing Association, NBC, Mobil Oil and Lincoln Center. He has produced many posters and illustrated for major book publishers.

Zimmer, Fred (b. 1923). Born in Pataskala, Ohio, he attended Ohio State University and PI. From 1953 to 1972 he illustrated for *Ford Times*. The winner of the Ohio Arts Council Award in Dayton in 1969, he had been the Fulbright Senior Researcher to India in 1966–1967. He is now a full professor at Ohio University. His work is owned by the Art Museum in Springfield, Missouri and the Butler Institute of American Art in Youngstown, Ohio.

Zoell, Robert (b. 1940). Born in Regina, Canada, where he began in the printing business, he moved to the United States in 1963, settling in Los Angeles. Though he first worked in the field of design, shortly thereafter he began illustrating for advertising and editorial clients. He now divides his time between illustration, design and fine art painting.

Zogbaum, Rufus (1849–1925). Born in Charleston, South Carolina, he studied at the ASL and in Paris. As an illustrator his chief subject matter was the military and his illustrations covered the Civil War, the Indian wars of the American West and the Spanish American War. His works appeared in *Scribner's* and in *the Century's Battles and Leaders*. In 1939, he participated in an exhibition at the Metropolitan Museum of Art in New York. The Corcoran Gallery, Kennedy Gallery and the Fine Arts Museum of Santa Fe all own examples of his illustrations

BIBLIOGRAPHY

Books

Abbott, Charles D., *Howard Pyle, A Chronicle*. New York and London. Harper & Brothers. 1935.

Allen, Douglas and Allen, Douglas Jr., *N. C. Wyeth, The Collected Paintings, Illustrations and Murals*. New York. Crown. 1972.

American Art Annual, Florence N. Levy, Editor. New York. American Art Annual, Inc. 1908-1951.

The American Historical Scene, depicted by Stanley Arthurs. Philadelphia. University of Pennsylvania Press. 1935.

American Watercolor and Winslow Homer, Minneapolis. The Walker Art Center. 1945.

Annual of Advertising and Editorial Art and Design, New York. The New York Art Directors Club Year Book. 1921 and annually.

Annual of American Illustration, The Society of Illustrators. New York. Hastings House. 1959 to present.

Benda, W. T., *Masks*. New York. Watson-Guptill. 1944.

Benezit, E., *Dictionnaire Des Peintres Sculpteurs Dessinateurs et Graveurs*. Paris. Librairie Gründ. 1976.

Bland, Theodore, *A History of Book Illustration*. Cleveland and New York. World Publishing Company. 1958.

Bolton, Theodore, *American Book Illustrators*. New York. R. R. Bowker Company. 1938.

Book of Notable American Illustrators, New York. The Walker Engraving Company. 1926. 1927.

Boudet, G., Editor, *Les Affiches Etrangères*. Paris. Librairie Artistique. 1897.

Calkins, Earnest Elmo, *Franklin Booth*. New York. Robert Frank. 1925.

Century of Illustration, Brooklyn. The Brooklyn Museum. 1972.

Cheever, Lawrence Oakley, *Edward A. Wilson, Book Illustrator*. Muscatine, Iowa. The Prairie Press. 1941.

Cortissoz, Royal, *American Artists*. New York and London. Charles Scribner's Sons. 1923.

Dallison, Ken, *When Zeppelins Flew*. New York. Time-Life Books. 1969.

Darton, F. S. Harvey, *Modern Book Illustration in Great Britain and America*. London. The Studio Limited.

Dodd, Loring Holmes, *A Generation of Illustrators and Etchers*. Boston. Chapman and Grimes. 1960.

Downey, Fairfax, *Portrait of an Era as Drawn by C. D. Gibson*. New York and London. Charles Scribner's Sons. 1936.

Dykes, Jeff, *Fifty Great Western Illustrators*. Flagstaff. Northland Press. 1975.

Ellis, Richard Williamson, *Book Illustration*. Kingsport, Tennessee. Kingsport Press. 1952.

Fawcett, Robert, *On the Art of Drawing*. New York. Watson-Guptill. 1958.

Flagg, James Montgomery, *Celebrities*. Watkins Glen, New York. Century House. 1951.

Frost, A. B., *A Book of Drawings*. New York. P. F. Collier and Son. 1904.

Gallatin, Albert Eugene, *Art and the Great War*. New York. E. P. Dutton and Co. 1919.

The Gibson Book, a collection of the published works of Charles Dana Gibson in two volumes. New York. Charles Scribner's Sons. 1907.

Groce, George C. and Wallace, David H., *The New-York Historical Society's Dictionary of Artists in America, 1564-1860*. New Haven and London. Yale University Press. 1957.

Guptill, Arthur L., *Drawing With Pen and Ink*, edited and revised by Henry C. Pitz. New York. Reinhold Publishing. 1961.

———— *Norman Rockwell–Illustrator*, New York. Watson-Guptill. 1946.

Haggerty, James J. and Smith, Warren Reiland, *The U.S. Air Force: A Pictorial History in Art*. New York. Spartan Books. 1966.

Halsey, Ashley Jr., *Illustrating for The Saturday Evening Post*. New York. Arlington House. 1946.

Harrison Fisher's American Beauties, Indianapolis. Bobbs-Merrill Company. 1909.

Holme, Charles, Editor, *Modern Pen-Drawing*. Special Winter Number of "The Studio", 1900-1901. London, Paris, New York. 1901.

Holme, Geoffrey, Editor, *Posters and Publicity*. London. The Studio Ltd. 1927.

Jones, James, *WWII*. New York. Grosset and Dunlap. 1975.

Jones, Sydney R., *Posters and Their Designers*. London. The Studio Ltd. 1924.

Kent, Norman, Editor, *The Book of Edward A. Wilson*. New York. The Heritage Press. 1948.

King, Ethel, *Darley, The Most Popular Illustrator of His Time*. Brooklyn. Theodore Gaus's Sons. 1964.

Lemman-Haupt, Hellmut, *The Book in America*. New York. R. R. Bowker Company. 1951.

Lucas, E. V., *Life and Work of Edwin Austin Abbey, R.A*. New York. Charles Scribner's Sons. London. Methuen and Company Ltd. 1921.

Mahony, Bertha E.; Latimer, Louise Payson; Folinsbee, Beulah, *Illustrators of Children's Books*. Boston. The Horn Book, Inc. 1947.

McConnell, Gerald, *Assemblage: Three Dimensional Picture Making*. New York. Van Nostrand Reinhold Company. 1976.

McCracken, Harold, *Portrait of the Old West*. New York. McGraw-Hill. 1952.

Meyer, Susan E., *James Montgomery Flagg*. New York. Watson-Guptill. 1974.

Miller, Bertha Mahony and Field, Eleanor Whitney, *Caldecott Medal Books: 1938-1957*. Boston. The Horn Book, Inc. 1957.

Morse, Willard S. and Brincklé, Gertrude, *Howard Pyle—A Record of his Illustrations and Writings*. Wilmington. The Wilmington Society of the Fine Arts. 1921.

Pennell, Joseph, *The Adventures of an Illustrator*. Boston. Little, Brown and Company. 1925.

———— *Modern Illustration*. London and New York. George Bell and Sons. 1895.

———— *Pen Drawing and Pen Draughtsmen*. New York. The Macmillan Company. 1920.

Pitz, Henry C., *A Treasury of American Book Illustration*. New York. Watson-Guptill and American Studio Books. 1947.

———— *The Practice of Illustration*. New York. Watson-Guptill. 1947.

———— *Illustrating Children's Books*. New York. Watson-Guptill. 1963.

———— *The Brandywine Tradition*. Boston. Houghton-Mifflin. 1969.

———— *Howard Pyle: Writer, Illustrator, Founder of the Brandywine Tradition*. New York. Clarkson Potter. 1975.

Price, Charles Matlack, *Poster Design*. New York. George W. Bricka. 1913. 1922.

Reed, Walt, *Harold Von Schmidt Draws and Paints The Old West*. Flagstaff. Northland Press. 1972.

———— *The Illustrator in America—1900-1960's*. New York. Reinhold Publishing. 1966.

Reid, Forrest, *Illustrators of the Sixties*. London. Faber and Gwyer Ltd. 1898.

Robinson, Jerry, *The Comics, An Illustrated History of Comic Strip Art*. New York. Berkley Publishing. 1974.

Rockwell, Norman, as told to Thomas Rockwell, *Norman Rockwell—My Adventures as an Illustrator*. New York. Doubleday and Company. 1960.

Rosner, Charles, *The Growth of the Book Jacket*. London. Sylvan Press. 1954.

Sears, Stephen W., Editor, *The American Heritage Century Collection of Civil War Art*. American Heritage Publishing Company. 1974.

Schau, Michael, *J. C. Leyendecker*. New York. Watson-Guptill. 1974.

Simon, Howard, *500 Years of Art in Illustration*. New York. World Publishing. 1942.

Stern, Philip Van Doren, *They Were There—The Civil War in Action as Seen by its Combat Artists*. New York. Crown Publishers. 1961.

Suarés, Jean-Claude, *Art of the Times*. New York. Avon Books. 1973.

Watson, Ernest W., *Forty Illustrators and How They Work*. New York. Watson-Guptill. 1946.

Waugh, Coulton, *The Comics*. New York. The Macmillan Company. 1947.

Weitenkampf, Frank, *The Illustrated Book*. Cambridge. The Harvard Press. 1938.

Whiting, John D., *Practical Illustration, A Guide for Artists*. New York and London. Harper and Brothers. 1920.

Who's Who in America, Chicago. Marquis-Who's Who. 1956-1957. Vol. 29.

Who's Who in American Art, Dorothy B. Gilbert, Editor. New York. R. R. Bowker Company. 1953 to present.

Articles, Catalogs, Pamphlets, etc.

Bolton, Theodore, "The Book Illustrations of Felix Octavius Darley." Worcester, Mass. *Proceedings* of the American Antiquarian Society. 1952.

Coffin, William A., "American Illustration of Today." New York. *Scribners Magazine*. March, 1892.

Contemporary Art of the United States, New York. International Business Machines Corporation. 1940.

Haas, Irvin, "A Bibliography of the Work of Edward A. Wilson." *Prints*. February, 1938.

Hawthorne, Julian, "Howard Pyle, Illustrator." New York. *Pearson's Magazine*. September, 1907.

Kent, Norman, "Edward A. Wilson: A Graphic Romancer." New York. *American Artist*. May, 1944.

Lunt, Dudley, "The Howard Pyle School of Art." *Delaware History*. Historic Society of Delaware. March, 1953.

Pitz, Henry C., "Alex Steinweiss: Advertising Designer." New York. *American Artist*. April, 1947. p. 33.

———— "27th Annual Exhibition: Art Directors Club of New York." September, 1948. p. 42.

———— "The Classics in New Dress." New York. *American Artist*. May, 1949. p. 32.

———— "Fashion Illustration as a Fine Art." New York. *American Artist*. June, 1949. p. 31.

———— "Whitney Darrow Jr." New York. *American Artist*. February, 1950. p. 32.

———— "Howard Pyle: American Illustrator." New York. *American Artist*. December, 1951. p. 44.

———— "American Book Illustration Today." London. *The Studio*. 1951.

———— "Isa Barnet." New York. *American Artist*. February, 1952. p. 44.

———— "Drugs and Art." New York. *American Artist*. May, 1952. p. 30.

———— "Nicholas Mordvinoff." Boston. *The Horn Book*. 1952.

———— "Foreign Invaders in the Field of Illustration." New York. *American Artist*. February, 1953. p. 29.

———— "Robert Fawcett." New York. *American Artist*. October, 1953. p. 28.

———— "The Limited Editions Club." New York. *American Artist*. October, 1954. p. 33.

———— "James Flora." New York. *American Artist*. January, 1955. p. 28.

———— "Al Parker." New York. *American Artist*. January, 1955. p. 30.

———— "The Illustrations of Lynd Ward." New York. *American Artist*. March, 1955. p. 35.

———— "Jacob Landau." New York. *American Artist*. October, 1956. p. 40.

———— "Albert Gold." New York. *American Artist*. November, 1956. p. 36.

———— "Charles Dana Gibson: Creator of a Mode." New York. *American Artist*. December, 1956. p. 50.

———— "The Design of the Paperback Book." New York. *American Artist*. March, 1957. p. 26.

———— "The Illustrators: Marie & Paul Nonnast." New York. *American Artist*. May, 1957. p. 38.

———— "George Harding." New York. *American Artist*. December, 1957. p. 29.

———— "The Book Illustrations of Edward Shenton." New York. *American Artist*. March, 1961. p. 22.

———— "American Illustration: Then and Now." New York. *American Artist*. June, 1961. p. 51.

———— "Millions of Pictures." (Two parts). New York. *American Artist*. November, 1961. p. 35. December, 1961. p. 52.

———— "Rudolf Freund: Scientific Illustrator." New York. *American Artist*. May, 1964. p. 20.

———— "Frank E. Schoonover: An Exampler of the Pyle Tradition." New York. *American Artist*. November, 1964. p. 64.

———— "N. C. Wyeth." New York. *American Heritage*. October, 1965. p. 34.

———— "N. C. Wyeth and the Brandywine Tradition." Harrisburg. William Penn Memorial Museum. 1965.

———— "The Resurgence of Robert Riggs." New York. *American Artist*. May, 1966. p. 50.

———— "Book Illustration since 1937." New York. *American Artist*. December, 1966. p. 64.

———— "The Brandywine Tradition." New York. *American Artist*. December, 1966. p. 43.

———— "Felix Darley: Early American Illustrator." New York. *American Artist*. June, 1968. p. 54.

———— "The Art of Illustration." Boston. *Horn Book Reflections*. 1969. p. 78.

Society of Illustrators, *37th Annual Exhibition Catalogue*. New York. 1939.

Society of Illustrators, "Robert McCall's Cosmic Mural." New York. *Illustrators Quarterly*. Winter 1976.

Trimble, Jessie, "The Founder of An American School of Art." New York. *The Outlook*. February, 1907.

Wasserman, Emily, "The Artist-Explorers." New York. *Art in America*. July, 1972. p. 48.

Watson, Ernest W., "Giant on a Hilltop." New York. *American Artist*. January, 1945.

Weitenkampf, Frank, "Illustrated by Darley." New York. *International Studio*. March, 1925.